# Shadows of the Messiah in the Torah

Volume Four
Revised Edition

*And beginning with Moses and all the prophets, He explained what was said in all the scriptures concerning Himself.*
Luke 24:27

Hebrew Roots Teachings for Home Studies
By
Dan and Brenda Cathcart

Scripture references used in this volume are from the following:

The New International Version, Copyright © 1973, 1978, 1984 by International Bible Society.

The New King James Version, Copyright © 1982 by Thomas Nelson, Inc.

Other Bible scripture versions as noted in the text.

Number references in the text i.e.: #1234, are from the Strong's Concordance, Copyright © 1890 James Strong, Madison, NJ

ISBN 978-1479282975

Copyright © 2012 Dan & Brenda Cathcart

Permission is given for the end user to print only the material contained in the PDF or other files on the enclosed CD or copy from the body of this book the Student Notes sections, discussion questions sections and the appendixes for the purpose of distributing to participants in your home study group. All other copyrights are reserved.

Cover Design: Dan Cathcart

A Note From the authors:

This material was compiled from a variety of sources including teachings from Pastor Mark Biltz at El Shaddai Ministries, Bonney Lake, WA where we attend. With a great love for the Torah and a desire to see Hebrew roots taught to the Nations, this volume has been compiled from studies conducted in our home over the last year. It is our sincere prayer that this study volume will enrich your life and those who attend your home study or small group. May the LORD bless you and your family.

Dan & Brenda Cathcart


Published by Moed Ministries, LLC

Office address:
3007 D Street SE
Auburn, WA 98002

Visit us on the web at www.moedministries.com

# Table of Contents

| | |
|---|---|
| Preface | 4 |
| Isaac: The Promised Seed | 7 |
| The Stone the Builders Rejected | 25 |
| Innocent until Proven Guilty | 41 |
| Grace and Truth in the Torah | 55 |
| Naomi and Ruth: Jew and Gentile | 71 |
| The Cities of Refuge, the Blood Avenger, and the High Priest | 91 |
| The Land of Israel | 105 |
| Hebron: The Promise of Resurrection | 119 |
| Shechem: Choose Life | 133 |
| Shechem: Decisions, Decisions! | 149 |
| Bethlehem: The City of Yeshua's Birth | 163 |
| Jerusalem: The Eternal City | 183 |
| Appendix A: The Hebrew Alphabet | 197 |
| Appendix B: The list of Names in the Book of Ruth | 199 |
| Appendix C: These are the Generations: The Story of Redemption | 200 |
| Appendix D: The Thirteen Attributes of God | 204 |
| Glossary | 205 |
| Additional Resources | 206 |

# Preface

As we get ready to publish this last volume (for now anyway) of the Shadows of Messiah, what words can we share that will inspire and encourage you, the reader? As we were pondering this question two people within a half hour of each other shared the same two scriptures with us. It just so happens they go beautifully with a teaching we watched just the previous day. The teaching was on the passage in Matthew 25 about the wise and foolish virgins. All ten virgins were waiting and watching for the coming of the bridegroom but they all fell asleep. They woke to the sounds of the imminent arrival of the bridegroom but five of the virgins had let their lamps go out and needed more oil. The oil is the teaching and power of the Holy Spirit; it cannot be shared in the sense that we can't use someone else's Holy Spirit in our own lives. We can only receive the teaching and power of the Holy Spirit from the One who gives it. Yeshua uses an analogy with the same message in the Book of Revelation. He tells the lukewarm church that they need to buy gold refined in the fire that can only be purchased from Him.

> Revelation 3:18 NKJV 18 "I counsel you to buy from Me gold refined in the fire, that you may be rich; and white garments, that you may be clothed, that the shame of your nakedness may not be revealed; and anoint your eyes with eye salve, that you may see.

Yeshua is not speaking to the world at large but to His own assembly, His congregation. Likewise the ten virgins were not unaware that the bridegroom was coming; they just did not actively have the presence of God in their lives. This brings us to the two passages of scripture that God led us to. The first is a warning that God's people are perishing because they don't know God's word and have rejected His Torah.

> Hosea 4:6 NKJV 6 My people are destroyed for lack of knowledge. Because you have rejected knowledge, I also will reject you from being priest for Me; Because you have forgotten the law (Torah) of your God, I also will forget your children.

The second one is stronger yet. It is a warning that even our prayers can be an abomination to God!

> Proverbs 28:9 KJV 9 He that turneth away his ear from hearing the law (Torah), even his prayer shall be abomination.

We have striven in these volumes to bring both the written and living Torah of God to life in the hearts and lives of believers, to return the knowledge of all His scriptures to those who are called by His name. Our goal has been and is to strengthen your faith through knowledge. But knowledge alone is not enough, faith is an action word. We must have an active presence of God in our lives, living and choosing each day to follow God. That very message just happens to resound through the lessons in this volume. We start with the faith of Abraham and Isaac with the offering of Isaac as an offering wholly dedicated to God, then contrast that with the lack of faith of the leaders of Yeshua's time as they reject the foundation stone. Moses, David, Ruth, Joshua and others are confronted time and time again with a choice. Some choose a path that leads to life while others choose a path that leads to death and destruction.

The first six lessons highlight God's grace and His identity as our redeemer. The lesson "Innocent until Proven Guilty" may bring you to your knees as you discover an incredible analogy of Yeshua taking the consequences of our sin on Himself in this ritual of a jealous husband who suspects his wife of adultery. The lesson "Grace and Truth in the Torah" may alter your entire perspective of the Tanakh or Old Testament.

The second six lessons all revolve around the land of Israel—the land of prophecy. We wrote these lessons as we prepared for a trip to Israel. Unfortunately, the trip didn't happen—yet. But the lessons that came out of that preparation reveal how the Promised Land is central to all prophecy. It seems strange that a location can be a shadow of Messiah, but Israel and each of these places in Israel have a role in the revelation and fulfillment of God's redemption plan. God brought His people to each of these places where He presented them with a choice. Learn about those choices and how each situation reveals Messiah.

We didn't set out to have a particular theme, we just wrote each lesson as God inspired us to write. But God knows what He is doing and we're sure He had it all planned. What better way could we end this series than with a call to remember and do God's commandments? We do them not as a means of salvation but because we love God and wish to obey Him. The Book of Revelation closes with Yeshua's words of encouragement to His followers.

> Revelation 22:14 KJV 14 Blessed are they that do his commandments, that they may have right to the tree of life, and may enter in through the gates into the city.

What are those commandments? Again, we look to the words of our Lord and Savior. On the eleventh of Nisan, three days before His crucifixion, one of the scribes asked Him which commandment was the first. He answers the scribe by citing two commandments after which no one dared question Him anymore.

> Mark 12:29-31 KJV 29 And Jesus answered him, The first of all the commandments is, Hear, O Israel; The Lord our God is one Lord: 30 And thou shalt love the Lord thy God with all thy heart, and with all thy soul, and with all thy mind, and with all thy strength: this is the first commandment. 31 And the second is like, namely this, Thou shalt love thy neighbour as thyself. There is none other commandment greater than these.

Shalom and be blessed,
Dan and Brenda Cathcart

## How to use these materials:

1. Pray! It's amazing how God opens our eyes and ears to see and understand when we ask Him. Pray before preparing and pray before teaching.

2. Choose a day and time. It can be weekly, monthly or bi-monthly. Invite friends, neighbors, family members. You might encourage them to bring a friend also. The materials included here are not sequential so new people can start any time. Be enthusiastic and positive. Let your excitement show; it's contagious. These study materials can be covered in about an hour. Extra time is good for questions, discussion and just getting to know each other.

3. Study for yourself. Leaders should read through all the material before teaching. It is especially helpful for the leader to be familiar with the contexts of the scriptures, so take some time and look up the scriptures and read the passages the scriptures are taken from. Leaders should also look up the Hebrew and/or Greek words and be familiar with their use in the scriptures.

4. Each lesson contains two parts. One part is a detailed guide for the use of the leader. We've found it easier to teach if all the scriptures are written out in the notes so we've written out all the scriptures. The second part consists of note pages for students. Make copies of the student notes and discussion questions for each participant. With the addition of discussion questions, each lesson can easily be extended to two sessions if desired. Some people have each person in the study purchase their own copy of the book and read through the lessons together using the student notes to record their own thoughts or insights as they go through each lesson. The discussion questions will make this method of using the materials both easier and more meaningful.

5. There are general handouts for all study participants included in the Appendices. The Hebrew Alphabet and Alphabet Chart should be available for all the sessions since most lessons have references to the Hebrew language or alphabet. The original Hebrew was written in pictographs. Each letter comes from a picture and retains the meaning of the picture. Many words make compelling "word pictures." Those are included in a separate text block. They may be used where they are inserted in the page or at the beginning or end of the lesson. The glossary is also useful especially for participants who drop in occasionally for a lesson.

6. Most of the lessons contain references to the original Hebrew or Greek. The number associated with the word is its reference in the Strong's Concordance and Dictionary. We use different versions of the Bible in our lessons; the version is noted at the beginning of each scripture passage. We use the New King James (NKJV) and Modern King James (MKJV) versions most often followed by the New International Version (NIV) and the King James Version (KJV). Other versions include the Young's Literal Translation (YLT) and the New American Standard Bible (NASB).

# Isaac: The Promised Seed

Isaac is perhaps the most easily recognized type of Messiah. God asks Abraham to offer up Isaac as a burnt offering, one given completely to God. But just as Abraham is going to kill Isaac, God intervenes and provides a ram instead. A ram is, of course, just a grown up lamb. The substituted ram represents Yeshua dying in our place and giving us eternal life. We easily see the symbolism in what Abraham was willing to do, God would actually do to redeem His people.

> Genesis 22:15-18 MKJV 15 And the Angel of the LORD called to Abraham out of the heavens the second time, 16 and said, I have sworn by Myself, says the LORD; because you have done this thing, and have not withheld your son, your only one; 17 that in blessing I will bless you, and in multiplying I will multiply your seed like the stars of the heavens, and as the sand which is upon the seashore. And your Seed shall possess the gate of His enemies. 18 And in your Seed shall all the nations of the earth be blessed, because you have obeyed My voice.

But by focusing on just this narrow incident in his life, we miss the incredible depth and richness of the prophecies contained in Isaac's life. So, let's start back at the beginning even before Isaac's birth.

**Part 1: Child of Promise**

**A.** Both Isaac's and Yeshua's births were eagerly awaited but a long time in coming. God promised Abraham or Abram, as he was then called, a son, a seed, who would inherit the land and the promises given to Abram.

> Genesis 15:4-5 MKJV 4 And behold, the word of the LORD came to him saying, This one shall not be your heir. But he that shall come forth out of your own bowels shall be your heir. 5 And He brought him outside and said, Look now toward the heavens and count the stars, if you are able to count them. And He said to him, So shall your seed be.

Abram was about 85 years old when God gave this promise to him. It had already been ten years since he left Haran to journey to the Promised Land. God had promised at that time that he would be a great nation but he still had no heir to pass anything on to. It would be another fourteen years before God would again appear before him and tell him that soon he would have a son by his wife Sarai.

> Genesis 17:1 MKJV 1 And when Abram was ninety-nine years old, the LORD appeared to Abram and said to him, I am the Almighty God! Walk before Me and be perfect.

> Genesis 17:15-16 MKJV 15 And God said to Abraham, As for Sarai your wife, you shall not call her name Sarai, but her name shall be Sarah. 16 And I will bless her,

Isaac: The Promised Seed

and give you a son also of her. Yes, I will bless her, and she shall be a mother of nations, kings of people shall be from her.

Abraham and Sarah waited for years before God gave them the promised seed. If we go back some 2000 years earlier, Eve was promised a "seed" that would crush the head of the serpent. Paul tells us that creation itself awaits the arrival of this seed.

> Romans 8:19-21 MKJV 19 For the earnest expectation of the creation waits for the manifestation of the sons of God. 20 For the creation was not willingly subjected to vanity, but because of Him who subjected it on hope 21 that the creation itself also shall be delivered from the bondage of corruption into the glorious liberty of the children of God.

In the days leading up to Yeshua's birth, there were those who were watching and eagerly expecting his birth. Anna and Simeon were two who watched for him their entire lives. God promised Simeon that he would see the birth of Messiah in his lifetime. Now he had reached the end of his life and finally, the Messiah is born.

> Luke 2:25-26 MKJV 25 And behold, there was a man in Jerusalem whose name was Simeon. And this man was just and devout, waiting for the Consolation of Israel. And the Holy Spirit was on him. 26 And it happened to him, being instructed by the Holy Spirit, he was not to see death before he would see the Christ of the Lord.

**B.** Isaac's birthday on the Biblical calendar is not obvious but there are clues that point to Passover and the time of the Feast of Unleavened Bread as the time of his birth. The promise to Sarah is that the birth would be at a "set time."

> Genesis 17:21 KJV 21 But my covenant will I establish with Isaac, which Sarah shall bear unto thee at this set time in the next year.

The word for set time is Moed the same word used for the Feasts of the LORD.

#4150. מועד mow`ed, mo-ade' or moled {mo-ade'} from 3259; properly, an appointment, i.e. a fixed time or season; specifically, a festival;

This promise is made during the visit of the angels warning of the destruction of Sodom and Gomorrah where Lot serves the angels unleavened bread pointing to the Feast of Unleavened Bread.

> Genesis 19:3 KJV And he pressed upon them greatly; and they turned in unto him, and entered into his house; and he made them a feast, and did bake unleavened bread, and they did eat.

From these hints in the scriptures, Isaac's birth is placed at Passover. In contrast, Yeshua was not born on Passover; instead his crucifixion was on Passover.

**C.** Both Isaac and Yeshua's births were the result of a miraculous conception. God repeatedly used a miraculous conception in the lives of the patriarchs to show specifically that God chooses the child. Isaac's own sons Jacob and Esau were born after he and Rebecca were married for 20 years. Even Jacob's wife Leah who eventually had six sons, was barren and God opened her womb. Jacob's wife Rachel continued barren for many years before she gave birth to Joseph. Other children that God chose through miraculous conception include Samson, Samuel, and John the Baptist.

How miraculous was the conception of Isaac? Abraham would be 100 years old and Sarah 90 years old when Isaac was born.

> Genesis 17:17 MKJV 17 And Abraham fell upon his face and laughed, and said in his heart, Shall a child be born to him that is a hundred years old? And shall Sarah, who is ninety years old, bear?

The Jewish sages say that God rejuvenated Abraham and Sarah's bodies so that they could have Isaac. In essence, they experience a type of resurrection. What evidence is there that this may have happened?

**1)** God gave Abram and Sarai new names.

> Genesis 17:5 MKJV 5 Neither shall your name any more be called Abram, but your name shall be Abraham. For I have made you a father of many nations.

> Genesis 17:15-16 MKJV 15 And God said to Abraham, As for Sarai your wife, you shall not call her name Sarai, but her name shall be Sarah. 16 And I will bless her, and give you a son also of her. Yes, I will bless her, and she shall be a mother of nations, kings of people shall be from her.

New names signify a change in status or destiny. Yeshua promises us a new name to go with our glorified bodies.

> Revelation 2:17 MKJV 17 He who has an ear, let him hear what the Spirit says to the churches. To him who overcomes I will give to eat of the hidden manna, and will give to him a white stone, and in the stone a new name written, which no man knows except he who receives it.

(The Lesson "Joshua: His Name and Mission" in <u>The Shadows of Messiah in the Torah, Volume 3</u> contains further details about God's appearance to Abram and Sarah in connection to receiving their new names.)

**2)** The second evidence that something new was about to happen is that Abraham was given circumcision as a sign of the covenant that Abraham was to be a father to many nations and that the Promised Land was to be his and his descendants and that God Himself had become their God.

> Genesis 17:10-11 MKJV 10 This is My covenant, which you shall keep, between Me and you and your seed after you. Every male child among you shall be circumcised. 11 And you shall circumcise the flesh of your foreskin. And it shall be a token of the covenant between Me and you.

**3)** Shortly after this event, Abimelech carried Sarah off to be his wife. Why would Abimelech want to take a 90 year old woman as his wife if she actually looked 90 years old?

> Genesis 20:2 MKJV 2 And Abraham said of Sarah his wife, She is my sister. And Abimelech the king of Gerar sent and took Sarah.

**4)** Paul seems to hint at new life for Abraham and Sarah. He says Abraham's body and Sarah's womb were as good as dead.

> Romans 4:17-19 MKJV 17 (as it has been written, "I have made you a father of many nations") --before God, whom he believed, who makes the dead live, and calls the things which do not exist as though they do exist. 18 For he who beyond hope believed on hope for him to become the father of many nations (according to that which was spoken, "So your seed shall be"). 19 And not being weak in faith, he did not consider his own body already dead (being about a hundred years old) or the deadening of Sarah's womb.

**5)** Abraham goes on to father six more sons after the death of Sarah. (Gen. 25:1) Whether or not God actually rejuvenated Abraham and Sarah, the conception of Isaac was truly miraculous. But as miraculous as that was, Yeshua's conception was even more amazing. Mary conceived without man's assistance.

> Luke 1:35 MKJV 35 And the angel answered and said to her, The Holy Spirit shall come on you, and the power of the Highest shall overshadow you. Therefore also that Holy One which will be born of you shall be called Son of God.

**Part 2: The Sacrifice**

**D.** Abraham's faith is tested when he is commanded to bring Isaac as a burnt offering.

> Genesis 22:1-2 MKJV 1 And it happened after these things that God tested Abraham, and said to him, Abraham! And he said, Behold me. 2 And He said, Take now your son, your only one, Isaac, whom you love. And go into the land of Moriah, and offer him there for a burnt offering upon one of the mountains which I will name to you.

In verse two, our English translations use the word "take" which implies that God is commanding Abraham to offer him as a sacrifice. In the Hebrew, the word is kach-nah. Kach means to take but with the ending "nah" the word is softened to a request. "Please take you son" better translates the implied meaning. God requested that Abraham bring his

Isaac: The Promised Seed

son and Abraham willingly complied. Because of Abraham's willing sacrifice, God swore a vow to Abraham to bless him.

> Genesis 22:15-18 MKJV 15 And the Angel of the LORD called to Abraham out of the heavens the second time, 16 and said, I have sworn by Myself, says the LORD; because you have done this thing, and have not withheld your son, your only one; 17 that in blessing I will bless you, and in multiplying I will multiply your seed like the stars of the heavens, and as the sand which is upon the seashore. And your Seed shall possess the gate of His enemies. 18 And in your Seed shall all the nations of the earth be blessed, because you have obeyed My voice.

God doesn't break His vows! This promise is sure!

What we don't realize, is that Isaac's faith was tested as well. We have the idea that Isaac was a young boy at the time of the offering because of the use of the English word "lad" in verse five.

> Genesis 22:5 KJV 5 And Abraham said unto his young men, Abide ye here with the ass; and I and the lad will go yonder and worship, and come again to you.

The word translated "lad" is na'ar which Strong's Dictionary defines as a male child from infancy to young adulthood.

#5288. נער na`ar, nah'-ar from 5287; (concretely) a boy (as active), from the age of infancy to adolescence; by implication, a servant; babe, boy, child, lad, servant, young (man).

What we don't see in English is that the phrase "young men" in verse 5 is also the Hebrew word na'ar. Later in Genesis, Judah uses the word na'ar in reference to Benjamin when pleading for his return in front of Joseph.

> Genesis 44:32 NKJV 32 "For your servant became surety for the lad to my father, saying, 'If I do not bring him back to you, then I shall bear the blame before my father forever.'

At this time, Benjamin is a father of ten sons and not at all a young boy! Likewise, Isaac was not a young boy except perhaps in the eyes of his father. Jewish tradition says that Isaac was 37 years old at the time he is bound for the offering. They assume that Sarah's death described in the next chapter occurred right after the offering. This is a crucial point. The offering of Isaac is done with Isaac's consent. There was no way a 137 year old Abraham could have forced a 37 year old Isaac to be bound and placed on an altar. We see this in the repeated phrase in verses six and eight, "and the two of them went together."

> Genesis 22:6 MKJV 6 And Abraham took the wood of the burnt offering and laid it on Isaac his son. And he took the fire in his hand, and a knife. And they both went together.

> Genesis 22:8 MKJV 8 And Abraham said, My son, God will provide Himself a lamb for a burnt offering. So they both went together.

The phrase translated went together is from the Hebrew word yachad referring to one unit. Abraham and Isaac were united in one purpose.

#3162. יחד yachad, yakh'-ad from 3161; properly, a unit, i.e. (adverb) unitedly:--alike, at all (once), both, likewise, only, (al-)together, withal.

Yeshua's age at the crucifixion was 33 years old. He, like Isaac, willingly offered his life in obedience to His father.

> John 10:17-18 NKJV 17 "Therefore My Father loves Me, because I lay down My life that I may take it again. 18 "No one takes it from Me, but I lay it down of Myself. I have power to lay it down, and I have power to take it again. This command I have received from My Father."

Like Isaac, if Yeshua had wanted to resist, no power on earth could have put him on the cross.

> Matthew 26:53-54 NKJV 53 "Or do you think that I cannot now pray to My Father, and He will provide Me with more than twelve legions of angels? 54 "How then could the Scriptures be fulfilled, that it must happen thus?"

In John 10:17-18, where Yeshua states that He lays down His life willingly, He goes on to state in verse 30 that He is one with His Father. Yeshua's prayer for us is that we also be one like He is one with the father.

> John 17:20-21 NKJV 20 "I do not pray for these alone, but also for those who will believe in Me through their word; 21 "that they all may be one, as You, Father, are in Me, and I in You; that they also may be one in Us, that the world may believe that You sent Me.

Now that we see Isaac as a man in the prime of life voluntarily offering to lay down his life, let's examine the details of his binding.

**E.** The instructions to Abraham were threefold. He was to (1) bring his son, (2) as a burnt offering, (3) to Moriah, a mountain God would show him.

> Genesis 22:2 MKJV 2 And He said, Take now your son, your only one, Isaac, whom you love. And go into the land of Moriah, and offer him there for a burnt offering upon one of the mountains which I will name to you.

**1)** Abraham was to bring his son but the phrasing in verse two is rather convoluted, "Take now your son, your only one, Isaac, whom you love."

Isaac: The Promised Seed

The father-son relationship is emphasized with Isaac referred to only in his relationship with Abraham. The *Talmud* describes this as an imaginary conversation between God and Abraham.

> God said, "Take your son."
> Abraham replied, "I have two sons."
> God said, "Your only son."
> Abraham replied, "They are both only sons of their mothers."
> God said, "The one you love."
> Abraham replied, "I love them both."
> God said, "Isaac."

The book of Hebrews says that Isaac is the only begotten of Abraham.

> Hebrews 11:17 NKJV 17 By faith Abraham, when he was tested, offered up Isaac, and he who had received the promises **offered up his only begotten son**,

Isaac is the only begotten son of Abraham in terms of the promise. Ishmael was born of the flesh. He and Sarah were trying to help God fulfill the promise of a son of Abraham's own body, but God already had it planned out and didn't need help. Isaac is the only son of the promise. When Sarah wanted to send away Hagar and Ishmael, God reassures Abraham that Isaac is the son who would inherit the promises.

> Genesis 21:12 NKJV 12 But God said to Abraham, "Do not let it be displeasing in your sight because of the lad or because of your bondwoman. Whatever Sarah has said to you, listen to her voice; for in Isaac your seed shall be called.

Yeshua is the only begotten son of the Father, the son of the promise.

> John 1:14 MKJV 14 And the Word became flesh, and tabernacled among us. And we beheld His glory, the glory as of the only begotten of the Father, full of grace and of truth.

> Acts 13:33 MKJV 33 this God has fulfilled to us their children, raising up Jesus, as also it is written in the second Psalm, "You are My Son, this day I have begotten You."

**2)** Genesis 22:2 said that Isaac was to be brought as a burnt offering. A burnt offering is one given entirely to God. In Hebrew the word translated as burnt offering is olah meaning to go up or to ascend. It is the only offering entirely burnt on the altar.

#5930. עלה `olah, o-law' or mowlah {o-law'}; a step or (collectively, stairs, as ascending); usually a holocaust (as going up in smoke):--ascent, burnt offering (sacrifice), go up to.

The Young's Literal Translation shows an interesting play on words. Isaac is to "ascend as a burnt offering."

> Genesis 22:2 YLT 2 And He saith, `Take, I pray thee, thy son, thine only one, whom thou hast loved, even Isaac, and go for thyself unto the land of Moriah, **and cause him to ascend there for a burnt-offering** on one of the mountains of which I speak unto thee.'

Even more literally, we can say that Isaac is "to ascend as an ascent."

The burnt offering is entirely devoted to God; it is a sweet scent to the LORD.

> Leviticus 1:9 MKJV 9 But its inward parts and its legs he shall wash in water. And the priest shall burn all on the altar, a burnt sacrifice, an offering made by fire, of a sweet savor to the LORD.

Yeshua was an olah offering. He was totally surrendered to God and came to do the will of His Father.

> John 6:38-40 MKJV 38 For I came down from Heaven, not to do My own will but the will of Him who sent Me.

After His resurrection, He ascended to the Father.

> John 20:17 MKJV 17 Jesus said to her, Do not touch Me, for I have not yet ascended to My Father. But go to My brothers and say to them, I ascend to My Father and Your Father, and to My God and your God.

Yeshua ascended to the Father as a voluntary offering totally dedicated to God, a sweet aroma to God.

**3)** The offering was to take place in the land of Moriah in the place God would show Abraham. The phrase "the place" is used repeatedly in this passage. They went to "the place" in verse 3, Abraham saw "the place" in verse 4, they came to "the place" in verse 9, and Abraham called "the place" in verse 14. Where is "the place?" It is the place David purchased for an altar to God and the place where Solomon would build the temple.

> 2 Chronicles 3:1 MKJV 1 And Solomon began to build the house of the LORD at Jerusalem in Mount Moriah, where He appeared to David his father, in the place that David had prepared in the threshing-floor of Ornan the Jebusite.

Like Abraham, the Israelites were to bring their sacrifices to "the place" he would show them.

> Deuteronomy 12:10-11 NKJV 10 "But when you cross over the Jordan and dwell in the land which the LORD your God is giving you to inherit, and He gives you rest

from all your enemies round about, so that you dwell in safety, 11 "then there will be **the place** where the LORD your God chooses to **make His name abide**. There you shall bring all that I command you: your burnt offerings, your sacrifices, your tithes, the heave offerings of your hand, and all your choice offerings which you vow to the LORD.

This place is the place where God would eventually place His name. That place was eventually revealed to be Jerusalem where Solomon built the house for God's name.

1 Kings 5:5 NKJV 5 And behold, I propose to build a house for the name of the LORD my God, as the LORD spoke to my father David, saying, "Your son, whom I will set on your throne in your place, he shall **build the house for My name**."

1 Kings 9:3 NKJV 3 And the LORD said to him: "I have heard your prayer and your supplication that you have made before Me; I have consecrated this house which you have built to put My name there forever, and My eyes and My heart will be there perpetually.

This place where Abraham would bring Isaac as an offering would eventually be the location of the Temple where all offerings were to be brought before the LORD.

**F.** Abraham's journey contains elements of the crucifixion.

**1)** On the third day of the journey, Abraham saw the place.

Genesis 22:4 MKJV 4 Then on the third day, Abraham lifted up his eyes and saw the place afar off.

Literally, Abraham saw Mt. Moriah in the distance. Since this happened on the third day, we can see this at a deeper level, Abraham saw Yeshua's crucifixion and resurrection far off in the future. Yeshua states that Abraham did indeed "see" His day.

John 8:56 KJV 56 Your father Abraham rejoiced to see my day: and he saw it, and was glad.

**2)** Abraham stated that he and Isaac would both return after worshipping God.

Genesis 22:5 MKJV 5 And Abraham said to his young men, You stay here with the ass. And I and the boy will go yonder and worship, and come again to you.

Abraham believed that God could and would bring Isaac back from the dead. Isaac was after all the child of the promise. God promised Abraham that he would be a father of many nations and that it was through Isaac that those descendants would be counted. Surely, the God who rejuvenated Abraham's seed and Sarah's womb could raise Isaac from the dead!

Hebrews 11:17-19 MKJV 17 By faith Abraham, being tested, offered up Isaac. And he who had received the promises offered up his only-begotten son, 18 of whom it was said that in Isaac your Seed shall be called, 19 concluding that God was able to raise him up, even from the dead, from where he even received him, in a figure.

God shows Himself as the covenant keeping God.

**G.** God would provide for Himself the lamb for the sacrifice.

> Genesis 22:7-8 MKJV 7 And Isaac spoke to Abraham his father and said, My father. And he said, Here am I, my son. And he said, Behold the fire and the wood. But where is the lamb for a burnt offering? 8 And Abraham said, My son, God will provide Himself a lamb for a burnt offering. So they both went together.

God would also provide for Himself a king for the nation of Israel. God is the one who provided David to be king of Israel.

> 1 Samuel 16:1 NKJV 1 Now the LORD said to Samuel, "How long will you mourn for Saul, seeing I have rejected him from reigning over Israel? Fill your horn with oil, and go; I am sending you to Jesse the Bethlehemite. For **I have provided Myself a king** among his sons."

The angel that appears to Mary promises that her child, conceived of her through the Holy Spirit would inherit David's throne.

> Luke 1:31-33 KJV 31 And, behold, thou shalt conceive in thy womb, and bring forth a son, and shalt call his name JESUS. 32 He shall be great, and shall be called the Son of the Highest: and the Lord God shall give unto him the throne of his father David: 33 And he shall reign over the house of Jacob for ever; and of his kingdom there shall be no end.

But before the ram was provided in Isaac's place, Isaac was bound and placed on the altar.

> Genesis 22:9 NKJV 9 Then they came to the place of which God had told him. And Abraham built an altar there and placed the wood in order; and he bound Isaac his son and laid him on the altar, upon the wood.

The word bound is from the Hebrew akod, עקד. Although the Strong's dictionary (#6123) defines it as "to bind," the Jewish understanding of the word is that it means ringed or striped. The Jewish sage Rashi explains that akod refers to the stripe-like marks left by the ropes. Yeshua, before His crucifixion, suffered the stripes of whips on His body.

> Matthew 27:26 NKJV 26 Then he released Barabbas to them; and when he had scourged Jesus, he delivered Him to be crucified.

Abraham bound Isaac on the altar but before he could slay Isaac, God called to him. Again, Abraham "lifted his eyes and saw."

Isaac: The Promised Seed

> Genesis 22:13 NKJV 13 Then Abraham lifted his eyes and looked, and there behind him was a ram caught in a thicket by its horns. So Abraham went and took the ram, and offered it up for a burnt offering instead of his son.

We've placed Abraham on the temple mount, but what is behind him? We know that the Tabernacle in the wilderness was set up so that it faced east. Those sacrificing in front of the tabernacle would face the entrance of the Tabernacle, so they would be facing west. The temple faced east with the altar east of the temple. Those bringing a sacrifice would face west, so behind them would be the Mt. of Olives. The Mt. of Olives is biblically the most likely place of Yeshua's crucifixion. All sacrifices were to be done before the LORD. That's why the altar was right outside the temple doors which were opened whenever offerings were brought. The Mt. of Olives is slightly higher than the temple mount and thus could be "seen" over the temple walls. (See the study *Ashes of the Red Heifer* in Volume 1 of Shadows of Messiah in the Torah for further details.) The ram would be caught in a thicket by his horns on the Mt. of Olives! Yeshua died on the Mt. of Olives with a crown of thorns on His head.

> Matthew 27:29 KJV 29 And when they had platted a crown of thorns, they put it upon his head, and a reed in his right hand: and they bowed the knee before him, and mocked him, saying, Hail, King of the Jews!

Abraham named "the place" of the offering calling it the LORD will provide or see. God did indeed provide the ram.

> Ge 22:14 And Abraham called the name of that place Jehovahjireh: as it is said to this day, In the mount of the LORD it shall be seen. (KJV)

#3070. יהוה ירה Yahovah yireh, yeh-ho-vaw' yir-eh' from 3068 and 7200; Jehovah will see (to it); Jehovah-Jireh, a symbolical name for Mount Moriah:--Jehovah- jireh.

The word yireh in its root form ra'ah (#7200) means either to see or to provide. Ra-ah is the word translated as provide when Abraham says that God Himself would provide the lamb and translated as looked when Abraham lifted his eyes and looked seeing the place and the ram. In fact, the name Moriah where God told Abraham to go contains the same root ra-ah and means seen or provided of God.

#4179. מוריה Mowriyah, mo-ree-yaw'; from 7200 and 3050; seen of Jah

God would both provide Yeshua, the lamb, and see the sacrifice.

The city of Jerusalem gets its name from this event. The city was originally called Salem when Melchizedek was king there. Combining Yireh with Shalem (Salem) forms the name Jerusalem which means peace or completeness will be seen or provided. God's eye is always on that place. When Yeshua comes again, He will establish His rule at Jerusalem. His reign will be marked with peace and righteous judgment. It will bring God's redemption plan to completion.

> Isaiah 9:6-7 KJV 6 For unto us a child is born, unto us a son is given: and the government shall be upon his shoulder: and his name shall be called Wonderful, Counsellor, The mighty God, The everlasting Father, **The Prince of Peace. 7 Of the increase of his government and peace there shall be no end**, upon the throne of David, and upon his kingdom, to order it, and to establish it with judgment and with justice from henceforth even for ever. The zeal of the LORD of hosts will perform this.

God provided the ram for the burnt offering and Abraham and Isaac worshipped the LORD. God will provide for the peace of Jerusalem and will see it established.

**H.** Abraham returned to his young men but there is no mention of Isaac.

> Genesis 22:19 MKJV 19 Abraham returned to his young men, and they rose up and went together to Beer-sheba. And Abraham lived at Beer-sheba.

Abraham told his young men to wait for them by the donkeys and that both he and Isaac would return. We must assume that both of them returned but no mention is made of Isaac returning. The scriptures instead skip ahead to focus on the selection of a bride for Isaac. Isaac disappears from the scriptures. The next time we see Isaac in the scriptures is when he greets his bride from the well of the Living One.

> Genesis 24:62-63 MKJV 62 And Isaac came from the way of the well, The Well of the Living One, my Beholder. For he lived in the south country. 63 And Isaac went out to meditate in the field at the beginning of the evening. And he lifted up his eyes, and looked. And behold, camels coming!

The word "Beholder" is once again the Hebrew word ra'ah. He is the Living One who sees and provides! (For more details about Isaac and his bride as a foreshadow of Yeshua and His bride, read "Isaac's Marriage and the Bride of Christ" in Shadows of Messiah in the Torah, Volume 1.)

After Yeshua's ascension, the Brit Chadashah scriptures turn their focus to the preparation of the bride for Yeshua. The next time we see Yeshua, it will be when He comes to claim His bride. He is the Living One providing the water of life; He sees us!

> Matthew 25:6 MKJV 6 And at midnight there was a cry made, Behold, the bridegroom comes! Go out to meet him.

> 1 Thessalonians 4:16-17 MKJV 16 For the Lord Himself shall descend from Heaven with a shout, with the voice of the archangel and with the trumpet of God. And the dead in Christ shall rise first. 17 Then we who are alive and remain shall be caught up together with them in the clouds, to meet the Lord in the air. And so we shall ever be with the Lord.

We see in this account of the binding of Isaac for sacrifice that both God and Yeshua are willing participants. God emphasizes that He is the one who provides the offering, that He sees the sacrifice and, finally, that it will be accomplished in Jerusalem.

## Student Notes for Isaac: The Promised Seed

Isaac is perhaps the most easily recognized type of Messiah. (Gen. 22:15-18)

**Part 1: Child of Promise**

**A.** Both Isaac's and Yeshua's births were eagerly awaited but a long time in coming. (Gen. 15:4-5, Gen. 17:1, Gen. 17:15-16, Rom. 8:19-21, Luke 2:25-26)

**B.** Passover—the Set Time (Gen. 17:21, Gen. 19:3)

Moed: #4150. מועד mow`ed, mo-ade' or moled {mo-ade'}; from 3259; properly, an appointment, i.e. a fixed time or season; specifically, a festival;

**C.** Both Isaac and Yeshua's births were the result of a miraculous conception. (Gen. 17:17)

The evidence for the rejuvenation of Abram and Sarai's bodies:

    1) God gave Abram and Sarai new names. (Gen. 17:5, Gen. 17:15-16, Rev. 2:17)

    2) God gave Abraham the covenant of circumcison. (Gen. 17:10-11)

    3) Shortly after this event, Abimelech carried Sarah off to be his wife. (Gen. 20:2)

4) Paul seems to hint at new life for Abraham and Sarah. (Rom. 4:17-19)

5) Abraham goes on to father six more sons after the death of Sarah. (Gen. 25:1)

Yeshua's conception was even more amazing. Mary conceived without man's assistance. (Luke 1:35)

**Part 2: The Sacrifice**
**D.** God tests Abraham and Isaac's faith. (Gen. 22:1-2, Gen. 22:15-18)

Isaac was not a young boy! (Gen. 22:5, Gen. 44:32)

#5288. נער na`ar, nah'-ar from 5287; (concretely) a boy (as active), from the age of infancy to adolescence; by implication, a servant; -- boy, child, lad, servant, young (man).

Abraham and Isaac were of one mind. (Gen. 22:6, Gen. 22:8)

#3162. יחד yachad, yakh'-ad from 3161; properly, a unit, i.e. (adverb) unitedly:--alike, at all (once), both, likewise, only.

Yeshua and His Father were of one mind. (John 10:17-18, Mat. 26:53-54, John 17:20-21)

Student Notes for Isaac: The Promised Seed

**E.** The instructions to Abraham were threefold. He was to (1) bring his son, (2) as a burnt offering, and (3) to Moriah, a mountain God would show him. (Gen. 22:2)

**1)** Abraham was to bring his son.

The *Talmud* describes this as an imaginary conversation between God and Abraham.
    God said, "Take your son."
    Abraham replied, "I have two sons."
    God said, "Your only son."
    Abraham replied, "They are both only sons of their mothers."
    God said, "The one you love."
    Abraham replied, "I love them both."
    God said, "Isaac."

The only begotten son of the promise: (Heb. 11:17, Gen. 21:12, John 1:14, Acts 13:33)

**2)** Isaac was to be brought as a burnt offering entirely devoted to God. (Lev. 1:9, John 6:38-40, John 20:17)

Burnt offering: #5930. עלה `olah, o-law' or mowlah {o-law'}; a step or (collectively, stairs, as ascending); usually a holocaust (as going up in smoke):--ascent, burnt offering (sacrifice), go up to.

Yeshua ascended to the Father as a voluntary offering totally dedicated to God, a sweet aroma to God.

**3)** The place God would show Abraham (2 Chr. 3:1, Deu. 12:10-11, 1 Kin. 5:5, 1 Kin. 9:3)

Student Notes for Isaac: The Promised Seed

**F.** Abraham's journey contains elements of the crucifixion.

**1)** On the third day of the journey, Abraham saw the place. (Gen. 22:4, John 8:56)

**2)** Abraham stated that he and Isaac would both return after worshipping God. (Gen. 22:5, Heb. 11:17-19)

**G.** God would provide for Himself the lamb. (Gen. 22:7-8, 1Sam. 16:1, Luke 1:31-33, Gen. 22:9)

#6123 akod, עקד. to bind

The Jewish understanding of the word is that it means ringed or striped. (Mat. 27:26)

Again, Abraham "lifted his eyes and saw." (Gen. 22:13, Matt. 27:29 Gen. 22:14)

Abraham named "the place" of the offering calling it the LORD will provide or see.

#3070. יהוה ירה Yehovah yireh, yeh-ho-vaw' yir-eh' from 3068 and 7200; Jehovah will see (to it); Jehovah-Jireh, a symbolical name for Mount Moriah:--Jehovah- jireh.

Ra'ah: #7200. har ra'ah, raw-aw' to see or to provide

Moriah: #4179. מוריה Mowriyah, mo-ree-yaw'; from 7200 and 3050; seen of Jah

Combining Yireh with Shalem (Salem) forms the name Jerusalem which means peace will be seen or provided. (Isa. 9:6-7)

**H.** Abraham returned to his young men but there is no mention of Isaac. (Gen. 22:19, Gen. 24:62-63, Mat. 25:6, 1The. 4:16-17)

Student Notes for Isaac: The Promised Seed

**Discussion Questions for Isaac: the Promised Seed**

1. God changed Abram and Sarai's names indicating their change in status. Read about God changing Jacob's name in Genesis 32:24-32 and about Yeshua changing Peter's name from Simon to Peter in Matthew 16:13018. What changes occurred in Jacob and Peter's lives to motivate their name changes?

2. Each of these people is referred to as na-ar or lad. Read the scripture about each person. About how old is each person when he is referred to as na-ar?

    Joseph: Gen. 37:2

    Joshua: Ex. 33:8-11, Ex. 17:8-10

    The spies sent to Jericho: Jos. 6:23, Num. 1:2-3

    Eli's sons: 2 Sam. 2:12-17, Num. 4:46-47

    The sons of Jesse: 1Sam. 16:8-11, 18

    David's followers: 1Sam. 21:4-5, 1Sam. 22:1-2

3. How does Paul instruct us to be like Isaac and Yeshua? (Rom. 12:1-2, Rom. 6:5-11)

4. Read John 3:13-15. How does Yeshua "ascend as an ascent?"

5. The first mention of the well of the Living One, My Beholder is when Hagar fled from Sarai. Read this account in Genesis 16. In what way did God "ra'ah" Hagar?

## The Stone the Builders Rejected

When Yeshua was in Jerusalem in the days leading up to the Passover, He addressed the chief priests and Pharisees calling Himself the stone the builders rejected.

> Matthew 21:42-45 MKJV 42 Jesus said to them, Did you never read in the Scriptures, "The stone which the builders rejected, this One has become the head of the corner; this is the Lord's doing, and it is marvelous in our eyes?" 43 Therefore I say to you, The kingdom of God shall be taken from you and given to a nation bringing out its fruits. 44 And he who falls on this Stone shall be broken, but on whomever it shall fall, it will grind him to powder. 45 And when the chief priests and Pharisees heard His parables, they knew that He spoke of them.

We will look at four parts in this passage, the builders and the head of the corner, the Stone itself, those who fall on the Stone, and those on whom it falls.

**A.** How did the chief priests and the Pharisees know that Yeshua spoke of them? Yeshua starts out by quoting a familiar Psalm which they read at every feast every year.

> Psalms 118:22-23 The stone which the builders rejected Has become the chief cornerstone. 23 This was the LORD'S doing; It is marvelous in our eyes. (NKJV)

Since Yeshua's teaching occurs in the days leading up to Passover, Yeshua's beginning statement "Did you never read" implies that the chief priests and Pharisees don't pay attention to the words they actually say and read. Yeshua goes on to quote a passage that the sages recognized as referring to the coming Messiah and the leaders of Israel as the "builders." The imagery of the builders comes from the prophet Isaiah. Isaiah specifically directs his words against the leaders of the people.

> Isaiah 28:14-17 MKJV 14 Therefore hear the word of the LORD, scornful men who **rule this people in Jerusalem**. 15 Because you have said, We have made a covenant with death, and we have made a vision with hell; when the overwhelming rod shall pass through, it shall not come to us; for we have made lies our refuge, and we have hidden ourselves under falsehood, 16 therefore so says the Lord Jehovah, Behold, I place in Zion a Stone for a foundation, a tried Stone, a precious Cornerstone, a sure Foundation; he who believes shall not hurry. 17 Also I will lay judgment to the line, and righteousness to the plummet; and the hail shall sweep away the refuge of lies, and the waters shall overflow the hiding place.

In the verses leading up to this passage, Isaiah states in verse 1 that the leaders are drunkards wearing the crown of pride, then, in verse 7, that they erred in both vision and judgment.

> Isaiah 28:7 MKJV 7 But they also have sinned through wine, and through strong drink are out of the way. The priest and the prophet have sinned through drink; they

are swallowed up by wine; they are out of the way through strong drink; they err in vision, they stumble in judgment.

Verse 15 elaborates on their error. Their vision is really that which leads to death; their judgment is perverted and false. Isaiah then uses the language of a builder to express the right foundation or vision, the precious cornerstone, and the coming righteous judgment in terms of the plumb line that measures true right angles and the straight line. A plumb line is a line with a weight on it. It is lowered to mark a vertical line. The weighted end has a point to mark in the dust or chalk to mark on other materials. It marks a vertical line and by extension, anything horizontal to it.

Staying with the imagery of the builder, the buildings of those days were made of stone without mortar. It was especially important that the stones selected fit together perfectly. Sometimes a stone was prepared but when they put it in place, it didn't fit right. The builders rejected that stone. The teachings of Yeshua didn't fit with the chief priest's and Pharisee's visions of what and who the Messiah should be. In the words of Isaiah, "They err in vision, they stumble in judgment." They rejected Messiah but He becomes the "head of the corner."

The phrase "head of the corner" in the context of a building is the capstone of an arch. The word corner is the Hebrew pinnah and the word head is rosh.

Corner: #6438. פנה pinnah, pin-naw'; an angle; by implication, a pinnacle; figuratively, a chieftain

Head: #7218. ראש ro'sh, roshe from an unused root apparently meaning to shake; the head (as most easily shaken), band, beginning, captain, chief(-est place, man, things), company, end, X every (man), excellent, first, forefront

The capstone of an arch is the most important stone of an arch. It balances all the forces holding the arch in place. It is the foundation only upside down. Without the capstone, the arch collapses. Yeshua, who is above all others, is also the foundation.

The word pinnah is also used to mean chief or ruler. We see that in 1 Samuel and in Judges.

> 1 Samuel 14:38 MKJV 38 And Saul said, Draw near here, all the **chief (pinnah)** of the people, and know and see what this sin has been today.

> Judges 20:2 MKJV 2 And the **leader (pinnah)** of all the people, of all the tribes of Israel, presented themselves in the assembly of the people of God, four hundred thousand footmen that drew sword.

The word rosh also means first. So, Yeshua becomes the first ruler, or the chief chieftain. Yeshua is the capstone; He is the pinnacle of God's redemption plan.

**B.** Not only is Yeshua the head of the corner; he is also the Stone. The word stone itself is the Hebrew word eben,

Eben: #68. אֶבֶן 'eben, eh'-ben from the root of 1129 through the meaning to build; a stone.

Isaiah calls Him the foundation stone and the tried stone in the passage we read in Isaiah 28. Yeshua became the tried stone after enduring temptation during His forty days in the wilderness. He is the foundation stone upon which He is building His assembly.

> Ephesians 2:19-22 MKJV 19 Now therefore you are no longer strangers and foreigners, but fellow citizens with the saints, and of the household of God, 20 and are built upon the foundation of the apostles and prophets, Jesus Christ Himself being the chief cornerstone, 21 in whom every building having been fitly framed together, grows into a holy sanctuary in the Lord; 22 in whom you also are built together for a dwelling place of God through the Spirit.

This isn't just any stone; it is a stone that has been prepared for the purpose of bringing life. The Hebrew word picture reveals this purpose.

---

Stone: Eben: אֶבֶן

אָב: Ab: Father

בֶן: Ben: Son

ב: Beit: House

The Father and Son are in the house.

א: Aleph: Abbreviation for Elohim, God

ב: Beit: House

ן: Nun: Life

Stone: God's house of life.

---

We see the meaning emphasized in the story of Jacob. When Jacob is on his way to his uncle's house to escape from Esau and find a bride, he spends the night in a place he will name Bethel. He uses a stone, eben, for his pillow.

> Genesis 28:11 NKJV 11 So he came to a certain place and stayed there all night, because the sun had set. And he took one of the stones of that place and put it at his head, and he lay down in that place to sleep.

During the night, Jacob had a dream that God promised Him the Land and that the Seed of Promise would come through him. When he wakes up, he takes the stone and pours oil on it and gives the place a new name.

> Genesis 28:18-19 NKJV 18 Then Jacob rose early in the morning, and took the stone that he had put at his head, set it up as a pillar, and poured oil on top of it. 19 And he called the name of that place Bethel; but the name of that city had been Luz previously.

Later, God reminds Jacob of this stone referring to it as an anointed pillar and says that Jacob anointed it.

> Genesis 31:13 NKJV 13 'I am the God of Bethel, where you anointed the pillar and where you made a vow to Me. Now arise, get out of this land, and return to the land of your family.'"

The word for anoint is mashach. The word messiah comes from mashach.

Mashach: #4886. משח mashach, maw-shakh' a primitive root; to rub with oil, i.e. to anoint.

Messiah: #4899. משיח mashiyach, maw-shee'-akh from 4886; anointed; usually a consecrated person (as a king, priest, or saint); specifically, the Messiah:--anointed, Messiah.

Jacob named the place Bethel which means the house of God.

Bethel: #1008. בית אל Beyth-'El, bayth-ale' from 1004 and 410; house of God.

The Stone is spoken of as a pillar which means memorial stone. This is like a roadside marker commemorating an historical event.

Pillar: #4676. מצבה matstsebah, mats-tsay-baw' something stationed, i.e. a column or (memorial stone); pillar.

There at Bethel, the house of God, Jacob anointed the stone which is the symbol of Messiah's presence in the house of God. Whenever anyone sees the stone, they remember God's promise of a Messiah.

When Jacob returned to the Promised Land after his exile, he was to go to Bethel. He was to return to the Messiah at the house of God, the anointed stone that is "God's house of life" as we saw from our word picture.

> Genesis 28:20-22 YLT 20 And Jacob voweth a vow, saying, `Seeing God is with me, and hath kept me in this way which I am going, and hath given to me bread to

eat, and a garment to put on-- 21 when I have turned back in peace unto the house of my father, and Jehovah hath become my God, 22 then **this stone which I have made a standing pillar is a house of God**, and all that Thou dost give to me-- tithing I tithe to Thee.'

**C.** Yeshua said in Matthew 21:44 that whoever falls on this stone, this eben, would be broken. This also comes from a passage in Isaiah.

> Isaiah 8:13-16 MKJV 13 Sanctify the LORD of hosts Himself, and let Him be your fear, and let Him be your dread. 14 And He shall be a sanctuary for you, but for a stone of stumbling, and for a rock of falling to both the houses of Israel, for a trap and for a snare to the people of Jerusalem. 15 And many among them shall stumble and fall and be broken, and be snared, and be taken. 16 Bind up the testimony, seal the law among My disciples.

God intended the stone to be a sanctuary, a holy place set aside for them. The word for sanctuary is the Hebrew word Miqdash.

Miqdash: #4720. מקדש miqdash, mik-dawsh' or miqqdash (Exod. 15:17) {mik-ked-awsh'}; from 6942; a consecrated thing or place, especially, a palace, sanctuary hallowed part, holy place, sanctuary.

God told the Israelites to build Him a sanctuary where He could live among them.

> Exodus 25:8 MKJV 8 And let them make Me a sanctuary, so that I may dwell among them.

God was and is a sanctuary for the remnant of Israel who believes but He became a stumbling stone to those who didn't believe. Peter quotes the passage in Isaiah 28.

> 1 Peter 2:6-8 MKJV 6 Therefore also it is contained in the Scripture: "Behold, I lay in Zion a chief corner Stone, elect, precious, and he who believes on Him shall never be ashamed." 7 Therefore to you who believe is the honor. But to those who are disobedient, He is the Stone which the builders rejected; this One came to be the Head of the corner, 8 and a Stone-of-stumbling and a Rock-of-offense to those disobeying, who stumble at the word, to which they also were appointed.

Paul also says they stumbled over the stumbling stone.

> Romans 9:31-33 MKJV 31 But Israel, who followed after a law of righteousness did not arrive at a law of righteousness. 32 Why? Because it was not of faith, but as it were by the works of the Law. For they stumbled at that Stumbling-stone; 33 as it is written, "Behold, I lay in Zion a Stumbling-stone and a Rock-of-offense, and everyone believing on Him shall not be put to shame."

He says they stumbled because they pursued righteousness by the Law and not by faith. This recalls the passage in Isaiah 28 where God said their vision and their judgment was faulty. Isaiah elaborates on their faulty vision.

> Isaiah 28:12-13 MKJV 12 To whom He said, This is the rest; cause the weary to rest; and this is the refreshing. Yet they were not willing to hear. 13 But the word of the LORD was to them precept on precept, precept on precept; line on line, line on line; here a little, there a little; that they might go, and fall backward, and be broken and snared and taken.

They viewed the Law as burdensome, as a set of rules to be followed. They didn't see it as part of larger Law of Righteousness and just judgment. They did not delight nor rest in the Law. Jeremiah tells them that rest is to be found in the "old ways."

> Jeremiah 6:16 MKJV 16 So says the LORD, Stand in the ways and see, and ask for the old paths where the good way is, and walk in it, and you shall find rest for your souls. But they said, We will not walk in it.

Yeshua said in Matthew that His burden was light and it gives rest to the soul.

> Matthew 11:28-30 MKJV 28 Come to Me all you who labor and are heavy laden, and I will give you rest. 29 Take My yoke on you and learn of Me, for I am meek and lowly in heart, and you shall find rest to your souls. 30 For My yoke is easy, and My burden is light.

Even when Peter points out to the chief priests and Pharisees that they are stumbling as prophesied by Isaiah, they do not see their error and repent.

> Acts 4:8-11 NKJV 8 Then Peter, filled with the Holy Spirit, said to them, "Rulers of the people and elders of Israel: 9 "If we this day are judged for a good deed done to a helpless man, by what means he has been made well, 10 "let it be known to you all, and to all the people of Israel, that by the name of Jesus Christ of Nazareth, whom you crucified, whom God raised from the dead, by Him this man stands here before you whole. 11 "This is the 'stone which was rejected by you builders, which has become the chief cornerstone.'

Luke, as the author of the Book of Acts, must have wanted us to make the connection between this passage and the one in Matthew 21:42-44 because he goes on to echo the words of Yeshua by saying that the council "marveled" at their words.

> Acts 4:13 MKJV 13 But seeing the boldness of Peter and John, and perceiving that they were unlearned and uneducated men, they **marveled**. And they recognized them, that they had been with Jesus.

The word marvel is the same word used in Matthew 21: 42, "this is the Lord's doing, and it is **marvelous** in our eyes." It was marvelous in their eyes, but they still didn't get it!

Yeshua also said (Matt. 21:43) that the kingdom would be given to a nation that would bring forth its fruit. Who did Yeshua give the kingdom to? The word translated nation is ethnos.

Nation: #1484. (Greek) ethnos, eth'-nos; a race (as of the same habit), i.e. a tribe; Gentile, heathen, nation, people.

Ethnos can mean a tribe or a people as well as a nation. Yeshua didn't give the kingdom to the Gentiles; He gave the kingdom to the apostles who in a sense mirror the original twelve tribes. In Ephesians 2:20, Paul said that the apostles and the prophets are part of the foundation built directly upon Him. When Yeshua changed Peter's name from Simon to Peter, He says that Peter will be a little rock in the foundation of His assembly.

> Matthew 16:16-18 MKJV 16 And Simon Peter answered and said, You are the Christ, the Son of the living God. 17 Jesus answered and said to him, You are blessed, Simon, son of Jonah, for flesh and blood did not reveal it to you, but My Father in Heaven. 18 And I also say to you that you are Peter, and on this rock I will build My church, and the gates of hell shall not prevail against it.

The name Peter is from the Greek petros #4074 meaning piece of rock. The word translated rock is from the Greek petra #4073 meaning mass of rock. So Peter is a piece of the mass of rock upon which Yeshua will build His assembly. We see this again in the foundation of the walls of the eternal Jerusalem

> Revelation 21:14 MKJV 14 And the wall of the city had twelve foundations, and in them were the names of the twelve apostles of the Lamb.

The twelve apostles, all Jewish, are the foundation of the holy Jerusalem which descends from heaven. They are the "people" to whom Yeshua gave the kingdom who brought forth the fruits of kingdom.

There is an interesting message in Peter's name change as recorded in the Matthew passage we just read. His original name was Simon son of Jonah. Simon comes from the Hebrew Shimown (#8095) meaning hearing. Jonah is the Hebrew for dove (#3123). The dove is a symbol of the Holy Spirit. At Jesus' baptism, the Holy Spirit falls on Yeshua like a dove. Simon's original name means "Hearing is the 'son' of the Spirit"; that is, hearing comes from the spirit of God. Matthew 16:17 can be read "You are blessed (Hearing comes from the spirit of God), for flesh and blood did not reveal it to you, but My Father in Heaven." Yeshua said that the Father Himself revealed to Simon that Yeshua was the Messiah the son of the Living God. Peter's testimony tells us that the massive rock, the foundation, is Yeshua HaMashiach.

**D.** Yeshua also said that the stone would crush those on whom it fell. This comes from the book of Daniel. King Nebuchadnezzar had a dream that greatly disturbed him. He wanted to know its meaning but wanted to make sure he heard the right interpretation. He set a challenge to his wise men and magicians to reward anyone who could tell him both the dream and its interpretation. Of course, none of them could tell the king his dream, so the king ordered all the wise men of the kingdom killed. This included the Hebrew wise men Daniel, Hananiah, Mishael, and Azariah (Shadrach, Meshach and Abednego). After they prayed, God revealed the dream and its interpretation to Daniel.

> Daniel 2:31-35 MKJV 31 You, O king, were seeing. And, behold! A great image! That great image, whose brightness was excellent, stood before you. And its form was dreadful. 32 This image's head was of fine gold; his breast and his arms were of silver; his belly and his thighs were of bronze; 33 his legs were of iron; his feet were part of iron and part of clay. 34 You watched until a **stone** was cut out without hands, which struck the image upon its feet which were of iron and clay, and broke them to pieces. 35 Then the iron, the clay, the bronze, the silver, and the gold were broken to pieces together. And they became like the chaff of the summer threshing floors. And the wind carried them away, so that no place was found for them. And the stone that struck the image became a great mountain and filled the whole earth.

The word stone is again the Hebrew word eben. This stone was not a manmade stone but one hewn by God alone. In contrast, the great image is something that would be manmade representing the kingdoms that man builds. When God commanded the children of Israel about building an altar, He said if they make it out of stone (eben), they are not to use any tools on it.

> Exodus 20:25 MKJV 25 And if you will make Me an altar of stone, you shall not build it of cut stone. For if you lift up your tool upon it, you have defiled it.

This differentiates it from man-made objects which we tend to honor above the purpose of the object. Think of all the cathedrals that tourists visit every year just to look at the structure and the images in the cathedrals. How many of these visitors even think about the fact that these cathedrals were supposedly built to honor and worship God? In the same way, God did not want the Israelites worshipping the altar instead of worshipping Him at the altar. We need to be careful not to elevate the son, the stone, above the father. Paul says that Yeshua reigns in submission to the Father.

> 1 Corinthians 15:28 NKJV 28 Now when all things are made subject to Him, then the Son Himself will also be subject to Him who put all things under Him, that God may be all in all.

Why does using a tool on the stone altar defile it? In Exodus 20:24, which is the verse before God gives them the instructions on how to build a stone altar, He told them to build an earthen altar. An earthen altar would not deflect worship to the altar itself and away from God. Similarly, the altar built for the Tabernacle was built of wood overlaid with bronze. Bronze is the metal representing judgment. Every time they brought an offering to this altar, the bronze would remind them of God's judgment.

Although the children of Israel may have made many stone altars to God, there is only one stone altar that they were commanded to make and that was the stone altar on Mt. Ebal after they came into the land.

> Deuteronomy 27:4-7 MKJV 4 Therefore it shall be when you have gone over Jordan, you shall set up these stones which I command you today, in Mount Ebal. And you shall plaster them with plaster. 5 And you shall build an altar there to the LORD your God, an altar of stones. You shall not lift up any iron tool on them. 6 You shall build the altar of the LORD your God of uncut stones, and you shall offer burnt offerings on it to the LORD your God. 7 And you shall offer peace offerings, and shall eat there, and rejoice before the LORD your God.

The picture presented by this altar is consistent with Daniel's vision of the stone representing the conquering Messiah smashing the kingdoms of men. We know that all the sacrifices brought to the altar represent Yeshua as our offering to God, but in this passage, we see the altar itself as a representation of Yeshua. When we try to use our tools on the stone of Messiah, we are attempting to change who He is by shaping Him in our image. Thus, we defile Him. We are to be conformed to His image not the other way around!

Daniel goes on to interpret Nebuchadnezzar's vision. We will focus on the part involving the stone.

> Daniel 2:41-45 MKJV 41 And as to that which you saw: the feet and toes, part of potters' clay and part of iron; the kingdom shall be divided. But there shall be in it the strength of the iron, because you saw the iron mixed with miry clay. 42 And as the toes of the feet were part of iron and part of clay, so the kingdom shall be partly strong and partly brittle. 43 And as you saw iron mixed with miry clay, they shall mix themselves with the seed of men. But they shall not cling to one another, even as iron is not mixed with clay. 44 And in the days of these kings, the God of Heaven shall set up a kingdom which shall never be destroyed. And the kingdom shall not be left to other peoples, but it shall crush and destroy all these kingdoms, and it shall stand forever. 45 Because you saw that the stone was cut out of the mountain without hands, and that it crushes the iron, the bronze, the clay, the silver, and the gold, the great God has made known to the king what shall occur after this. And the dream is certain, and its meaning is sure.

In the days of the kingdoms represented by the toes, God will set up His eternal kingdom. The stone crushes all the previous kingdoms; all those empires set up by man. What does it mean that "they will mix themselves with the seed of men?" The word for man here is the Aramaic 'enash which comes from the Hebrew word "enosh."

Men: #582. אנוש 'enowsh, en-oshe' from 605; properly, a mortal (and thus differing from the more dignified 120 a-dam)

#605. אנש 'anash, aw-nash' a primitive root; to be frail, feeble, or (figuratively) melancholy:--desperate(-ly wicked), incurable, sick, woeful.

This word for man, enosh, means mortal. It comes from anash which means to be feeble, frail, or sick. The emphasis is not on the life but on the inevitable death. In contrast, other words sometimes translated as man are iysh, which is literally man, and nephesh which is also translated as soul. Nephesh means to breathe or live. The seed of men (enosh) then, are those destined to die. These are not the seed of Abraham. The phrase the Seed of Abraham, although literally referring to the physical descendants of Abraham, refers more specifically to those of the faith of Abraham. Yeshua said that those who are true children of Abraham would do the acts of Abraham (John 8:35). Paul referred to this in his letter to the Romans.

> Romans 9:7-8 MKJV 7 nor because they are the seed of Abraham are they all children. But, "In Isaac shall your Seed be called." 8 That is, not the children of the flesh are children of God; but the children of the promise are counted for a seed.

There is no way Isaac could have been born through the agency of man. Only God could restore Abraham's seed. The seed of men then would refer to those who either count on works of the flesh for salvation or look to the works of men elevating man above God. They are destined for death. David writes of the Lord at the right hand of God striking down kings and setting up His authority over the nations.

> Psalms 110:5-6 MKJV 5 The Lord at Your right hand shall strike through kings in the day of His wrath. 6 He shall judge among the nations, He shall fill them with dead bodies; He shall shatter heads over much of the earth.

The kingdoms of men that are broken to pieces become like chaff. The Book of Revelation uses the metaphor of the harvest to describe the days after the sounding of the seventh trumpet.

> Revelation 14:15-16 MKJV 15 And another angel came out of the temple, crying in a great voice to Him sitting on the cloud, Thrust in Your sickle and reap, for the time has come for You to reap, for the harvest of the earth was dried. 16 And He sitting on the cloud thrust in His sickle on the earth, and the earth was reaped.

Unlike the nations of men, Yeshua will rule with perfect justice and mercy. His kingdom will stand forever.

> Psalms 89:13-14 MKJV 13 You have a mighty arm; Your hand is strong, and Your right hand is high. 14 Justice and judgment are the foundation of Your throne; mercy and truth shall go before Your face.

## Student Notes for the Stone the Builders Rejected

Matthew 21:42-45 MKJV 42 Jesus said to them, Did you never read in the Scriptures, "The stone which the builders rejected, this One has become the head of the corner; this is the Lord's doing, and it is marvelous in our eyes?" 43 Therefore I say to you, The kingdom of God shall be taken from you and given to a nation bringing out its fruits. 44 And he who falls on this Stone shall be broken, but on whomever it shall fall, it will grind him to powder. 45 And when the chief priests and Pharisees heard His parables, they knew that He spoke of them.

We will look at four parts in this passage, the builders and the head of the corner, the Stone, those who fall on the Stone, and those on whom it falls.

**A.** The builders: Yeshua quoted a passage that the sages recognized as referring to the coming Messiah and the leaders of Israel as the "builders." (Psa. 118:22-23, Isa. 28:14-17, Isa. 28:7)

Head of the corner: the capstone of an arch.

Corner: #6438. פנה pinnah, pin-naw'; an angle; by implication, a pinnacle; figuratively, a chieftain

Head: #7218. ראש ro'sh, roshe from an unused root apparently meaning to shake; the head (as most easily shaken), band, beginning, captain, chief(-est place, man, things), company, end, X every (man), excellent, first, forefront

The word pinnah is also used to mean chief or ruler. (1Sam. 14:38, Jdg. 20:2)

**B.** Yeshua is also the Stone. (Eph. 2:19-22)

Stone: Eben: #68. אבן 'eben, eh'-ben from the root of 1129 through the meaning to build; a stone.

> Stone: Eben: אבן
>
> אב: Ab: Father
>
> בן: Ben: Son
>
> ב: Beit: House
>
> The Father and Son are in the house.
>
> א: Aleph: Abbreviation for Elohim, God
>
> ב: Beit: House
>
> ן: Nun: Life
>
> Stone: God's house of life.

We see the meaning emphasized in the story of Jacob. (Gen. 28:11, Gen. 28:18-19, Gen. 31:13)

Annoint: Mashach: #4886. משח mashach, maw-shakh' a primitive root; to rub with oil, i.e. to anoint.

Messiah: #4899. משיח mashiyach, maw-shee'-akh from 4886; anointed; usually a consecrated person (as a king, priest, or saint); specifically, the Messiah:--anointed, Messiah.

Bethel: #1008. בית אל Beyth-'El, bayth-ale' from 1004 and 410; house of God.

Jacob was to return to the Messiah at the house of God, the stone that is "God's house of life." (Gen. 28:20-22)

Pillar: #4676. מצבה matstsebah, mats-tsay-baw' something stationed, i.e. a column or (memorial stone); pillar.

**C.** Yeshua said in Matthew 21:44 that whoever falls on this stone, this eben, would be broken. (Isa. 8:13-16, Exo. 25:8, 1Pet. 2:6-8, Rom. 9:31-33, Isa. 28:12-13, Jer. 6:16, Mat. 11:28-30, Acts 4:8-11, Acts 4:13)

Sanctuary: Miqdash: #4720. מקדש miqdash, mik-dawsh' or miqqdash (Exod. 15:17) {mik-ked-awsh'}; from 6942; a consecrated thing or place, especially, a palace, sanctuary hallowed part, holy place, sanctuary.

Who did Yeshua give the kingdom to? (Mat. 16:16-18, Rev. 21:14)

Nation: #1484. (Greek) ethnos, eth'-nos; a race (as of the same habit), i.e. a tribe; Gentile, heathen, nation, people.

Peter Greek petros #4074 piece of rock. The word translated rock is from the Greek petra.

Rock: Greek petra #4073 meaning mass of rock.

Simon son of Jonah:
Simon: #8095. שמעון Shim`own, shim-one' hearing.
Jonah: #3123. יונה yownah, yo-naw' dove

**D.** Yeshua also said that the stone would crush those on whom it fell. (Dan. 2:31-35, Exo. 20:25, 1Cor. 15:28, Deu. 27:4-7, Rom. 9:7-8, Dan. 2:41-45, Psa. 110:5-6, Rev. 14:15-16, Psa.89:13-14)

Men: #582. אנוש 'enowsh, en-oshe' from 605; properly, a mortal (and thus differing from the more dignified 120 a-dam)

#605. אנש 'anash, aw-nash' a primitive root; to be frail, feeble, or (figuratively) melancholy:--desperate(-ly wicked), incurable, sick, woeful.

Student Notes for The Stone the Builders Rejected

**Discussion Questions for the Stone the Builders Rejected**

1. The leaders of the Jewish people rejected Yeshua, the stone which God intended to be a sanctuary for them. But God didn't totally reject His people. Read Ezekiel 11:16-20. How is God's presence still with them?

2. The angel that came to Samson's father to announce the upcoming birth of Samson said his name was Wonderful which has the same root as the Hebrew word for marvelous. Read the account of Samson's birth in Judges 13. What evidence is there that this Angel is really a pre-incarnate Yeshua?

3. Isaiah 28:15 is about the covenant the rulers of Judah made with death. Discuss this covenant with death.

4. Yeshua is the stone which is not fashioned by man. Read Exodus 32:1-4. Contrast Yeshua with the golden calf Aaron "fashioned with an engraving tool." Read Galatians 1:6-12. How is following another gospel like building a golden calf?

5. Read Isaiah 45:9-13, Ephesians 2:10 and 2 Corinthians 3:18. What does God say about the works of man versus His works?

6. Read Isaiah 29:13-24. Verse 14 says that God will again do a marvelous work. What is the marvelous work and what happens as a result?

## Innocent until Proven Guilty
Numbers 5:11-31

This passage in Numbers details the provisions for a jealous husband to have his wife judged before the LORD to determine whether or not she has been faithful to him. This seems a bit unfair to say the least. A husband can have his wife subjected to this ritual while there are no provisions for her to bring her husband before the LORD. But the sages interpret the last verse in the passage to mean that God judges the woman guilty only if the man himself is innocent of transgression.

> Numbers 5:31 KJV 31 Then shall the man be guiltless from iniquity, and this woman shall bear her iniquity.

But whether this is fair or not in our eyes, we see that God values the marriage relationship and goes to great lengths to provide a means for a woman to prove her fidelity to her husband. For, while the penalty for her guilt in this ritual is a painful death if she is indeed guilty, she can avoid this death by just confessing her guilt. Because there are no witnesses to her adultery, her husband can divorce her but he cannot have her killed. So, the intent of this ritual is to prove her innocence and restore the relationship. When her innocence is established, God blesses her with children.

The ritual itself is one that makes little sense to us. Like all such rituals in the scriptures, it has layers of meaning. The husband and wife relationship is at the heart of God's relationship with man. It is the first institution established by God, and He uses it repeatedly as He reveals His redemption plan. We will look at three layers of meaning within this passage.

First, God describes His relationship with Israel as that of husband and wife. God also describes Himself as a jealous God even as He is establishing the covenant with Israel.

> Exodus 20:4-5 KJV 4 Thou shalt not make unto thee any graven image, or any likeness of any thing that is in heaven above, or that is in the earth beneath, or that is in the water under the earth: 5 Thou shalt not bow down thyself to them, nor serve them: for I the LORD thy God am a jealous God, visiting the iniquity of the fathers upon the children unto the third and fourth generation of them that hate me;

We will examine instances in which God establishes the fidelity and infidelity of His people through a ritual similar to this one.

Second, Yeshua takes on all our sins and punishments. All of us have been guilty of infidelity to God and would be judged guilty under this ritual. We will see how Yeshua underwent this ritual for us taking on our iniquity. This is one of the many ways God shows that Yeshua took our punishment for us.

Third, Paul describes the assembly of believers as the bride of Christ. We, as His bride, must be pure and without blemish. Each of us faces standing before God and having our hearts and actions judged at the judgment seat of Christ.

> 2 Corinthians 5:10 KJV 10 For we must all appear before the judgment seat of Christ; that every one may receive the things done in his body, according to that he hath done, whether it be good or bad.

**A.** In this ritual, God is the one who judges. The husband brings his wife to the priest and the priest brings her before God with an offering of jealousy.

> Numbers 5:15 NKJV 15 'then the man shall bring his wife to the priest. He shall bring the offering required for her, one-tenth of an EPHAH of barley meal; he shall pour no oil on it and put no frankincense on it, because it is a grain offering of jealousy, an offering for remembering, for bringing iniquity to remembrance.

The offering is without oil or frankincense. The oil beautifies an offering, symbolizing prosperity and gladness. Frankincense gives the offering a sweet aroma. Neither of these are present here because the offering is one asking for God's judgment not mercy. It is not a time of gladness or prosperity. The purpose of the offering is to cause both God and the wife to remember iniquity.

Ezekiel writes that God judged Israel in the wilderness and He will do it again before bringing them back into the covenant and the Promised Land.

> Ezekiel 20:36-37 NIV 36 As I judged your fathers in the desert of the land of Egypt, so I will judge you, declares the Sovereign LORD. 37 I will take note of you as you pass under my rod, and I will bring you into the bond of the covenant.

When He brings them back into the covenant, God will cause them to remember their iniquities.

> Ezekiel 20:43 NKJV 43 "And there you shall remember your ways and all your doings with which you were defiled; and you shall loathe yourselves in your own sight because of all the evils that you have committed.

If, before the ritual begins, the wife confesses, there will be no further punishment. The husband is free to divorce her. God, however, forgives His people if they will repent.

> Jeremiah 3:13-14 NKJV 13 Only acknowledge your iniquity, That you have transgressed against the LORD your God, And have scattered your charms To alien deities under every green tree, And you have not obeyed My voice,' says the LORD. 14 "Return, O backsliding children," says the LORD; "for I am married to you. I will take you, one from a city and two from a family, and I will bring you to Zion.

**B.** The priest uncovers the head of the wife.

> Numbers 5:18 NKJV 18 'Then the priest shall stand the woman before the LORD, uncover the woman's head, and put the offering for remembering in her hands, which is the grain offering of jealousy. And the priest shall have in his hand the bitter water that brings a curse.

The only place in the Torah that mentions uncovering the head is in connection with mourning. For the guilty, this judgment will result in death. For both innocent and guilty, it represents that all things will be revealed before God.

> Jeremiah 16:17 NKJV 17 "For My eyes are on all their ways; they are not hidden from My face, nor is their iniquity hidden from My eyes.

> Ecclesiastes 12:14 NKJV 14 For God will bring every work into judgment, Including every secret thing, Whether good or evil.

> Mark 4:22 NKJV 22 "For there is nothing hidden which will not be revealed, nor has anything been kept secret but that it should come to light.

If the wife is guilty, her iniquities will be revealed; she will be shamed in front of God and man. Yeshua suffered for our iniquities bearing our shame. A Psalm of David prophesies about this.

> Psalms 69:5-9 NKJV 5 O God, You know my foolishness; And my sins are not hidden from You. 6 Let not those who wait for You, O Lord GOD of hosts, be ashamed because of me; Let not those who seek You be confounded because of me, O God of Israel. 7 Because for Your sake I have borne reproach; Shame has covered my face. 8 I have become a stranger to my brothers, And an alien to my mother's children; 9 Because zeal for Your house has eaten me up, And the reproaches of those who reproach You have fallen on me.

> Romans 15:3 NKJV 3 For even Christ did not please Himself; but as it is written, "The reproaches of those who reproached You fell on Me."

**C.** The bitter water that brings a curse is at the heart of the ritual. The three things that make up the bitter water are holy water from the laver in the tabernacle, dust from the floor of the tabernacle and ink from the written words of the curse.

> Numbers 5:17 NKJV 17 'The priest shall take holy water in an earthen vessel, and take some of the dust that is on the floor of the tabernacle and put it into the water.

> Numbers 5:23 NKJV 23 'Then the priest shall write these curses in a book, and he shall scrape them off into the bitter water.

The water from the laver is the same water the priests used to wash their hands and feet to become ritually pure before appearing before the LORD. It was set apart for God's purposes. In this case it serves to emphasize that the judgment is from God. The dust from the tabernacle served the same purpose to emphasize the divine nature of the judgment. The priests served barefoot in the Tabernacle and the temple because the ground was holy ground. The dust along with the earthenware vessel in which the water was served was also a reminder of the wife's mortality.

> Genesis 3:19 NKJV 19 In the sweat of your face you shall eat bread Till you return to the ground, For out of it you were taken; For dust you are, And to dust you shall return."

We will examine the significance of the words of the curse a little later in the study. For now, we will turn our attention to other instances where God proved the fidelity of His people.

**D.** The incident at Mara is the first place where we see God test Israel with bitter water. After crossing the Red Sea, they traveled three days arriving at a place where there was only bitter water. With around two million people and all the livestock, this situation is desperate. The bitter water meant sure death.

> Exodus 15:23-26 NKJV 23 Now when they came to Marah, they could not drink the waters of Marah, for they were bitter. Therefore the name of it was called Marah. 24 And the people complained against Moses, saying, "What shall we drink?" 25 So he cried out to the LORD, and the LORD showed him a tree. When he cast it into the waters, the waters were made sweet. There He made a statute and an ordinance for them. And there He tested them, 26 and said, "If you diligently heed the voice of the LORD your God and do what is right in His sight, give ear to His commandments and keep all His statutes, I will put none of the diseases on you which I have brought on the Egyptians. For I am the LORD who heals you."

What is the test? What is the significance of the tree? The tree represents the cross of Yeshua. It makes the waters sweet providing life. Yeshua is the living water that we can drink from only because of His death and resurrection. The sages say the waters were bitter because of the bitterness that Israel brought with them out of Egypt due to the bitterness of their lives as slaves.

> Exodus 1:14 NKJV 14 And they made their lives bitter with hard bondage-in mortar, in brick, and in all manner of service in the field. All their service in which they made them serve was with rigor.

The question voiced in verse 24 is the test. "What shall they drink?" Will they drink the bitter water or the sweet? We can compare this to the test of fidelity of the wife. If she is faithful, then the bitter waters will be life giving. She will conceive and have children and her flesh will not rot away. If the Israelites will obey God, He will not put on them any of the plagues that He put on the Egyptians. He goes on to say that He will heal them. They will no longer carry the bitterness of their slavery in Egypt. On a deeper level, we see the offering of the living water through Yeshua who dies on the cross for them and for us which offers healing. For Yeshua, the water was bitter; for us, it is sweet.

> Isaiah 53:5 NKJV 5 But He was wounded for our transgressions, He was bruised for our iniquities; The chastisement for our peace was upon Him, And by His stripes we are healed.

**E.** The second place where God tests them with bitter waters is after the incident of the golden calf.

> Exodus 32:20 NKJV 20 Then he took the calf which they had made, burned it in the fire, and ground it to powder; and he scattered it on the water and made the children of Israel drink it.

The Bible doesn't tell us directly the consequences of having to drink the water but we can infer it from the test of fidelity. If they were guilty of worshipping the golden calf, that is committing adultery, their flesh would rot. If they were innocent, the water would not harm them. Further on in the chapter, God said He blotted out the names of the guilty and sent a plague as punishment.

> Exodus 32:33-35 NKJV 33 And the LORD said to Moses, "Whoever has sinned against Me, I will blot him out of My book. 34 "Now therefore, go, lead the people to the place of which I have spoken to you. Behold, My Angel shall go before you. Nevertheless, in the day when I visit for punishment, I will visit punishment upon them for their sin." 35 So the LORD plagued the people because of what they did with the calf which Aaron made.

So, those who were guilty failed the test of drinking the water and God sent judgment directly!

**F.** Mary, the mother of Yeshua could have been subjected to the ritual of the bitter waters. A betrothal was just as binding as a marriage and Mary was clearly guilty of adultery in man's eyes. But Joseph did not want to subject her to a public examination and was planning to put her aside as was his right. Instead, God revealed His judgment to Joseph.

> Matthew 1:18-20 NKJV 18 Now the birth of Jesus Christ was as follows: After His mother Mary was betrothed to Joseph, before they came together, she was found with child of the Holy Spirit. 19 Then Joseph her husband, being a just man, and not wanting to make her a public example, was minded to put her away secretly. 20 But while he thought about these things, behold, an angel of the Lord appeared to him in a dream, saying, "Joseph, son of David, do not be afraid to take to you Mary your wife, for that which is conceived in her is of the Holy Spirit.

Innocent until Proven Guilty

Even though Joseph chose not to bring Mary before the priests, God acted as if he had revealing the secrets of Mary's heart. As an added point, Mary's Hebrew name was Miriam which means bitter. The word picture reveals Miriam as the bitter water.

מרים  Miryam from #4805. מרי , mer-ee' from 4784; bitterness, i.e. (figuratively) rebellion; concretely, bitter, or rebellious:--bitter, (most) rebel(-lion, -lious).

> Hebrew Word  מרים מאירים הרטתניף
>
> מרי: Yood-Reysch-Mem: Mer-ee': bitter, bitternes
>
> מ : Mem: Water
>
> Miriam is bitter water.

Mary passed the test of the bitter waters. When Mary and Joseph brought Yeshua to the temple to present Him to God and to redeem Him according to the commandment, a prophet named Simeon met them.

> Luke 2:34-35 NKJV 34 Then Simeon blessed them, and said to Mary His mother, "Behold, this Child is destined for the fall and rising of many in Israel, and for a sign which will be spoken against 35 "(yes, a sword will pierce through your own soul also), that the thoughts of many hearts may be revealed."

Simeon prophesied about both Yeshua and Mary. The words about Yeshua call to mind the words of Psalm 69 that we read earlier, "The reproaches of those who reproached You fell on Me." Simeon says this occurs so "that the thoughts of many hearts may be revealed." To Mary, he says that she will also taste of the bitterness of his crucifixion. She, as Yeshua's mother, experienced in part, the bitterness that Yeshua experienced.

G. Yeshua went through this ritual symbolically proving Himself and us faithful to God. We read of Yeshua's inner agony as the hour of his crucifixion approaches.

> Matthew 26:37-39 NKJV 37 And He took with Him Peter and the two sons of Zebedee, and He began to be sorrowful and deeply distressed. 38 Then He said to them, "My soul is exceedingly sorrowful, even to death. Stay here and watch with Me." 39 He went a little farther and fell on His face, and prayed, saying, "O My Father, if it is possible, let this cup pass from Me; nevertheless, not as I will, but as You will."

Yeshua shows His faithfulness to God by His obedience to God's will.

> Hebrews 3:5-6 NIV 5 Moses was faithful as a servant in all God's house, testifying to what would be said in the future. 6 But Christ is faithful as a son over God's

house. And we are his house, if we hold on to our courage and the hope of which we boast.

At Mara, God tested the Israelites by telling them to heed the voice of God and do what is right in God's sight. This is what Yeshua did proving His faithfulness to God. Just before He dies, Yeshua is given a cup of bitter wine and immediately dies.

> John 19:30 NKJV 30 So when Jesus had received the sour wine, He said, "It is finished!" And bowing His head, He gave up His spirit.

He drank of the bitter wine and God's judgment fell on Him for our adulteries against God.

**H.** We said earlier that the cup of bitter water that causes a curse contained holy water, dust from the tabernacle and ink from the curse. What exactly was written in the curse that was in the cup? To the guilty, the curse brought rotting of the flesh.

> Numbers 5:20-22 NKJV 20 "But if you have gone astray while under your husband's authority, and if you have defiled yourself and some man other than your husband has lain with you" - 21 'then the priest shall put the woman under the oath of the curse, and he shall say to the woman-"the LORD make you a curse and an oath among your people, when the LORD makes your thigh rot and your belly swell; 22 "and may this water that causes the curse go into your stomach, and make your belly swell and your thigh rot." Then the woman shall say, "Amen, so be it."

The curse makes the thigh rot. The thigh is a euphemism for the reproductive organs. We see this usage when Abraham has his servant swear by placing his hand "under his thigh" not to take Isaac out of the Promised Land.

> Genesis 24:2-3 NKJV 2 So Abraham said to the oldest servant of his house, who ruled over all that he had, "Please, put your hand under my thigh, 3 "and I will make you swear by the LORD, the God of heaven and the God of the earth, that you will not take a wife for my son from the daughters of the Canaanites, among whom I dwell;

The servant swore by Abraham's progeny that he would do as Abraham commanded. So, the curse starts by destroying the woman's ability to have children.

In contrast, if the woman was innocent, she would have children. The sages elaborate on this and say that not only will she have children, she will have an easy time bearing children and that the child would be physically perfect.

> Numbers 5:28 NKJV 28 'But if the woman has not defiled herself, and is clean, then she shall be free and may conceive children.

Innocent until Proven Guilty

Having children is a further testimony of her faithfulness. We see again that Mary passed the test for faithfulness. God blessed her with at least four other sons, James, Joses, Simon and Judas, as well as daughters.

But, perhaps the most significant part of the curse is that God's name, Yah-weh, is written in the curse twice. It is washed, along with the other words of the curse, off the parchment and into the water. Literally, the priest blots out the words.

> Numbers 5:23 KJV 23 And the priest shall write these curses in a book, and he shall blot them out with the bitter water:

Blot: #4229. מחה machah, maw-khaw' a primitive root; properly, to stroke or rub; by implication, to erase;--abolish, blot out, destroy, full of marrow, put out, reach unto, X utterly, wipe (away, out).

God is willing to have His name blotted out in order for a wife to prove her faithfulness to her husband, in order to restore peace and trust to the relationship. When the Israelites sinned by making and worshipping the golden calf, God said He would destroy them in His wrath and establish a nation from Moses. But Moses pleads on behalf of the Israelites.

> Exodus 32:32 NKJV 32 "Yet now, if You will forgive their sin-but if not, I pray, blot me out of Your book which You have written."

Moses was willing to have his name blotted out in order to bring forgiveness to Israel. Paul was also willing to drink of the bitter waters that cause a curse to bring more of his fellow Jews to know Christ.

> Romans 9:1-3 NKJV 1 I tell the truth in Christ, I am not lying, my conscience also bearing me witness in the Holy Spirit, 2 that I have great sorrow and continual grief in my heart. 3 For I could wish that I myself were accursed from Christ for my brethren, my countrymen according to the flesh,

Because Yeshua drank of the cup, God counts us as innocent, as faithful.

> Galatians 3:13 NKJV 13 Christ has redeemed us from the curse of the law, having become a curse for us (for it is written, "Cursed is everyone who hangs on a tree"),

We know that this scripture refers to the manner of Yeshua's death but if we look at it in the context of the bitter water at Mara, we see that it says the same thing in another way. His death on the tree makes our bitter water sweet. Instead of death, we are blessed with fruitfulness and the love of God. The tree that Moses threw into the bitter water made the water sweet!

The offering brought for the remembrance of iniquity is an offering of barley. Barley is the offering brought at the Feast of Firstfruits during the Feast of Unleavened Bread. The first sheaf of barley is cut and threshed during the time that Yeshua was in the grave. Yeshua says that He is the barley offering of the Feast of Firstfruits.

> John 12:24 NIV 24 I tell you the truth, unless a kernel of wheat falls to the ground and dies, it remains only a single seed. But if it dies, it produces many seeds.

This verse appears to say that Yeshua compares Himself to a kernel of wheat but the word for wheat is sitos which is a generic word for grain.

#4621. σιτoω sitos, see'-tos of uncertain derivation; grain

These words of Yeshua were also spoken at the time of the Passover when the barley harvest is just beginning, so He is most likely referring to Himself as the kernel of barley. Yeshua, then, is the barley offering brought for the remembrance of iniquity.

In an offering, the blood or smoke ascends to God bringing the offering into God's presence. Yeshua as the offering and the offerer is both the one who accuses and intercedes. All judgment has been entrusted to His hands.

> John 5:22 NKJV 22 "For the Father judges no one, but has committed all judgment to the Son,

The offering for the remembrance of iniquity no longer brings our sins to remembrance; they died with Yeshua.

> Romans 6:6 NKJV 6 knowing this, that our old man was crucified with Him, that the body of sin might be done away with, that we should no longer be slaves of sin.

> Isaiah 43:25 NKJV 25 "I, even I, am He who blots out your transgressions for My own sake; And I will not remember your sins.

> Psalms 103:12 NKJV 12 As far as the east is from the west, So far has He removed our transgressions from us.

We can be confident on the Day of Judgment that we will be judged worthy. Yeshua's sacrifice is sufficient to cleanse us of all our iniquities.

> Psalms 19:12-13 NKJV 12 Who can understand his errors? Cleanse me from secret faults. 13 Keep back Your servant also from presumptuous sins; Let them not have dominion over me. Then I shall be blameless, And I shall be innocent of great transgression.

Paul puts his entire faith in the judgment of the LORD. Let us be like Paul and rest in the confidence we have in Yeshua our Messiah.

1 Corinthians 4:1-5 NKJV 1 Let a man so consider us, as servants of Christ and stewards of the mysteries of God. 2 Moreover it is required in stewards that one be found faithful. 3 But with me it is a very small thing that I should be judged by you or by a human court. In fact, I do not even judge myself. 4 For I know nothing against myself, yet I am not justified by this; but He who judges me is the Lord. 5 Therefore judge nothing before the time, until the Lord comes, who will both bring to light the hidden things of darkness and reveal the counsels of the hearts. Then each one's praise will come from God.

# Student Notes Innocent until Proven Guilty
Numbers 5:11-31

God judges the woman guilty only if the man himself is innocent of transgression. (Nu. 5:31)

We will look at three layers of meaning within this passage:
First: God describes his relationship with Israel as that of a husband and wife. (Exo. 20:4-5)

Second: Yeshua takes on all our sins and punishments.

Third: Paul describes the assembly of believers as the bride of Christ. (2Cor. 5:10)

**A.** God is the one who judges. (Num 5:15, Eze. 20:36-38, Eze. 20:43, Jer. 3:13-14)

**B.** The priest uncovers the head of the wife. (Num. 5:18, Jer. 16:17, Ecc. 12:14, Mark 4:22, Psa. 69:5-9, Rom. 15:3)

**C.** The bitter water that brings a curse is at the heart of the ritual. (Num. 5:17, 23, Gen. 3:19)

Student Notes for Innocent until Proven Guilty

**D.** The incident at Mara is the first place where we see God test Israel with bitter water. (Exo. 15:23-26, Exo. 1:14, Isa. 53:5)

**E.** The second place where God tests them with bitter waters is after the incident of the golden calf. (Exo. 32:20, Exo. 32:33-35)

**F.** Mary, the mother of Yeshua could have been subjected the ritual of the bitter water. (Mat. 1:18-20)

מרים Miryam from #4805. מרי , mer-ee' from 4784; bitterness, i.e. (figuratively) rebellion; concretely, bitter, or rebellious:--bitter, (most) rebel(-lion, -lious).

> Hebrew Word Picture: Miriam מרים
>
> מרי: Yood-Reysch-Mem: Mer-ee': bitter, bitternes
>
> מ : Mem: Water
>
> Miriam is bitter water.

Bitterness experienced by Yeshua and Mary: (Luke 2:34-35)

Student Notes for Innocent until Proven Guilty

**G.** Yeshua went through this ritual symbolically proving Himself and us faithful to God. (Mat. 26:37-39, Heb. 3:5-6, John 19:30)

**H.** What exactly was written in the curse that was in the cup? (Num. 5:20-22, Gen. 24:2-3, Num. 5:28)

The most significant part of the curse is that God's name, Yah-weh, is in it twice. (Num. 5:23, Ex. 32:32, Rom. 9:1-3, Gal. 3:13)

Blot: #4229. מחה machah, maw-khaw' a primitive root; properly, to stroke or rub; by implication, to erase;--abolish, blot out, destroy, full of marrow, put out, reach unto, X utterly, wipe (away, out).

The offering brought for the remembrance of iniquity is an offering of barley. (John 12:24, John 5:22)

#4621. σιτοω sitos, see'-tos of uncertain derivation; grain

The offering brought for the remembrance of iniquity no longer brings our sins to remembrance. (Rom. 6:6, Isa. 43:25, Psa. 103:12, Psa. 19:12-13)

Paul puts his entire faith in the judgment of the LORD. (1Cor. 4:1-5)

Student Notes for Innocent until Proven Guilty

**Discussion Questions for Innocent Until Proven Guilty**

1. In the millennium, the water that flows from the temple brings life. In what circumstances will the water that the woman drinks bring life?

2. God told the Israelites when they went into the Promised Land that they were to blot out the names of the pagan gods but not to do so with the name of God. Yet God willingly blots out His name to establish the innocence of a wife. Discuss the importance God places on the marriage relationship. Since we are the bride of Messiah, how important is our relationship with Messiah to God?

3. The third trumpet judgment turns one-third of the water on Earth bitter. Read Revelation 9:10-11. Compare this to the trial by bitter water.

4. Joseph's Egyptian name, Zaphenath-Paneah, means revealer of secrets. Read about Joseph's encounters with his brothers in Egypt in Genesis 42:20-24 and Genesis 44:14-45:5. How did Joseph look into the hearts of his brothers revealing their secrets? What verdict did he reach?

5. The bitter water could bring death or life with the blessing of many children. Torah is compared to water that flows from heaven to earth. Read Romans 7:7-8:11. How is Torah like the bitter water? Why was it necessary that Yeshua drank the bitter water in our place?

6. What are the elements of the bitter water? Are they holy or profane (common)? How is this like Torah?

# Grace and Truth in the Torah

In the gospel of John, John seems to contrast the law or Torah with grace and truth.

> John 1:17 KJV 17 For the law was given by Moses, but grace and truth came by Jesus Christ.

What we don't see is that the word "but" was not in the Greek manuscripts; it is added to make the sentence flow smoothly. Without the word "but," the sentence doesn't quite make sense; the initial word "For" needs a contrast. The problem, then, is with the word translated "for." It is the Greek word #3754 οτι hoti hot'-ee neuter of #3748 as conjunction; demonstrative, that; causative, because. Hoti is a conjunctive indicating cause not contrast. This verse should start with the word "because." If we look at a couple of other Greek words, we see even deeper into this verse.

By: #1223. δια dia, dee-ah' a primary preposition denoting the channel of an act; through

Came: 1096. γινομαι ginomai, ghin'-om-ahee a prolongation and middle voice form of a primary verb; to cause to be ("gen"-erate), i.e. (reflexively) to become (come into being)

The literal translation then of John 1:17 is, "Because the law through the channel of Moses was given, grace and truth through the channel Jesus Christ came into being."

There is not a contrast here; there is a cause and effect! So, how does giving the Law through Moses bring about grace and truth through Yeshua? John goes on to point to the very passage in which this occurs. The next verse says that only the Son has seen the Father and the Son is the one who declares Him.

> John 1:18 NKJV 18 No one has seen God at any time. The only begotten Son, who is in the bosom of the Father, He has declared Him.

Wait a minute! Didn't Moses see God? Let's go back to that passage in Exodus where God declares His name to Moses and we will see a surprising connection. We will see that John 1:14-18 is a direct reference to Exodus 33:1 through Exodus 34:9. We've already read verses 17 and 18 in John 1; verses 14 through 16 are about Yeshua's glory, grace and truth, His pre-existence, and that by His fullness we receive grace upon grace.

> John 1:14-18 NKJV 14 And the Word became flesh and dwelt among us, and we beheld His glory, the glory as of the only begotten of the Father, full of grace and truth. 15 John bore witness of Him and cried out, saying, "This was He of whom I said, 'He who comes after me is preferred before me, for He was before me.'" 16 And of His fullness we have all received, and grace for grace.

The passage in Exodus 33:1 to 34:9 takes place after the sin of the golden calf when only God's grace can save them. God had already given the children of Israel the Ten Commandments and the people had accepted them. They had a covenant ratification ceremony with offerings of bulls on the altar and blood sprinkled on the congregation and on the altar. The only thing left to accomplish was for Moses to bring back the Tablets with the Ten Commandments written on them, the signed contract.

But the people, by the hand of Aaron, the one whom Moses left in charge, built a carved image of a calf and called it God. By the letter of the commandments, the people's lives were forfeit. They broke the commandment.

> Exodus 20:4-5 NKJV 4 "You shall not make for yourself a carved image, or any likeness of anything that is in heaven above, or that is in the earth beneath, or that is in the water under the earth; 5 you shall not bow down to them nor serve them. For I, the LORD your God, am a jealous God, visiting the iniquity of the fathers on the children to the third and fourth generations of those who hate Me …

If all that Moses accomplished was to bring the law, Israel would have been finished right here. In fact, God said He would kill them all off and make Moses into a great nation.

> Exodus 32:9-10 KJV 9 And the LORD said unto Moses, I have seen this people, and, behold, it is a stiffnecked people: 10 Now therefore let me alone, that my wrath may wax hot against them, and that I may consume them: and I will make of thee a great nation.

How did Israel know that they had sinned? It was in the Commandments that they had just agreed to follow forty days earlier. Paul says that the law or Torah brings knowledge of sin.

> Romans 3:20 NKJV 20 Therefore by the deeds of the law no flesh will be justified in His sight, for by the law is the knowledge of sin.

Through Moses bringing the Law, people are now aware of their sins. But even in the Law, there is provision for unintentional sins against God. In fact, we will see that the promise of mercy is in the Law from the beginning! Moses was God's chosen channel through which He revealed His law and His mercy.

Moses didn't intercede on the behalf of the children of Israel based on their deserving forgiveness or on their works, but instead, Moses interceded based on God's promise to Abraham, Isaac and Israel to give them the Land.

> Exodus 32:13 NKJV 13 "Remember Abraham, Isaac, and Israel, Your servants, to whom You swore by Your own self, and said to them, 'I will multiply your descendants as the stars of heaven; and all this land that I have spoken of I give to your descendants, and they shall inherit it forever.'"

Abraham received these promises through obedience in faith.

> Genesis 26:4-5 NKJV 4 "And I will make your descendants multiply as the stars of heaven; I will give to your descendants all these lands; and in your seed all the nations of the earth shall be blessed; 5 "because Abraham obeyed My voice and kept My charge, My commandments, My statutes, and My laws."

Notice that even before Moses brought the Law, Abraham knew and followed them! He knew all God's commandments, statutes and laws. Abraham obeyed because of his faith.

> Hebrews 11:8-9 NKJV 8 By faith Abraham obeyed when he was called to go out to the place which he would receive as an inheritance. And he went out, not knowing where he was going. 9 By faith he dwelt in the land of promise as in a foreign country, dwelling in tents with Isaac and Jacob, the heirs with him of the same promise;

So, based on His own promises, God relented and promised to send His angel or messenger along with them.

> Exodus 33:1-2 NKJV 1 Then the LORD said to Moses, "Depart and go up from here, you and the people whom you have brought out of the land of Egypt, to the land of which I swore to Abraham, Isaac, and Jacob, saying, 'To your descendants I will give it.' 2 "And I will send My Angel before you, and I will drive out the Canaanite and the Amorite and the Hittite and the Perizzite and the Hivite and the Jebusite.

That was good, but Moses wasn't satisfied. He wanted to know just who this angel was that God was going to send with them.

> Exodus 33:12-13 NKJV 12 Then Moses said to the LORD, "See, You say to me, 'Bring up this people.' But You have not let me know whom You will send with me. Yet You have said, 'I know you by name, and you have also found grace in My sight.' 13 "Now therefore, I pray, if I have found grace (chen) in Your sight, show me now Your way, that I may know You and that I may find grace (chen) in Your sight. And consider (ra-ah) that this nation is Your people."

As we dig deeper into verse 13, we see that Moses wants to understand what God is doing. Notice how Moses uses God's grace as the reason for his request wanting to know God's "way." The word translated "way" is "derek" which means road or mode of action. The word translated "consider" is "ra'ah" meaning to see or provide. This word "ra'ah" is the root word for the name Yehovah Yireh in Genesise 22:14. This is the name of the place where Abraham offered up Isaac and means Yehovah provides. And the word translated "grace" is "chen" which comes from the word "chanan" meaning to stoop in kindness.

#1870. דרך derek, deh'-rek from 1869; a road (as trodden); figuratively, a course of life or mode of action

#7200. ראה ra'ah, raw-aw' a primitive root; to see, provide

Grace and Truth in the Torah

#2603. חנן chanan, khaw-nan' a primitive root (compare 2583); properly, to bend or stoop in kindness to an inferior; to favor, bestow

Moses asks that, since God has chosen to stoop in kindness to him, He would also show him His mode of action. Moses wants to know not only what God is doing but why He is doing it. In the broad picture, Moses wants to know God better and find further favor with Him. More specifically, he wants to know who God is sending with them. He finishes by reminding God once again to consider, that is to see or provide, that the children of Israel are His people.

God responds with an incredible outpouring of who He is starting with the revelation that the angel that will go with them is the Angel of His Presence.

> Exodus 33:14 NKJV 14 And He said, "My Presence will go with you, and I will give you rest."

In answer to Moses' question, "Whom will you send with us," God said He would send the Angel of His presence. In answer to Moses' request that God see to it that the children of Israel are His people, God says He will give Moses rest.

Just who is the Angel of God's presence? Earlier in Exodus, God revealed more about this Angel.

> Exodus 23:20-23 NKJV 20 "Behold, I send an Angel before you to keep you in the way and to bring you into the place which I have prepared. 21 "Beware of Him and obey His voice; do not provoke Him, for He will not pardon your transgressions; for My name is in Him. 22 "But if you indeed obey His voice and do all that I speak, then I will be an enemy to your enemies and an adversary to your adversaries. 23 "For My Angel will go before you and bring you in to the Amorites and the Hittites and the Perizzites and the Canaanites and the Hivites and the Jebusites; and I will cut them off.

This is the Angel who stood between Israel and Pharaoh's army. God's name is in Him and He has the power to forgive or withhold forgiveness for their sins. The Angel of God's presence is a pre-incarnate Yeshua who was with them as they crossed the Red Sea and continued to go with them as He led them into the Promised Land. This is what Moses wanted to know. He wanted to know that God would go with them, not just an angel, but the actual presence of God!

This is all good, but the word "you" in Exodus 33:14 is in the singular. God told Moses He would go with him and give him rest. Moses tells God that if He doesn't go with all of them, then not to bother taking them up to the Promised Land. It is only by God's presence with His people that His people are separate from the nations. Again, God reassures Moses that He will go with all of them. Moses then takes it one step further and asks God to show him His glory. This is where it really gets interesting.

Grace and Truth in the Torah

> Exodus 33:19-23 NKJV 19 Then He said, "I will make all My goodness pass before you, and I will proclaim the name of the LORD before you. I will be gracious (chanan) to whom I will be gracious (chanan), and I will have compassion (racham) on whom I will have compassion (racham)." 20 But He said, "You cannot see My face; for no man shall see Me, and live." 21 And the LORD said, "Here is a place by Me, and you shall stand on the rock. 22 "So it shall be, while My glory passes by, that I will put you in the cleft of the rock, and will cover you with My hand while I pass by. 23 "Then I will take away My hand, and you shall see My back; but My face shall not be seen."

In the first phrase of this passage, God again uses the word chanan, to stoop in kindness. He then takes His grace with Moses one step further and states He will have compassion on whom He will have compassion. The word translated "compassion" is "racham" meaning to fondle or love. The Hebrew word for womb comes from this same word.

#7355. רחם racham, raw-kham' a primitive root; to fondle; by implication, to love, especially to compassionate

#7358. רחם rechem, rekh'-em from 7355; the womb

God will not only stoop down and show kindness to His people, He will love them as a mother loves the child of her womb. How does God show His love, His racham for us?

> John 1:12-13 NKJV 12 But as many as received Him, to them He gave the right to become children of God, to those who believe in His name: 13 who were born, not of blood, nor of the will of the flesh, nor of the will of man, but of God.

God wills to adopt us into His family and consider or see to it that we are His children! He shows us racham.

Here is where the words of Yeshua in the gospel of John connect. Yeshua said that no one sees the Father except Him and that He is the one who declares that Father. Further, John said that Yeshua is the glory of the Father.

> John 1:14 NKJV 14 And the Word became flesh and dwelt among us, and we beheld His glory, the glory as of the only begotten of the Father, full of grace and truth.

Yeshua's glory, the glory of the Father, is full of grace and truth. He is the Angel of God's Presence with the children of Israel in the wilderness! He is one with the Father; He is the one declaring the name of the LORD to Moses in the wilderness!

John said that he had seen the glory of the Son of God. He along with Peter and his brother James saw Yeshua transfigured before them.

> Matthew 17:1-5 NKJV 1 Now after six days Jesus took Peter, James, and John his brother, led them up on a high mountain by themselves; 2 and He was transfigured before them. His face shone like the sun, and His clothes became as white as the light. 3 And behold, Moses and Elijah appeared to them, talking with Him. 4 Then Peter answered and said to Jesus, "Lord, it is good for us to be here; if You wish, let us make here three tabernacles: one for You, one for Moses, and one for Elijah." 5 While he was still speaking, behold, a bright cloud overshadowed them; and suddenly a voice came out of the cloud, saying, "This is My beloved Son, in whom I am well pleased. **Hear Him**!"

This event also took place on a high mountain. The cloud of God's presence descended and a voice out of the cloud spoke. Now, look at what Moses does next. Moses was to cut two new tablets of stone and present himself to God on Mt. Sinai.

> Exodus 34:4-5 NKJV 4 So he cut two tablets of stone like the first ones. Then Moses rose early in the morning and went up Mount Sinai, as the LORD had commanded him; and he took in his hand the two tablets of stone. 5 Now the LORD descended in the cloud and stood with him there, and proclaimed the name of the LORD.

The voice of God declared the name of Yehovah to Moses. At Yeshua's transfiguration, the voice declared that Yeshua was the prophet like Moses whose voice they are to hear.

> Deuteronomy 18:15 NKJV 15 "The LORD your God will raise up for you a Prophet like me from your midst, from your brethren. **Him you shall hear**,

> Deuteronomy 18:18 NKJV 18 'I will raise up for them a Prophet like you from among their brethren, and will put My words in His mouth, and **He shall speak to them all that I command Him.**

The word "hear" is the Hebrew word "Sh'ma" which means to hear and obey not just to hear.

#8085. שמע shama`, shaw-mah' a primitive root; to hear intelligently (often with implication of attention, obedience

Peter, James, and John heard that Yeshua was the prophet like Moses who would speak all that God commanded Him to speak. Moses heard the proclamation of the name of Yehovah. These are Yeshua's words since He is the only one who has seen the Father and He declares His name! These are the words of grace and truth that came into being through Yeshua because Moses brought God's law.

> Exodus 34:6-7 NKJV 6 And the LORD passed before him and proclaimed, "The LORD, the LORD God, merciful and gracious, longsuffering, and abounding in goodness and truth, 7 "keeping mercy for thousands, forgiving iniquity and transgression and sin, by no means clearing the guilty, visiting the iniquity of the

fathers upon the children and the children's children to the third and the fourth generation."

God starts by proclaiming His name Yehovah twice. In Hebrew, when a word is repeated, it serves to emphasize that word, to communicate intensity. In English, we add adjectives or adverbs such as "very," "surely," or "diligently" to add emphasis. When we encounter these adjectives or adverbs as we read scripture, we can be fairly certain that the Hebrew contains a double word. For example, at the end of Genesis when Joseph is speaking to the children of Israel, he says that God will surely visit them. The words translated "surely visit" are from a repetition of the word "paqad" meaning to visit. Literally, the phrase would read, "God will visiting visit you."

So, this repetition of God's name serves to emphasize that He alone is God; there is no other. This passage, is in fact an emphasis of an earlier passage in which God declared His name and that He alone is God. Just forty days earlier, God came down in the presence of all the people and spoke His ten Words beginning with the statement, "I am the LORD your God."

> Exodus 20:1-6 NKJV 1 And God spoke all these words, saying: 2 "I am the LORD your God, who brought you out of the land of Egypt, out of the house of bondage. 3 "You shall have no other gods before Me. 4 "You shall not make for yourself a carved image, or any likeness of anything that is in heaven above, or that is in the earth beneath, or that is in the water under the earth; 5 you shall not bow down to them nor serve them. For I, the LORD your God, am a jealous God, visiting the iniquity of the fathers on the children to the third and fourth generations of those who hate Me, 6 but showing mercy to thousands, to those who love Me and keep My commandments.

Remember the context of God declaring His name in the Exodus 34 passage is that the children of Israel built a graven image and called it LORD.

> Exodus 32:4-5 NKJV 4 And he received the gold from their hand, and he fashioned it with an engraving tool, and made a molded calf. Then they said, "This is your god, O Israel, that brought you out of the land of Egypt!" 5 So when Aaron saw it, he built an altar before it. And Aaron made a proclamation and said, "Tomorrow is a feast to the LORD."

Aaron's words are a direct violation of God's Words in which He spoke to them about who He is and how they were to live in relationship with Him. God pronounced judgment on them but, through the intercession of Moses, God forgave them. Let's look at a direct comparison of these two passages.

Grace and Truth in the Torah

| Exodus 34 | Exodus 20 |
|---|---|
| The LORD, the LORD God… | I am the LORD your God, who brought you out of the land of Egypt, out of the house of bondage. You shall have no other gods before Me. |
| …merciful and gracious, longsuffering, and abounding in goodness (checed) and truth, 7 "keeping mercy (checed) for thousands, forgiving iniquity and transgression and sin | …showing mercy (checed) to thousands, to those who love Me and keep My commandments. |
| … by no means clearing the guilty, visiting the iniquity of the fathers upon the children and the children's children to the third and the fourth generation." | …visiting the iniquity of the fathers on the children to the third and fourth generations of those who hate Me |

In Exodus 34, the word translated goodness is the same Hebrew word in Exodus 20 that is translated mercy. This Hebrew word is checed which is most frequently translated as kindness or loving kindness.

#2617. חסד checed, kheh'-sed from 2616; kindness; by implication (towards God) piety: favour, good deed(-liness, -ness), kindly, (loving-)kindness, merciful (kindness), mercy, pity.

It comes from a word meaning to bow the neck as to an equal.

#2616. חסד chacad, khaw-sad' a primitive root; properly, perhaps to bow (the neck only in courtesy to an equal)

It holds the connotation of upholding an agreement, showing respect. For example, when God destroyed Sodom, He spared Lot, not based on Lot's righteousness, but based on His promise to Abraham.

> Genesis 19:29 NKJV 29 And it came to pass, when God destroyed the cities of the plain, that God remembered Abraham, and sent Lot out of the midst of the overthrow, when He overthrew the cities in which Lot had dwelt.

Lot knew this and pleaded with God on this basis to allow him to flee to another city.

> Genesis 19:19 NKJV 19 "Indeed now, your servant has found favor in your sight, and you have increased your mercy (checed) which you have shown me by saving my life; but I cannot escape to the mountains, lest some evil overtake me and I die.

When the spies that Joshua sent out to Jericho took refuge in Rehab's house, she asked them to spare her based on her actions of sparing them.

Grace and Truth in the Torah

> Joshua 2:12-14 NKJV 12 "Now therefore, I beg you, swear to me by the LORD, since I have shown you kindness (checed), that you also will show kindness (checed) to my father's house, and give me a true token, 13 "and spare my father, my mother, my brothers, my sisters, and all that they have, and deliver our lives from death." 14 So the men answered her, "Our lives for yours, if none of you tell this business of ours. And it shall be, when the LORD has given us the land, that we will deal kindly (checed) and truly with you."

In this passage, the understanding of kindly would be "according to our agreement with respect." We also see that this word checed is paired with the word truth or "emet." Emet means truth as reality or certainty as opposed to something that is artificial or not real.

#571. אמת 'emeth, eh'-meth contracted from 539; stability; (figuratively) certainty, truth, trustworthiness:--assured(-ly), establishment, faithful, right, sure, true (-ly, -th), verity

We see this pairing again when Jacob is about to die and seeks Joseph's promise to bury him in the Promised Land.

> Genesis 47:29 NKJV 29 When the time drew near that Israel must die, he called his son Joseph and said to him, "Now if I have found favor in your sight, please put your hand under my thigh, and deal kindly (checed) and truly with me. Please do not bury me in Egypt,

In the declaration of God's name, God says He is abounding in goodness (checed) and truth. In respect to God, this word checed can be viewed as covenant devotion. In Exodus 34:7, God goes onto say that He keeps mercy (checed) for thousands of generations. The word "keeps" is from the Hebrew word "natzar" meaning to guard and protect.

#5341. נצר natsar, naw-tsar' a primitive root; to guard, in a good sense (to protect, maintain, obey, etc.) observe, preserve(-r)

God will guard and protect His mercy, kindness, and covenant devotion for thousands of generations to those who love Him. When the children of Israel were getting ready to enter the Promised Land forty years later, Moses summarized God's actions over those forty years. He pairs God's covenant keeping nature with His mercy (checed) that He keeps for thousands of generations.

> Deuteronomy 7:9 NKJV 9 "Therefore know that the LORD your God, He is God, the faithful God who keeps covenant and mercy (checed) for a thousand generations with those who love Him and keep His commandments;

God extends that mercy to those who love Him and keep His commandments. There is an implied contrast that mercy will not be extended to those who don't love Him or keep His commandments. In the Exodus 34 passage, God says that He won't clear the guilty. In the original declaration of His name in Exodus 20, God says that those who are not cleared are those who hate him. To those who do not repent, who continue in their rebellion and hatred of God, their iniquity lingers into the third and fourth generation. It seems unfair to us that God would visit the iniquity onto the children but that is the nature of iniquity. Children of child abusers tend to be child abusers; children of those who do evil tend to do evil themselves. But if any children of those generations love God and keep His commands, God will keep mercy for them.

David understood this concept well. In Psalm 25, he, like Moses, asked God to show him His way. Like Moses, he wanted God and no one else to lead him. God's mercy is not a new thing; it is from of old!

> Psalms 25:1-10 NKJV 1 <<A Psalm of David.>> To You, O LORD, I lift up my soul. 2 O my God, I trust in You; Let me not be ashamed; Let not my enemies triumph over me. 3 Indeed, let no one who waits on You be ashamed; Let those be ashamed who deal treacherously without cause. 4 Show me Your ways, O LORD; Teach me Your paths. 5 Lead me in Your truth and teach me, For You are the God of my salvation; On You I wait all the day. 6 Remember, O LORD, Your tender mercies and Your lovingkindnesses (checed), For they are from of old. 7 Do not remember the sins of my youth, nor my transgressions; According to Your mercy (checed) remember me, For Your goodness' sake, O LORD. 8 Good and upright is the LORD; Therefore He teaches sinners in the way. 9 The humble He guides in justice, And the humble He teaches His way. 10 All the paths of the LORD are mercy (checed) and truth, To such as keep His covenant and His testimonies.

God has mercy on those who are humble and repent. He doesn't leave them in their sin but teaches them His way. This is that word "derek" again meaning road, path, course of life. And all the paths of the LORD are of covenant devotion and certainty.

After hearing the name of Yehovah, Moses bowed and worshipped Yehovah. He then reminds God of God's own words about the Israelites after they had sinned with the golden calf.

> Exodus 34:8-9 NKJV 8 So Moses made haste and bowed his head toward the earth, and worshiped. 9 Then he said, "If now I have found grace (chen) in Your sight, O Lord, let my Lord, I pray, go among us, even though we are a stiff-necked people; and pardon our iniquity and our sin, and take us as Your inheritance."

We see here the incredible revelation of God's mercy, grace and forgiveness. Even though they are a stiff-necked people, God chooses to forgive. This is the righteousness of God; that He keeps mercy for all those who love Him even though we have sinned.

> Romans 3:21-24 NKJV 21 But now the righteousness of God apart from the law is revealed, being witnessed by the Law and the Prophets, 22 even the righteousness of God, through faith in Jesus Christ, to all and on all who believe. For there is no difference; 23 for all have sinned and fall short of the glory of God, 24 being justified freely by His grace through the redemption that is in Christ Jesus,

Grace and Truth in the Torah

All Israel had sinned and fallen short of God's glory; this is the glory demonstrated in the cloud that descended on both Moses and Yeshua. And this glory declared Yehovah's name of grace and truth. Does this then nullify the Torah or the law? Paul answers this question.

> Romans 3:31 NKJV 31 Do we then make void the law through faith? Certainly not! On the contrary, we establish the law.

Again, we look to the words of David in Psalm 25. He writes that because God is good and upright, He teaches sinners His way.

The next words God speaks to Moses in Exodus 34 are a reiteration of the covenant! God has not cast aside His people nor has He changed His standards! When Moses went up Mt. Sinai, God told him to carve out and bring two stone tablets. Now He tells Moses what to carve on those tablets.

> Exodus 34:27-28 NKJV 27 Then the LORD said to Moses, "Write these words, for according to the tenor of these words I have made a covenant with you and with Israel." 28 So he was there with the LORD forty days and forty nights; he neither ate bread nor drank water. And He wrote on the tablets the words of the covenant, the Ten Commandments.

God writes the same commandments on the second set of tablets. Moses then brings the tablets down the mountain; they were a replacement for the tablets that Moses broke when he saw the behavior of the Israelites with the golden calf. God forgave their iniquity and their sin and restored the Commandments; He didn't do away with the commandments! Should the Israelites build another golden calf and worship it so God could have grace on them again? Paul poses this very question to the believers in Rome.

> Romans 6:1-2 KJV 1 What shall we say then? Shall we continue in sin, that grace may abound? 2 God forbid. How shall we, that are dead to sin, live any longer therein?

Yeshua tells His followers, "If you love me, keep my commandments." Obedience follows faith.

When Moses came down the mountain, his face shone with the glory of God.

> Exodus 34:29-30 NKJV 29 Now it was so, when Moses came down from Mount Sinai (and the two tablets of the Testimony were in Moses' hand when he came down from the mountain), that Moses did not know that the skin of his face shone while he talked with Him. 30 So when Aaron and all the children of Israel saw Moses, behold, the skin of his face shone, and they were afraid to come near him.

When Yeshua was transfigured on the high mountain, Matthew recorded that "His face shone like the sun, and His clothes became as white as the light."

Isaiah writes of Yeshua, the Angel of God's Presence. He is our salvation and redeemer.

> Isaiah 63:7-9 NKJV 7 I will mention the lovingkindnesses (checed) of the LORD And the praises of the LORD, According to all that the LORD has bestowed on us, And the great goodness toward the house of Israel, Which He has bestowed on them according to His mercies (racham), According to the multitude of His lovingkindnesses (checed). 8 For He said, "Surely they are My people, Children who will not lie." So He became their Savior. 9 In all their affliction He was afflicted, And the Angel of His Presence saved them; In His love and in His pity He redeemed them; And He bore them and carried them All the days of old.

He bestows His checed, His covenant devotion, on Israel according the certainty of His adoption of them (racham) as His people.

Here in the midst of the Torah, God revealed the Angel of His Presence, a pre-incarnate Yeshua full of grace and truth, their redeemer and savior. "Because the law through Moses was given, grace and truth through Jesus Christ came into being."

# Student Notes for Grace and Truth in the Torah

In the gospel of John, John seems to contrast the law or Torah with grace and truth. (John 1:17)

By: #1223. δια dia, dee-ah' a primary preposition denoting the channel of an act; through

Came: 1096. γινομαι ginomai, ghin'-om-ahee a prolongation and middle voice form of a primary verb; to cause to be ("gen"-erate), i.e. (reflexively) to become (come into being)

The literal translation then of John 1:17 is, **"Because the law through Moses was given, grace and truth through Jesus Christ came into being."**

So, how does giving the Law through Moses bring about grace and truth through Yeshua? (John 1:18)

John 1:14-18 is a direct reference to Exodus 33 through Exodus 34:9. (John 1:14-18)
They broke the commandment. What did God say He would do as a result? (Exo. 20:4-5, Exo. 32:9-10)

What did Moses do? (Exo. 32:31-32, Rom. 3:20, Gen. 26:4-5, Heb. 11:8-9)

So God relented and promised to send His angel or messenger along with them. What did Moses want from God? (Exo. 33:1-2, Exo. 33:12-13)

Way: #1870. דרך derek, deh'-rek from 1869; a road (as trodden); figuratively, a course of life or mode of action

Consider: #7200. ראה ra'ah, raw-aw' a primitive root; to see

Grace: #2603. חנן chanan, khaw-nan' a primitive root (compare 2583); properly, to bend or stoop in kindness to an inferior; to favor, bestow

Student Notes for Grace and Truth in the Torah

What is God's answer? (Exo. 33:14, Exo. 33:19-23, Rom 5:8)


Compassion: #7355. רחם racham, raw-kham' a primitive root; to fondle; by implication, to love, especially to compassionate

Womb: #7358. רחם rechem, rekh'-em from 7355; the womb

How does Yeshua's words in John 1:14-18 connect? (John 1:14, Exo. 34:4-5, Mat. 17:1-5, Deu. 18:15, 18)




Hear: #8085. שמע shama`, shaw-mah' a primitive root; to hear intelligently (often with implication of attention, obedience

The Declaration of Yehovah's name is full of grace and truth: (Exo. 34:6-7)

What is Moses' response? (Exo. 34:8-9, Rom. 3:23-25)



Does grace then nullify the Torah? (Rom. 3:31, Exo. 34:27-28, Rom. 6:1-2)



The glory of God on Moses and Yeshua: (Exo. 34:29-30, Exo. 23:20-23, Isa. 63:7-9)


Here in the midst of the Torah, God revealed the Angel of His Presence, a pre-incarnate Yeshua full of grace and truth.

Student Notes for Grace and Truth in the Torah

**Discussion Questions for Grace and Truth in the Torah**

1. What did Moses have with Him when God declared His name, Yehovah, the name of grace and mercy (Ex. 34:1-2)? Discuss the significance of these items and the fact that Moses held them when God revealed His name.

2. Read Exodus 32:11-14 which contains Moses' reply to God when God said He would destroy the children of Israel and replace them with Moses. Compare Moses' reply with the doctrine that the Gentile church replaced Israel.

3. In Exodus 33:13, Moses asks God to "consider" that the nation of Israel is His people. The word translated "consider" is the Hebrew word ra-ah #7200 in Strong's Concordance. It means to see or provide. This is the same word used to refer to the place where God provided the ram as the sacrifice instead of Isaac which Abraham named "Yehovah-yireh," the LORD-Will-Provide. What are the implications if we read this request of Moses that God "make provision" that the nation of Israel is His people?

4. The word translated "by" in John 1:17 is the Greek word "dia" meaning the channel of an act. How was Moses a channel for giving the Torah as well as a channel for extending grace to the children of Israel?

5. Read Psalm 32 and 1 John 1:5-10. To whom does God extend mercy?

## Naomi and Ruth: Jew and Gentile

The story of Naomi and Ruth is the story of Jew and Gentile joined together in one family. It is the story of the Jewish nation that abandons their God, and in the wilderness of the nations, returns to their faith. It is the story of the Gentile grafted into the Jewish nation, guided by Jewish learning, introducing the Messiah to that same Jewish nation. The framework of the story is the physical needs of bread and water. Yeshua spoke of Himself as the living water and the bread of life and so we can read this account and see its spiritual significance.

*Since each name in this story is significant to the story, we've provided a list of the names and their meanings in Appendix B. Refer to this list as we go through the study.*

**A.** We begin with the family of Elimelech who represents Israel.

> Ruth 1:2 MKJV 2 And the name of the man was Elimelech, and the name of his wife Naomi, and the name of his two sons Mahlon and Chilion, Ephrathites of Bethlehem-Judah. And they came to the fields of Moab and stayed there.

The names of the family members show their fall from faith to apostasy. The parents' names Elimelech and Naomi honor God and His blessings. Elimelech means God is king and Naomi means pleasantness, grace, or beauty.

#458. אלימלך 'Eliymelek, el-ee-meh'-lek from 410 and 4428; God of (the) king; Elimelek, an Israelite:--Elimelech.

#5281. נעמי No`omiy, no-om-ee' from 5278; pleasant; Noomi, an Israelitess:--Naomi.

#5278. נעם no`am, no'-am from 5276; agreeableness, i.e. delight, suitableness, splendor or grace:--beauty, pleasant(-ness).

There is delight where God is king! They are Ephrathites of Bethlehem-Judah which means "they are fruitful in the house of bread where God is praised!" But there is a famine in the land and the family departs for the wilderness of the nations.

> Ruth 1:1 MKJV 1 And it happened in the days when the judges ruled, there was a famine in the land. And a certain man of Bethlehem-Judah went to live in the country of Moab, he and his wife and his two sons.

Amos writes of a similar famine in the land.

> Amos 8:11 MKJV 11 Behold, the days come, says the Lord Jehovah, that I will send a famine in the land; not a famine of bread nor a thirst for water, but of hearing the words of the LORD.

This famine is a famine of hearing the words of the LORD. They suffer from lack of hearing God's word. When there is famine in the land, they are no longer fruitful and leave the house of bread.

Elimelech's family leave to live in Moab. Moab is the son of Lot through an incestuous relationship with one of his daughters. The name Moab means from her father and Lot's name means to cover, veil or wrap up. This is the same word Isaiah uses to describe the covering blocking both Jew and Gentile from seeing the truth about God.

> Isaiah 25:7 NKJV 7 And He will destroy on this mountain The surface of the **covering** cast over all people, And the veil that is spread over all nations.

From this incestuous relationship with Lot, Lot's daughter achieves a son out of Lot from whom knowledge of God is now covered. Elimelech and Naomi come to this nation formed by Moab. They left the Promised Land and entered a land that covered their eyes. They abandon God's word and embrace the teachings of the world whether that takes the form of following tradition as opposed to God or lifting up man above God. Ruth 1:2 says that they came to the **fields** of Moab and **stayed there**. (Some versions translate the verse as the **country** of Moab but the word is #7704 שדה sadah, field.) The symbolism of the book of Ruth is in agricultural terms. Elimelech's family left the fields of Israel and worked in the fields of the pagans. Their fallen spiritual state is further evident in the names of their sons. The names of their sons mean sickness and destruction.

#4248. מחלון Machlown, makh-lone' from 2470; sick, weak, afflicted, to grieve; Machlon, an Israelite:--Mahlon.

#3630. כליון Kilyown, kil-yone' a form of 3631 pining, destruction: -consumption, failing.

The offspring of "Delight" and "God is King" are "Sickness" and "Destruction." Naomi and Elimelech bear sickness and destruction there in the fields of Moab. Job writes of the pain and destruction that comes on the wicked.

> Job 21:17 NKJV 17 "How often is the lamp of the wicked put out? How often does their destruction come upon them, The sorrows God distributes in His anger?

The family of Elimelech has fallen; they grieve and pine for what they have lost. Elimelech, Mahlon and Chilion all die. There is no one left to carry on the name of Elimelech; he has been cut off from his brothers. Again, we see that the family of Elimelech represents the branch of Israel, the branch of the olive tree which has been broken off. Naomi is the only one who is left. Her name doesn't just mean pleasantness or delight, it also means grace. When all else is gone, only grace remains. Paul says that what has been broken off can be grafted in again.

> Romans 11:23 MKJV 23 And those also, if they do not continue in unbelief, will be grafted in. For God is able to graft them in again.

Naomi and Ruth: Jew and Gentile

When destruction came, Naomi heard that God had visited His people and given them bread.

> Ruth 1:6 NKJV 6 Then she arose with her daughters-in-law that she might return from the country of Moab, for she had heard in the country of Moab that the LORD had visited His people by giving them bread.

Yeshua is the bread of life provided by the Father to His people.

> John 6:35 NKJV 35 And Jesus said to them, "I am the bread of life. He who comes to Me shall never hunger, and he who believes in Me shall never thirst.

Amos wrote that the famine was spiritual; the people could not hear the word of God. Yeshua, the Living Word of God breaks the famine; He is the bread that brings life.

**B.** All was not totally without hope for Naomi. While in the wilderness of the people, she gained two daughters-in-law, Orpah and Ruth. Gentiles had joined themselves to the family of Israel. Orpah whose name means back of the neck turned back to Moab. But Ruth, whose name means friend in the sense of tending a flock, cleaved to Naomi.

> Ruth 1:14 NKJV 14 Then they lifted up their voices and wept again; and Orpah kissed her mother-in-law, but Ruth clung to her.

The word translated clung is the Hebrew word dabak.

#1695. דבק dabeq, daw-bake' from 1692; adhering:--cleave, joining, stick closer.

This is the same word Adam uses when describing the relationship between husband and wife, and the same word used by Moses five times in his exhortation of the Israelites to hold on to God. One example is Deuteronomy 10:20.

> Deuteronomy 10:20 KJV 20 Thou shalt fear the LORD thy God; him shalt thou serve, and to him shalt thou **cleave**, and swear by his name.

Ruth has joined herself to Naomi. She is the Gentile grafted into Israel!

> Ruth 1:16-17 MKJV 16 And Ruth said, Do not beg me to leave you, to return from following after you. For where you go, I will go. Where you stay, I will stay. Your people shall be my people, and your God my God. 17 Where you die, I will die, and there I will be buried. May the LORD do so to me, and more also, if anything but death parts you and me.

> Romans 11:17 MKJV 17 And if some of the branches were broken off, and you, being a wild olive tree, were **grafted in among them**, and became a sharer of the root and the fatness of the olive tree with them,

Orphah, on the other hand represents those Gentiles who, though grafted in, are broken off.

> Romans 11:19-21 MKJV 19 You will say then, The branches were broken off so that I might be grafted in. 20 Well, because of unbelief they were broken off, and you stand by faith. Do not be high-minded, but fear. 21 For if God did not spare the natural branches, fear lest He also may not spare you either!

At this time, Naomi is a branch that has been broken off yet it is through her that Ruth comes to God. Paul is clear; the Messiah comes from the Jews.

> Romans 9:3-5 NKJV 3 For I could wish that I myself were accursed from Christ for my brethren, my countrymen according to the flesh, 4 who are Israelites, to whom pertain the adoption, the glory, the covenants, the giving of the law, the service of God, and the promises; 5 of whom are the fathers and from whom, according to the flesh, Christ came, who is over all, the eternally blessed God. Amen.

**C.** Naomi doesn't see the hope yet. Although Naomi has physically returned to Bethlehem, she has yet to partake once again of the house of bread. Naomi is caught up in her bitterness.

> Ruth 1:20-21 NKJV 20 But she said to them, "Do not call me Naomi; call me Mara, for the Almighty has dealt very bitterly with me. 21 "I went out full, and the LORD has brought me home again empty. Why do you call me Naomi, since the LORD has testified against me, and the Almighty has afflicted me?"

The name Mara means bitter. The afflictions of the curse have come upon Naomi and Israel. Moses warned the Israelites before they even went into the Land that if they turned from God, failing to cleave to Him, the curses would come on them.

> Deuteronomy 28:15 NKJV 15 "But it shall come to pass, if you do not obey the voice of the LORD your God, to observe carefully all His commandments and His statutes which I command you today, that all these curses will come upon you and overtake you:

Those curses came on Naomi but now she is returning home. Moses also wrote of the return of Israel.

> Deuteronomy 30:1-3 NKJV 1 "Now it shall come to pass, when all these things come upon you, the blessing and the curse which I have set before you, and you call them to mind among all the nations where the LORD your God drives you, 2 "and you return to the LORD your God and obey His voice, according to all that I command you today, you and your children, with all your heart and with all your soul, 3 "that the LORD your God will bring you back from captivity, and have compassion on you, and gather you again from all the nations where the LORD your God has scattered you.

Naomi had heard that God was with His people. It was only when things were at their lowest that she began to look again toward God. Naomi says that she was full and now she is empty. It is only when we are emptied of ourselves that God can fill us. This whole idea is present in the name El Shaddai or God Almighty. It is this name of God that Naomi uses in verse 20 that the Almighty has dealt bitterly with her.

The Almighty comes from the Hebrew word "Shaddai."

#7706. שדי Shadday, shad-dah'-ee from 7703; the Almighty:--Almighty.

Strong's Lexicon says it comes from the root word shadad.
#7703. שדד shadad, shaw-dad' a primitive root; properly, to be burly, i.e. (figuratively) powerful (passively, impregnable); by implication, to ravage:--dead, destroy(-er), oppress, robber, spoil(-er), X utterly, (lay) waste.

Others say it comes from the root word shood.

#7736. שוד shuwd, shood a primitive root; properly, to swell up, i.e. figuratively (by implication of insolence) to devastate:--waste.

It is in the second possibility that we see the emptying and filling. The Hebrew word for breast, שד, also comes from the root shood. A breast is filled with milk to nurture the young. But shood also means to waste. God, who filled Naomi and Israel when they walked with Him, emptied them when they turned away. He will fill them once again when they accept Yeshua as their Messiah.

This process begins when Naomi returns to the Land at the time of the barley harvest.

> Ruth 1:22 MKJV 22 And Naomi returned; and Ruth, who was of Moab, her daughter-in-law, was with her, returning out of the fields of Moab. And they came to Bethlehem in the beginning of barley harvest.

We can see that this return is beginning to be more than the physical. Naomi returns out of the fields of Moab! She has turned her back on the things of the world. She does this at the beginning of the barley harvest. In agricultural terms, this is the first harvest of the year. Symbolically, the harvest of the end times is beginning. This is the beginning of redemption for Israel.

According to the Biblical calendar, this is the first month of the redemption cycle corresponding to the redemption of Israel from slavery in Egypt. The yearly cycle of the Feasts of the LORD is beginning. It starts with the spring feasts of Passover, the Feast of Unleavened Bread, and the Feast of Firstfruits as the barley harvest begins. Specifically, the barley harvest refers to the Feast of Firstfruits that occurs during the week of the Feast of Unleavened Bread.

> Leviticus 23:10-11 MKJV 10 Speak to the sons of Israel and say to them, When you have come into the land which I give to you, and shall reap the harvest of it, then you shall bring a sheaf of the firstfruits of your harvest to the priest. 11 And he shall wave the sheaf before the LORD to be received for you. On the next day after the sabbath the priest shall wave it.

This feast is the day that Yeshua rose from the grave beginning the harvest of souls for the kingdom of God. So, Naomi returns to Israel at the time of the barley harvest representing her redemption.

This harvest continues until Yeshua's return at the end of the harvest season when we celebrate the fall feasts culminating in the Feast of Tabernacles. The Feast of Tabernacles is a rehearsal for the wedding supper of the lamb and the time when God will once again dwell with man.

**D.** Ruth goes out to glean in the field of Boaz. Boaz represents the Messiah redeemer. No longer is Ruth in the fields of Moab; she is working the field of the King. The name Boaz means "in him is strength."

The name Boaz comes from an unused Hebrew root the meaning of which is in doubt. Some say it means fleetness (Brown, Driver, Griggs, Gesenius Lexicon) others say it means strength. The two pillars next to the door of Solomon's Temple were named Jachin and Boaz. Jachin means Yah establishes. The Septuagint renders Boaz as a Greek word meaning "with strength" in 2 Chron. 3:17. (Source Jewish Encyclopedia) So the pillars would read "Yah establishes with strength."

When we come to God in our weakness, He is our strength.

> 2 Corinthians 12:10 NKJV 10 Therefore I take pleasure in infirmities, in reproaches, in needs, in persecutions, in distresses, for Christ's sake. For when I am weak, then I am strong.

Boaz is a kinsman of Naomi and Ruth. Paul reminds us in his letter to the Hebrews that Yeshua is our brother.

> Hebrews 2:11 MKJV 11 For both He who sanctifies and they who are sanctified are all of One, for which cause He is not ashamed to call them brothers,

Boaz like Yeshua came from Bethlehem the house of bread.

> Ruth 2:4 MKJV 4 And behold, Boaz came from Bethlehem and said to the reapers, The LORD be with you. And they answered him, The LORD bless you.

It's interesting that even though everyone working in the fields including Ruth came from Bethlehem, the scriptures specifically mention that Boaz came from Bethlehem. Boaz is

## Naomi and Ruth: Jew and Gentile

visiting his fields of grain. This calls to mind the words of Naomi that she heard that God had visited His people by providing bread. And so, Boaz comes from the house of bread and sees Ruth working in his field. The verses that follow record Boaz's first encounter with Ruth and are a shadow of Yeshua and His instructions to us.

> Ruth 2:8-14 NKJV 8 Then Boaz said to Ruth, "You will listen, my daughter, will you not? Do not go to glean in another field, nor go from here, but stay close by my young women. 9 "Let your eyes be on the field which they reap, and go after them. Have I not commanded the young men not to touch you? And when you are thirsty, go to the vessels and drink from what the young men have drawn." 10 So she fell on her face, bowed down to the ground, and said to him, "Why have I found favor in your eyes, that you should take notice of me, since I am a foreigner?" 11 And Boaz answered and said to her, "It has been fully reported to me, all that you have done for your mother-in-law since the death of your husband, and how you have left your father and your mother and the land of your birth, and have come to a people whom you did not know before. 12 "The LORD repay your work, and a full reward be given you by the LORD God of Israel, under whose wings you have come for refuge." 13 Then she said, "Let me find favor in your sight, my lord; for you have comforted me, and have spoken kindly to your maidservant, though I am not like one of your maidservants." 14 Now Boaz said to her at mealtime, "Come here, and eat of the bread, and dip your piece of bread in the vinegar." So she sat beside the reapers, and he passed parched grain to her; and she ate and was satisfied, and kept some back.

1. Boaz instructs Ruth to stay in his field. We are to be workers in Yeshua's field.

> Luke 10:2 MKJV 2 Then He said to them, The harvest truly is great, but the laborers are few. Therefore pray to the Lord of the harvest that He may send forth laborers into His harvest.

2. Ruth is to keep her eyes on the task at hand following after Boaz's maidens. Paul tells us we are to keep our eyes on the prize following after the great men of faith.

> Hebrews 12:1 MKJV 1 Therefore since we also are surrounded with so great a cloud of witnesses, let us lay aside every weight and the sin which so easily besets us, and let us run with patience the race that is set before us,

3. Boaz's word provides protection for her. Yeshua provides protection for us.

> 2 Samuel 22:3 MKJV 3 The God who is my Rock, in Him will I trust. He is my Shield, and the Horn of my salvation, my High Tower, and my Refuge, my Savior. You save me from violence.

4. He provides water for her thirst. Yeshua is our living water. When we drink from Him, we do not thirst anymore.

> John 4:14 MKJV 14 but whoever drinks of the water that I shall give him shall never thirst, but the water that I shall give him shall be in him a well of water springing up into everlasting life.

5. Boaz blesses her because of the way she treated her Jewish mother-in-law. God promised Abraham that He would bless those who blessed him and his descendants. Ruth, the Gentile, blesses Naomi, the Israelite. Also, Naomi is her parent and Paul reminds us that honoring our parents is the first commandment with a promise.

> Ephesians 6:2-3 MKJV 2 Honor your father and mother (which is the first commandment with a promise), 3 so that it may be well with you, and that you may live long on the earth.

Yeshua says He will know those who provide for others in distress.

> Matthew 25:38-40 MKJV 38 When did we see You a stranger, and took You in? Or naked, and clothed You? 39 Or when did we see You sick, or in prison, and came to You? 40 And the King shall answer and say to them, Truly I say to you, Inasmuch as you did it to one of the least of these My brothers, you have done it to Me.

> James 1:27 MKJV 27 Pure religion and undefiled before God and the Father is this, to visit orphans and widows in their afflictions, and to keep oneself unspotted from the world.

6. Boaz blesses her because she left her old life behind. Yeshua blesses us with eternal life when we leave our old lives behind.

> Matthew 19:29 MKJV 29 And everyone who left houses, or brothers, or sisters, or father, or mother, or wife, or children, or lands, for My name's sake, shall receive a hundredfold, and shall inherit everlasting life.

Paul tells us that we are new creations in Yeshua.

> 2 Corinthians 5:17 MKJV 17 So that if any one is in Christ, that one is a new creature; old things have passed away; behold, all things have become new.

7. Boaz blesses her in the name of the LORD God of Israel under whose wings she has taken refuge. The Psalmist writes of God's loving kindness to those who take refuge under His wing.

> Psalms 36:7-9 MKJV 7 How precious is Your loving-kindness, O God! And the sons of men take refuge under the shadow of Your wing. 8 They shall be satisfied with the fatness of Your house; and You shall make them drink of the river of Your pleasures. 9 For with You is the fountain of life; in Your light we shall see light.

Malachi reminds us that there is healing in His wings.

> Malachi 4:2 MKJV 2 But to you who fear My name, the Sun of Righteousness shall arise, and healing will be on His wings. And you shall go out and frisk like calves of the stall.

8. Boaz provides bread for her that satisfies. The Psalmist writes that the meek shall eat and be satisfied.

> Psalms 22:26 MKJV 26 The meek shall eat and be satisfied; those who seek the LORD shall praise Him; your heart shall live forever.

Ruth has now been "filled." Yeshua is our bread of life that satisfies.

> John 6:35 MKJV 35 And Jesus said to them, I am the bread of life. He who comes to Me shall never hunger, and he who believes on Me shall never thirst.

Ruth was filled with the bread of life and she takes some back to Naomi! In verse 14, Ruth "kept some back" after she was satisfied and in verse 18, we read that she gave it to Naomi. (Some versions just say she left but the Hebrew word is yathar which in verse 18 is translated as "she had kept back.") Ruth offers the chance to be full to Naomi who is empty.

> Ruth 2:18 NKJV 18 Then she took it up and went into the city, and her mother-in-law saw what she had gleaned. So she brought out and gave to her what she had kept back after she had been satisfied.

**E.** Ruth worked right up until the end of the harvest season all through the spring and summer. It is time for the final threshing and winnowing.

> Ruth 2:23 MKJV 23 And she kept close by the maidens of Boaz to glean until the end of barley harvest and of wheat harvest. And she lived with her mother-in-law.

We read that Boaz himself is on the threshing floor winnowing the barley.

> Ruth 3:2 NKJV 2 "Now Boaz, whose young women you were with, is he not our relative? In fact, he is winnowing barley tonight at the threshing floor.

Yeshua told a parable about the final judgment being like the winnowing of the harvest.

> Matthew 3:12 NKJV 12 "His winnowing fan is in His hand, and He will thoroughly clean out His threshing floor, and gather His wheat into the barn; but He will burn up the chaff with unquenchable fire."

There on the threshing floor, Ruth basically asks Boaz to marry her. She repeats Boaz's own words back to him. Boaz said she had taken shelter under the wings of the God of Israel. Ruth takes shelter under Boaz's "wings."

> Ruth 3:9 NKJV 9 And he said, "Who are you?" So she answered, "I am Ruth, your maidservant. Take your maidservant under your wing, for you are a close relative."

Some English translations say she requested that Boaz take her under his skirt or garment but the Hebrew word both in this verse and in Ruth 2:12 is Kanaph.

#3671. כנף kanaph, kaw-nawf' from 3670; an edge or extremity; specifically (of a bird or army) a wing,

So Ruth places herself under God's protection through Boaz who represents Messiah. When we accept Yeshua as our redeemer, we are taking refuge under God's wing through Yeshua our redeemer. Boaz's response to Ruth's request is that she is blessed of the LORD. We who take refuge in Yeshua are blessed of the LORD! Ruth, as a symbol for the bride of Christ, is found to be faithful in Boaz's town, the house of bread. She did not go after false gods, idols or the doctrines of prosperity or poverty.

> Ruth 3:10-11 NKJV 10 Then he said, "Blessed are you of the LORD, my daughter! For you have shown more kindness at the end than at the beginning, in that you did not go after young men, whether poor or rich. 11 "And now, my daughter, do not fear. I will do for you all that you request, for all the people of my town know that you are a virtuous woman.

We also are to be steadfast and blameless.

> Colossians 1:21-23 NKJV 21 And you, who once were alienated and enemies in your mind by wicked works, yet now He has reconciled 22 in the body of His flesh through death, to present you holy, and blameless, and above reproach in His sight-- 23 if indeed you continue in the faith, grounded and steadfast, and are not moved away from the hope of the gospel which you heard, which was preached to every creature under heaven, of which I, Paul, became a minister.

Ruth, who was from an enemy nation, persevered to the end showing more kindness at the end than the beginning. She continued in the faith and Boaz proclaims that she is a virtuous woman. But this word virtuous doesn't mean without sin or blameless. It is from the Hebrew word chayil, חיל, #2428 a force of men, means or other resources; an army, wealth, virtue, valor, or strength. She is a woman of strong character.

Contrast this with God's words of condemnation for Israel through the prophet Ezekiel.

> Ezekiel 16:15-16 NKJV 15 "But you trusted in your own beauty, played the harlot because of your fame, and poured out your harlotry on everyone passing by who would have it. 16 "You took some of your garments and adorned multicolored high

> places for yourself, and played the harlot on them. Such things should not happen, nor be.

> Ezekiel 16:19 NKJV 19 "Also My food which I gave you-the pastry of fine flour, oil, and honey which I fed you-you set it before them as sweet incense; and so it was," says the Lord GOD.

Israel looked everywhere but to God who provided for them. Even the bread He provided, they set before their idols. But God still offers forgiveness to His people and through Ruth, Naomi will be restored.

**F.** Boaz desires to be Ruth's kinsman redeemer but there is a closer relative who must release her first. When Ruth brought this word to Naomi, Naomi replied that Boaz would certainly accomplish his desire. She used the phrase "he will not rest."

> Ruth 3:18 NKJV 18 Then she said, "Sit still, my daughter, until you know how the matter will turn out; for the man will not rest until he has concluded the matter this day."

We know that Yeshua did not rest until He accomplished what He came to do. After His death and resurrection, He sits at the right hand of the father.

> Hebrews 10:12 NKJV 12 But this Man, after He had offered one sacrifice for sins forever, sat down at the right hand of God,

But Yeshua has one more task, to establish Jerusalem and her inhabitants as His bride.

> Isaiah 62:1 MKJV 1 For Zion's sake I will not be silent, and for Jerusalem's sake I will not rest, until its righteousness goes out as brightness, and her salvation as a burning lamp.

When Yeshua comes and takes His bride, the New Jerusalem, after the millennial reign, He will truly rest.

> Revelation 21:2 MKJV 2 And I, John, saw the holy city, New Jerusalem, coming down from God out of Heaven, prepared as a bride adorned for her Husband.

But what did Yeshua need to accomplish when He was here in physical form? He needed to pay the penalty of the Law, the Torah, so that though we were dead, we could have new life.

> Galatians 3:13 NKJV 13 Christ has redeemed us from the curse of the law, having become a curse for us (for it is written, "Cursed is everyone who hangs on a tree"),

Part of the job of the kinsman redeemer is to marry the widow of his dead kinsman and through her, restore the "life" of the dead kinsman by providing children for him. The kinsman who was nearer in relation to Naomi said he could not fulfill that part of the role of kinsman redeemer.

> Ruth 4:5-6 NKJV 5 Then Boaz said, "On the day you buy the field from the hand of Naomi, you must also buy it from Ruth the Moabitess, the wife of the dead, to perpetuate the name of the dead through his inheritance." 6 And the close relative said, "I cannot redeem it for myself, lest I ruin my own inheritance. You redeem my right of redemption for yourself, for I cannot redeem it."

The closer kinsman then represents the Law that would like to redeem us but cannot.

> Romans 7:10 NKJV 10 And the commandment, which was to bring life, I found to bring death.

The Law is holy, spiritual and good but it cannot bring life because man, through Adam, is subject to the weakness of the flesh.

> Romans 8:3 NKJV 3 For what the law could not do in that it was weak through the flesh, God did by sending His own Son in the likeness of sinful flesh, on account of sin: He condemned sin in the flesh,

> Hebrews 10:1 NKJV 1 For the law, having a shadow of the good things to come, and not the very image of the things, can never with these same sacrifices, which they offer continually year by year, make those who approach perfect.

This kinsman passed on the right and responsibility to Boaz. He passes the sandal to Boaz, "in him is strength," and says buy it or redeem it yourself. Boaz has the strength, as did Yeshua, to pay the price redeeming the property of Elimelech. He marries Ruth restoring the line of Elimelech. The line of Elimelech representing Israel is grafted back in!

> Ruth 4:8-10 NKJV 8 Therefore the close relative said to Boaz, "Buy it for yourself." So he took off his sandal. 9 And Boaz said to the elders and all the people, "You are witnesses this day that I have bought all that was Elimelech's, and all that was Chilion's and Mahlon's, from the hand of Naomi. 10 "Moreover, Ruth the Moabitess, the widow of Mahlon, I have acquired as my wife, to perpetuate the name of the dead through his inheritance, that the name of the dead may not be cut off from among his brethren and from his position at the gate. You are witnesses this day."

What exactly did Boaz purchase? Boaz's statement in verse 9 with the meaning of the names inserted reads, "I have bought all that was God the king's, all that was afflicted and grieving, all that was destroyed and pining from the hand of grace." He marries the widow of Mahlon whose name means sickness and grieving, thus restoring his line. Yeshua pays the redemption price. He heals our sicknesses and comforts those who grieve. He marries His bride and restores the line of Adam through whom death once came to all mankind.

Ruth bears a son to Boaz whom they name Obed. Obed means to serve. We know that Yeshua said that the greatest in God's kingdom are those who serve. Obed, the servant, is the one who restores Elimelech's line. Elimelech's position at the gate is restored. The gates of the New Jerusalem bear the names of the tribes of Israel (Eze 48:31-34).

Naomi who was empty is now full.

> Ruth 4:14-15 MKJV 14 And the women said to Naomi, Blessed be the LORD, who has not left you this day without a redeemer, so that his name may be famous in Israel. 15 And he shall be to you as a restorer of life, and one who cheers your old age. For your daughter-in-law who loves you has borne him, she who is better to you than seven sons.

Praise God that He has sent Yeshua as not only the kinsman redeemer of the Gentiles but the kinsman redeemer of Israel. May we be like Ruth to Naomi and bring the message of salvation to Israel through love and respect.

*(Appendix C: These are the Generations: The Story of Our Redemption includes supplemental material for this lesson.)*

# Student Notes for Naomi and Ruth: Jew and Gentile

The story of Naomi and Ruth is the story of Jew and Gentile joined together in one family. It is the story of the Jewish nation who abandons their God, and in the wilderness of the nations, returns to their faith. It is the story of the Gentile grafted into the Jewish nation, guided by Jewish learning, introducing the Messiah to that same Jewish nation. The framework of the story is the physical needs of bread and water. Yeshua spoke of Himself as the living water and the bread of life and so we can read this account and see its spiritual significance.

*Since each name in this story is significant to the story, we've provided a list of the names and their meanings in Appendix B. Refer to this list as we go through the study.*

**A.** We begin with the family of Elimelech that represents Israel. (Ruth 1:2, Isa. 25:7)


Fall from faith to apostasy: (Ruth 1:1, Amos 8:11)


Elimelech's family left the fields of Israel and worked in the fields of the pagans:
**Fields**: #7704 שׂדה sadah, field.)


Their fallen spiritual state is further evident in the names of their sons. (Job 21:17, Rom. 11:23)


Naomi heard that God had visited His people given them bread. (Ruth 1:6, John 6:35)


**B.** Gentiles had joined themselves to the family of Israel. (Ruth 1:14, Deu. 10:20)

**Clung:** #1695. דבק dabeq, daw-bake' from 1692; adhering:--cleave, joining, stick closer.

Ruth represents: (Ruth 1:16-17, Rom. 11:17)

Orpah represents: (Rom. 11:19-21)

Messiah comes from the Jews: (Rom. 9:3-5)

**C.** Naomi returns home in bitterness after the curses have come upon her: (Ruth 1:20-21, Deu. 28:15, Deu. 30:1-3)

It is only when we are emptied of ourselves that God can fill us. This whole idea is present in the name El Shaddai or God Almighty.

#7706. שׁדי Shadday, shad-dah'-ee from 7703; the Almighty:--Almighty.

Strong's Lexicon says it comes from the root word shadad.
#7703. שׁדד shadad, shaw-dad' a primitive root; properly, to be burly, i.e. (figuratively) powerful (passively, impregnable); by implication, to ravage:--dead, destroy(-er), oppress, robber, spoil(-er), X utterly, (lay) waste.

Others say it comes from the root word shood.

#7736. שׁוד shuwd, shood a primitive root; properly, to swell up, i.e. figuratively (by implication of insolence) to devastate:--waste.

This process begins when Naomi returns to the Land at the time of the barley harvest. (Ruth 1:22)

The Feast of Firstfruits: (Lev. 23:10-11)

**D.** No longer is Ruth in the fields of Moab; she is working the field of the King. (2Cor. 12:10)

Boaz is a kinsman from Bethlehem: (Heb. 2:11, Ruth 2:4)

The verses that follow record Boaz's first encounter with Ruth and are a shadow of Yeshua and His instructions to us. (Ruth 2:8-14)

    1. We are to be workers in Yeshua's field. (Luke 10:2)

    2. Paul tells us we are to keep our eyes on the prize following after the great men of faith. (Heb. 12:1)

    3. Boaz's word provides protection for her. (2Sam. 22:3)

    4. He provides water for her thirst. Yeshua is our living water. (John 4:14)

    5. Boaz blesses her because of the way she treated her Jewish mother-in-law. (Eph. 6:2-3, Mat. 25:38-40, Jam. 1:27)

    6. Boaz blesses her because she left her old life behind. (Mat. 19:29, 2Cor. 5:17)

    7. Boaz blesses her in the name of the LORD God of Israel under whose wings she has taken refuge. (Psa. 36:7-9, Mal. 4:2)

    8. Boaz provides bread for her that satisfies. The Psalmist writes that the meek shall eat and be satisfied. (Psa. 22:26, John 6:35, Ruth 2:18)

Verse 14, Ruth "kept some back": Yathar
Verse 18, "She had kept back": Yathar

Student Notes for Naomi and Ruth: Jew and Gentile

**E.** Ruth worked right up until the end of the harvest season all through the spring and summer. It is time for the final threshing and winnowing. (Ruth 2:23, Ruth 3:2, Mat. 3:12, Ruth 3:9)

**Wings:** #3671. כנף kanaph, kaw-nawf' from 3670; an edge or extremity; specifically (of a bird or army) a wing,

So Ruth places herself under God's protection through Boaz who represents Messiah. (Ruth 3:10-11, Col. 1:21-23)

Ruth continued in the faith and Boaz proclaims that she is a virtuous woman: (Eze. 16:15-16, 19)

**Virtuous:** #2428:chayil חיל a force of men, means or other resources; an army, wealth, virtue, valor, or strength.

**F.** Boaz desires to be her kinsman redeemer but there is a closer relative who must release her first. (Ruth 3:18)

He will not rest until he accomplishes his goal: (Heb. 10:12, Isa. 62:1, Rev. 21:2, Gal. 3:13)

The kinsman who was nearer in relation to Naomi said he could not fulfill that part of the role of kinsman redeemer. (Ruth 4:5-6, Rom. 7:10, Rom. 8:3, Heb. 10:1)

The line of Elimelech, representing Israel, is grafted back in! (Ruth 4:8-10, Ruth 4:14-15)

"I have bought all that was God the king's, all that was afflicted and grieving, all that was destroyed and pining from the hand of grace."

*(Appendix C: These are the Generations: The Story of Our Redemption includes supplemental material for this lesson.*

**Discussion Questions for Naomi and Ruth: Jew and Gentile**

1. Ruth gave birth to a son who restores the line of Elimelech. Read Isaiah 49:18-23. How is the account of Ruth a pattern for the fulfillment of this prophecy?

2. Naomi and Elimelech left Israel for the fields of Moab. How is this a pattern of the believer who is walking in the world? What is the "offspring" of such a lifestyle?

3. Boaz went out from Bethlehem to visit the harvesters. Read Luke 10:1-2. How does Yeshua go out from Bethlehem to visit His harvesters?

4. Ruth ate the grain that Boaz provided and was satisfied. She even had more than enough to share with Naomi. Read John 6:4-14 and John 4:32-36. How does Yeshua provide the bread that satisfies?

5. Obed means to serve. Read Revelation 22:3. What is our role in the New Jerusalem?

6. Moab means from my father and Moab's father was Lot. Lot means to cover or veil. How does the fact that Lot chose to live in Sodom amongst some of the wickedest people of his day show that his understanding was veiled? (Read Genesis 13:8-13 and 2 Corinthians 3:12-18.)

## The Cities of Refuge, the Blood Avenger and the High Priest

> Numbers 35:6 NKJV 6 "Now among the cities which you will give to the Levites you shall appoint six cities of refuge, to which a manslayer may flee...

This verse begins an interesting passage near the end of the book of Numbers. This takes place near the end of the exile in the wilderness as the Children of Israel are finally about to enter the Promised Land. God gives Moses some final instructions about an important administrative matter that is a powerful shadow of the promised Messiah.

> Numbers 35:9-14 NKJV 9 Then the LORD spoke to Moses, saying, 10 "Speak to the children of Israel, and say to them: 'When you cross the Jordan into the land of Canaan, 11 'then you shall appoint cities to be cities of refuge for you, that the manslayer who kills any person accidentally may flee there. 12 'They shall be cities of refuge for you from the avenger, that the manslayer may not die until he stands before the congregation in judgment. 13 'And of the cities which you give, you shall have six cities of refuge. 14 'You shall appoint three cities on this side of the Jordan, and three cities you shall appoint in the land of Canaan, which will be cities of refuge.

These cities of refuge were set apart from among the Levitical cities spread out within the boundaries of the twelve tribes with three cities on the East side of the Jordan and three cities on the West.

The cities on the Western side of the Jordan were Kadesh, Shechem and Hebron. The Eastern cities were Betzer, Ramoth Gilead and Golan. These six cities were to be a refuge for someone who unintentionally takes the life another person. The person could flee to one of these cities and ask for judgment about their guilt in causing the death of the other person.

> Numbers 35:15-16 NKJV 15 'These six cities shall be for refuge for the children of Israel, for the stranger, and for the sojourner among them, that anyone who kills a person accidentally may flee there. 16 'But if he strikes him with an iron implement, so that he dies, he is a murderer; the murderer shall surely be put to death.

If the person was judged guilty of murder, that is intentionally killing another, then they were banished from the city to face the "blood avenger" who could kill them on sight. If they are judged to have killed another unintentionally, then they were to remain in the city until the death of the High Priest.

God originally provided for three cities but, even before they entered the Promised Land, God enlarged their territory and established three more cities.

> Deuteronomy 19:8-10 NKJV 8 "Now if the LORD your God enlarges your territory, as He swore to your fathers, and gives you the land which He promised to give to your fathers, 9 "and if you keep all these commandments and do them,

which I command you today, to love the LORD your God and to walk always in His ways, then you shall add three more cities for yourself besides these three, 10 "lest innocent blood be shed in the midst of your land which the LORD your God is giving you as an inheritance, and thus guilt of bloodshed be upon you.

God established these three extra cities to enable the manslayer to reach a city of refuge so the avenger of blood would not catch up to him and slay him before he reached refuge, and, thus, spilling additional innocent blood.

While the manslayer remained in one of these cities, he is protected from the "blood avenger." This almost reminds us of the Wild West of the movies where there was no established system of justice except for an individual taking revenge themselves. Or like the Sharks and Jets of West Side Story. The cities of refuge provided a safe haven and a kind of covering or atonement for the manslayer. The manslayer is one who was judged not guilty of intentionally killing another, but was still guilty of shedding blood.

**A.** The "avenger of blood" or "revenger" as some translations put it is a close relative of the murder victim, perhaps a brother or father. The Hebrew word used in this passage and translated as "avenger" is ga'al:

> #1350. גאל ga'al, gaw-al' A primitive root, to redeem (according to the Oriental law of kinship), i.e. to be the next of kin (and as such to buy back a relative's property, marry his widow), **avenger**, deliver, (do, perform the part of near, next) kinsfolk(-man), purchase, ransom, redeem(-er), **revenger.**

This is one of those interesting cases where the same Hebrew word has what appears to be opposite meanings depending on the context in which it is used. This word, גאל ga'al is most often used in reference to a redeemer or the action of being redeemed.

> Job 19:25 NKJV 25 For I know that my **Redeemer** (גאל ga'al) lives, And He shall stand at last on the earth;

> Psalms 77:15 NKJV 15 You have with Your arm **redeemed** (גאל ga'al) Your people, The sons of Jacob and Joseph. Selah

Ga'al is also translated as "kinsman" as well, referring to the one who has the potential to redeem such as in the book of Ruth.

> Ruth 2:20 NIV 20 "The LORD bless him!" Naomi said to her daughter-in-law. "He has not stopped showing his kindness to the living and the dead." She added, "That man is our close relative (kinsman גאל ga'al); he is one of our kinsman-redeemers."

An avenger and a redeemer have apparently opposite purposes, but with גאל ga'al as with many other words with apparently opposing definitions, we will see that these opposing concepts are not as "opposite" as they might seem at first glance. A person who redeems and another who avenges are actually taking the same action. And it is only a kinsman who may take this action. We will see that the blood avenger, the redeemer and the kinsman are all tied together.

**B.** The redeemer is a close relative. This close relative is the only one who can redeem the property of another.

> Leviticus 25:24-25 NKJV 24 'And in all the land of your possession you shall grant redemption of the land. 25 'If one of your brethren becomes poor, and has sold some of his possession, and if his redeeming relative comes to redeem it, then he may redeem what his brother sold.

If a person has financial trouble and is forced to sell his possessions, a close relative or kinsman can step in to redeem his property. Should a man die, as in the story of Ruth, it is the kinsman redeemer who is the only one able to restore the inheritance to the family of the one who died. Ruth is the story of a Moabite woman who left her homeland and came to the Land of Israel as a convert. She gave up the idolatry of her homeland and clung to her elderly, widowed mother in-law Naomi who was an Israelite from Bethlehem in Judah. It is Naomi's deceased husband Elimelech's inheritance and property that is in need of redemption. Boaz is the close relative who comes to redeem Elimelech's inheritance by taking Ruth as his wife.

> Ruth 4:9-10 NKJV 9 And Boaz said to the elders and all the people, "You are witnesses this day that I have bought all that was Elimelech's, and all that was Chilion's and Mahlon's, from the hand of Naomi. 10 "Moreover, Ruth the Moabitess, the widow of Mahlon, I have acquired as my wife, to perpetuate the name of the dead through his inheritance, that the name of the dead may not be cut off from among his brethren and from his position at the gate. You are witnesses this day."

We see that it is the kinsman who takes possession of the property, and restores it to its original status. A kinsman is the only one who has the right to restore or redeem the property of a family member. In the case of Ruth, this redemption results in the restoration of an important family line which, in just three generations, leads to Israel's greatest King and ultimately to the Messiah himself.

> Ruth 4:13, 16-17 NKJV 13 So Boaz took Ruth and she became his wife; and when he went in to her, the LORD gave her conception, and she bore a son... 16 Then Naomi took the child and laid him on her bosom, and became a nurse to him. 17 Also the neighbor women gave him a name, saying, "There is a son born to Naomi." And they called his name Obed. He is the father of Jesse, the father of David.

**C.** I am sure that we can all agree that murder is sin. It is, of course, one of the Ten Commandments or Ten Words. To transgress the Torah is to sin. And the penalty for sin is death. Redemption can only come through the sin offering, but only for an unintentional sin. If a man kills another intentionally, escape to a city of refuge would do him no good. As stated before, these cities provided for judgment of his crime.

As with the "kinsman redeemer," the "blood avenger" or revenger is also a kinsman. Only a kinsman has the right, and indeed requirement, to require the blood of a murderer. Remember that "kinsman" and "avenger" are the same word in Hebrew (ga'al). If a man is judged guilty of murder, then he is to be put to death at the hand of the avenger (ga'al) who is a kinsman (ga'al) of the murder victim. The cities of refuge offer no protection for one who is guilty of intentional murder.

> Numbers 35:19 NKJV 19 'The avenger of blood himself shall put the murderer to death; when he meets him, he shall put him to death.

> Deuteronomy 19:11-13 NKJV 11 "But if anyone hates his neighbor, lies in wait for him, rises against him and strikes him mortally, so that he dies, and he flees to one of these cities, 12 "then the elders of his city shall send and bring him from there, and deliver him over to the hand of the avenger of blood, that he may die. 13 "Your eye shall not pity him, but you shall put away the guilt of innocent blood from Israel, that it may go well with you.

The death of the person guilty of murder was necessary for the well being of the entire nation of Israel. But if a person is judged to be guilty of only manslaughter which is an unintentional killing of another man, then he is to be protected from the avenger by remaining in a city of refuge. He is to remain there until the death of the High Priest.

> Numbers 35:22-25 NKJV 22 'However, if he pushes him suddenly without enmity, or throws anything at him without lying in wait, 23 'or uses a stone, by which a man could die, throwing it at him without seeing him, so that he dies, while he was not his enemy or seeking his harm, 24 'then the congregation shall judge between the manslayer and the avenger of blood according to these judgments. 25 'So the congregation shall deliver the manslayer from the hand of the avenger of blood, and the congregation shall return him to the city of refuge where he had fled, and he shall remain there until the death of the high priest who was anointed with the holy oil.

**D:** So what does the death of the High priest have to do with the atonement of the manslayer? First, we must address what the consequences are for the shedding of blood. The shedding of blood has a profound impact on the land itself! When Cain killed Abel, the consequence was that the land would no longer produce crops for Cain.

> Genesis 4:11-12 NKJV 11 "So now you are cursed from the earth, which has opened its mouth to receive your brother's blood from your hand.12 "When you till the ground, it shall no longer yield its strength to you. A fugitive and a vagabond you shall be on the earth."

So, blood spilled on the ground cuts a person off from the land and causes it to withhold its "strength." The word translated "strength" is koach which means force or vigor.

Strength: #3581. כֹּחַ koach, ko'-akh to be firm; vigor, literally (force, in a good or a bad sense) or figuratively (capacity, means, produce); -ability, able, chameleon, force, fruits, might, power(-ful), strength, substance, wealth.

In not producing fruit for the person, the land would not give of its life-sustaining vigor. The land is defiled. This is the situation that existed at the time of Noah. The whole earth was corrupt because of the evil and violence of men.

> Genesis 6:11 NKJV 11 The earth also was corrupt before God, and the earth was filled with violence.

The word corrupt is from the Hebrew word "shachath" meaning to decay or ruin.

Corrupt: #7843. שָׁחַת shachath, shaw-khath' a primitive root; to decay, i.e. (causatively) ruin (literally or figuratively):--batter, cast off, corrupt

Mankind's violence caused the decay and ruin of the earth. After the flood, God gave instructions to Noah that all bloodshed must be atoned for.

> Genesis 9:5-7 NKJV 5 "Surely for your lifeblood I will demand a reckoning; from the hand of every beast I will require it, and from the hand of man. From the hand of every man's brother I will require the life of man. 6 "Whoever sheds man's blood, By man his blood shall be shed; For in the image of God He made man. 7 And as for you, be fruitful and multiply; Bring forth abundantly in the earth And multiply in it."

The instructions are twofold. First, blood must be shed to atone for shedding blood and second, Noah was to bring forth abundantly from the earth. Noah could only accomplish the second, bringing forth from the earth, if he adhered to the first, shedding blood for shed blood. God also gave Noah the instruction not to eat meat with the blood still in it. He repeated these instructions to Moses giving the reason; life is in the blood.

> Deuteronomy 12:23-24 NKJV 23 "Only be sure that you do not eat the blood, for the blood is the life; you may not eat the life with the meat. 24 "You shall not eat it; you shall pour it on the earth like water.

The blood is so important that God gave detailed instructions about where they were to slaughter animals of the flock as well as wild animals suitable for food. This is the reason there was to be no ransom for the one who sheds blood.

> Numbers 35:31-34 NKJV 31 'Moreover you shall take no ransom for the life of a murderer who is guilty of death, but he shall surely be put to death. 32 'And you shall take no ransom for him who has fled to his city of refuge, that he may return

to dwell in the land before the death of the priest. 33 'So you shall not pollute the land where you are; for blood defiles the land, and no atonement can be made for the land, for the blood that is shed on it, except by the blood of him who shed it. 34 'Therefore do not defile the land which you inhabit, in the midst of which I dwell; for I the LORD dwell among the children of Israel.'"

Because of the defiling of the land, the murderer must be put to death making atonement for the shedding of blood. The manslayer must stay in the city of refuge; no ransom can be paid to release him. But atonement must still be made for the shedding of that innocent blood.

> Hebrews 9:22 NKJV 22 And according to the law almost all things are purified with blood, and without shedding of blood there is no remission.

There must be an atonement of blood for the spilling of blood. But as long as the manslayer lives that atoning blood is not shed. This is where the High Priest comes in. Atonement is postponed; as long as the manslayer remains in the city of refuge, he is under the protection or covering of the High Priest.

> Numbers 35:26-28 NKJV 26 'But if the manslayer at any time goes outside the limits of the city of refuge where he fled, 27 'and the avenger of blood finds him outside the limits of his city of refuge, and the avenger of blood kills the manslayer, he shall not be guilty of blood, 28 'because he should have remained in his city of refuge until the death of the high priest. But after the death of the high priest the manslayer may return to the land of his possession.

The words ransom and atonement are related to each other. The word ransom is the Hebrew word kopher which is from the word kaphar, the word for atonement. No ransom (kopher) can be made for the manslayer to leave the city of refuge, but by staying in the city, he is under the atonement or covering (kaphar) of the High Priest.

There is a special sin offering and sacrifice that the High Priest performs on Yom Kippur. Yom Kippur is the one time each year when the High Priest himself performs a sin offering and takes the blood into the Holy of Holies making atonement for all the people and their unintentional sins. The High Priest, in a sense, takes the sins of the community upon himself then takes them to God offering himself in their stead.

> Leviticus 16:21-22 NKJV 21 "Aaron shall lay both his hands on the head of the live goat, confess over it all the iniquities of the children of Israel, and all their transgressions, concerning all their sins, putting them on the head of the goat, and shall send it away into the wilderness by the hand of a suitable man. 22 "The goat shall bear on itself all their iniquities to an uninhabited land; and he shall release the goat in the wilderness.

According to the Sages as recorded in the Talmud in Makkot 11a, by the act of the High Priest in protecting the manslayer residing in a city of refuge, the High Priest is, in effect, taking the place of the guilty party or taking on the guilt of the manslayer. The High Priest provides a substitution at his annual sacrificial atonement before the LORD on Yom Kippur, but the atonement is incomplete because the sin can only be truly and ultimately atoned for by the death of the guilty party. Therefore the sin is not fully atoned for until the High Priest dies in the place of the manslayer. Only then can the manslayer go free.

This is telling us exactly why the manslayer, the one who sheds the blood of another, is released at the death of the High Priest. The High Priest is both the intercessor while he is alive and the redeemer providing the necessary blood atonement at his death. Thus, he redeems the lives of those who have fled to the cities of refuge. His blood is the substitute for the manslayer's guilt of the blood of the one whom he killed!

**E.** Yeshua said the generation that was alive at His death would be held accountable for the bloodshed of the righteous people from the very beginning of creation.

> Matthew 23:34-36 NKJV 34 "Therefore, indeed, I send you prophets, wise men, and scribes: some of them you will kill and crucify, and some of them you will scourge in your synagogues and persecute from city to city, 35 "that on you may come all the righteous blood shed on the earth, from the blood of righteous Abel to the blood of Zechariah, son of Berechiah, whom you murdered between the temple and the altar. 36 "Assuredly, I say to you, all these things will come upon this generation.

Judgment did fall on Israel because of the sin of her leaders. The temple was destroyed and the Jewish people scattered throughout the nations. The land was desolate for centuries because of the innocent blood shed on her. This reminds us of the curse on Cain for killing his brother Abel that he would be cut off from the land. But there was a second provision on the curse on Cain; anyone who harmed Cain would receive back sevenfold for the vengeance.

> Genesis 4:15 NKJV 15 And the LORD said to him, "Therefore, whoever kills Cain, vengeance shall be taken on him sevenfold." And the LORD set a mark on Cain, lest anyone finding him should kill him.

God will not stay angry with Israel forever. For the sake of His name, He will restore them and anyone who harmed Israel will face the blood avenger.

> Ezekiel 35:5-6 NKJV 5 "Because you have had an ancient hatred, and have shed the blood of the children of Israel by the power of the sword at the time of their calamity, when their iniquity came to an end, 6 "therefore, as I live," says the Lord GOD, "I will prepare you for blood, and blood shall pursue you; since you have not hated blood, therefore blood shall pursue you.

God will restore Israel and lift the curse. The mountains of Israel will once again provide her vigor for her people.

> Ezekiel 36:8 NKJV 8 "But you, O mountains of Israel, you shall shoot forth your branches and yield your fruit to My people Israel, for they are about to come.

**F.** As you know, all the statutes regarding the tabernacle and priesthood here on earth are but a shadow of that which is in the heavenly tabernacle. Yeshua is our High Priest. He is in the heavenly Holy of Holies making intercession for us before the Father. At his death we were released from the death sentence of our sin, but only so long as we remain under His protection.

> Hebrews 9:24-28 NKJV 24 For Christ has not entered the holy places made with hands, which are copies of the true, but into heaven itself, now to appear in the presence of God for us; 25 not that He should offer Himself often, as the high priest enters the Most Holy Place every year with blood of another-- 26 He then would have had to suffer often since the foundation of the world; but now, once at the end of the ages, He has appeared to put away sin by the sacrifice of Himself. 27 And as it is appointed for men to die once, but after this the judgment, 28 so Christ was offered once to bear the sins of many. To those who eagerly wait for Him He will appear a second time, apart from sin, for salvation.

The book of Hebrews illustrates in dramatic fashion the role of Yeshua as our High Priest, but not a High Priest of the earthly kind.

> Hebrews 5:1 NKJV 1 For every high priest taken from among men is appointed for men in things pertaining to God, that he may offer both gifts and sacrifices for sins.

Yeshua is our High Priest of a higher order:

> Hebrews 6:20 NKJV 20 where the forerunner has entered for us, even Jesus, having become High Priest forever according to the order of Melchizedek.

> Hebrews 8:1 NKJV 1 Now this is the main point of the things we are saying: We have such a High Priest, who is seated at the right hand of the throne of the Majesty in the heavens,

> Hebrews 9:11 NKJV 11 But Christ came as High Priest of the good things to come, with the greater and more perfect tabernacle not made with hands, that is, not of this creation.

His death released us of our guilt. Blood restitution is complete!

When Yeshua returns, he himself will be both the redeemer of Israel and the "blood avenger" who cleanses the earth. The nations, for millennia have shed the blood of Israel and that blood will be avenged. Psalms 79 contains this prayer:

> Psalms 79:7-11 NKJV 7 For they (the nations) have devoured Jacob, And laid waste his dwelling place. 8 Oh, do not remember former iniquities against us! Let Your tender mercies come speedily to meet us, For we have been brought very low. 9 Help us, O God of our salvation, For the glory of Your name; And deliver us, and **provide atonement for our sins**, For Your name's sake! 10 Why should the nations say, "Where is their God?" Let there be known among the nations in our sight **The avenging of the blood of Your servants which has been shed**. 11 Let the groaning of the prisoner come before You; According to the greatness of Your power Preserve those who are appointed to die;

The blood of the nations will be required to cleanse the land of Israel. The land must be sanctified before the LORD can once again dwell there.

> Revelation 14:19-20 NKJV 19 So the angel thrust his sickle into the earth and gathered the vine of the earth, and threw it into the great winepress of the wrath of God. 20 And the winepress was trampled outside the city, and blood came out of the winepress, up to the horses' bridles, for one thousand six hundred furlongs.

Remember what it says in Numbers 35:19, the avenger, the Ga'al of blood himself, will put the murderer to death. The LORD Himself will slay or bring vengeance on the adversary.

> Isaiah 35:3-4 NKJV 3 Strengthen the weak hands, And make firm the feeble knees. 4 Say to those who are fearful-hearted, "Be strong, do not fear! Behold, your God will come with vengeance, With the recompense of God; He will come and save you."

In the latter days the people will be divided into two camps, those who follow the LORD and identify with Yeshua, and those who follow the beast and identify with Satan. In the Gospel of John, Yeshua tells us that Satan is a murderer from the beginning.

> John 8:44 NKJV 44 "You are of your father the devil, and the desires of your father you want to do. He was a murderer from the beginning, and does not stand in the truth, because there is no truth in him. When he speaks a lie, he speaks from his own resources, for he is a liar and the father of it.

For a murderer there is no refuge from the blood avenger who is justified in taking that one's life.

> Revelation 19:20-21 NKJV 20 Then the beast was captured, and with him the false prophet who worked signs in his presence, by which he deceived those who received the mark of the beast and those who worshiped his image. These two were cast alive into the lake of fire burning with brimstone. 21 And the rest were killed with the sword which proceeded from the mouth of Him who sat on the horse. And all the birds were filled with their flesh.

We are also brothers and sisters with Yeshua. He is our kinsman (ga'al), our avenger (ga'al) and our redeemer (ga'al).

> Galatians 3:26 NKJV 26 For you are all sons of God through faith in Christ Jesus.

He comes to avenge and redeem all those He counts as kinsman.

# Student Notes for the Cities of Refuge, the Blood Avenger and the High Priest

The cities of refuge: (Num. 35:6, Num. 35:9-14, Num. 35:15-16, Deu. 19:8-10)

Levitical cities: Three on the western side of the Jordan and three on the eastern side.

To protect the unintentional slayer from the "blood avenger"

The manslayer is one who was judged not guilty of intentionally killing another, but was still guilty of shedding blood.

**A.** The "avenger of blood" or "revenger"

Avenger: #1350. גאל ga'al, gaw-al' A primitive root, to redeem, i.e. to be the next of kin (and as such to buy back a relative's property, marry his widow), **avenger**, deliver, (do, perform the part of near, next) kinsfolk(-man), purchase, ransom, redeem(-er), **revenger**.

Redeemer: גאל ga'al (Job 19:25, Psa. 77:15)

Ga'al is also translated as "kinsman" (Ruth 2:20)

The blood avenger, the redeemer and the kinsman are all tied together.

**B.** The redeemer is a close relative. (Lev. 25:24-25, Ruth 4:9-10)

A kinsman is the only one who has the right to restore or redeem the property of a family member (Ruth 4:13, 16-17)

**C.** The "blood avenger" or revenger is also a kinsman. Only a kinsman has the right to require the blood of a murderer.

   Intentional murder: (Num. 35:19, Deu. 19: 11-13)

   Unintentional killing: (Num. 35:22-25)

**D.** So what does the death of the High priest have to do with atonement of the manslayer? First, we must address the consequences for shedding blood. (Gen. 4:11-12, Gen 6:11)

Strength: #3581. כח koach, ko'-akh to be firm; vigor, literally (force, in a good or a bad sense) or figuratively (capacity, means, produce); -ability, able, chameleon, force, fruits, might, power(-ful), strength, substance, wealth.

Corrupt: #7843. שחת shachath, shaw-khath' a primitive root; to decay, i.e. (causatively) ruin (literally or figuratively):--batter, cast off, corrupt

There must be an atonement of blood for the shedding of blood. (Gen. 9:5-7, Deu. 12:23-24, Num. 35:31-34, Heb. 9:22, Num. 35:26-28)

The atonement offering on Yom Kippur: (Lev. 16:21-22)

According to the Sages as recorded in the Talmud in Makkot 11a, the High Priest is, in effect, taking the place of the guilty party or taking on the guilt of the manslayer. The High Priest provides a substitution at his annual sacrificial atonement before the LORD on Yom Kippur, but the atonement is incomplete because the sin can only be truly and ultimately atoned for by the death of the guilty party. (Num. 35:33-34)

Student Notes for The Cities of Refuge, the Blood Avenger and the High Priest

**E.** Who will be held accountable for shedding the blood of all the righteous people from the beginning of creation? (Mat. 23:34-36, Gen. 4:15, Eze. 35:5-6, Eze. 36:8)

**F.** Yeshua is our High Priest (Heb. 9:24-28, Heb. 5:1, Heb. 6:20, Heb. 8:1, Heb. 9:11)

When Yeshua returns, he himself will be the "blood avenger" who cleanses the earth. (Psa. 79:7-11, Rev. 14:19-20)

The avenger, the Ga'al of blood himself will put the murderer to death. (Isa. 35:3-4)

Yeshua tells us that Satan is a murderer from the beginning. (John 8:44, Rev. 19:20-21)

We are also brothers and sisters with Yeshua. He is our kinsman (ga'al), our avenger (ga'al) and our redeemer (ga'al). (Gal. 3:26)

Student Notes for The Cities of Refuge, the Blood Avenger and the High Priest

**Discussion Questions for the Cities of Refuge, the Blood Avenger and the High Priest**

1. Read Revelation 18:21-24 about the destruction of Babylon. What has Babylon been judged guilty of and what is her sentence?


2. Read Genesis 15:15-16 about God who delayed in giving Abram the Promised Land. What is the reason for the delay? Compare this with the reason the angels visited Sodom before its destruction (Gen. 18:20-23) and God's warning to His people who live in Babylon (Rev. 18:4-5).


3. Read Revelation 6:9-11. How does this apply to the blood avenger?


4. After Israel is restored to the Promised Land, Gog comes against Israel. Read Ezekiel 38:14-23. What will the avenger of blood do to Gog?


5. Read Deuteronomy 21:1-9 about the procedure for cleansing the land after an unsolved murder. Why does the land need "cleansing?" How does this relate to the blood avenger?


6. Read Leviticus 26:3-8. What is the response of the Land when Israel keeps the covenants of God? What is the response of the Land when Israel does not keep the covenants (Lev. 18 and 20)? What are the two main sins listed in these two chapters?

## The Land of Israel

The land of Israel is a shadow of the Garden of Eden and may have been the actual location of the Garden of Eden. So, the story of the Land of Israel begins in the Garden of Eden after Adam and Eve ate of the tree of the knowledge of good and evil. God exiles Adam and Eve from the Garden of Eden, and curses the land and the serpent who had tempted them.

> Genesis 3:17 NKJV 17 Then to Adam He said, "Because you have heeded the voice of your wife, and have eaten from the tree of which I commanded you, saying, 'You shall not eat of it': "Cursed is the ground for your sake; In toil you shall eat of it All the days of your life.

> Genesis 3:15 NKJV 15 And I will put enmity Between you and the woman, And between your seed and her Seed; He shall bruise your head, And you shall bruise His heel."

The curse on the serpent contains a promise of redemption; a seed from Eve would crush his head. God promises redemption to both man and the land.

With Abraham, God began to enact His plan for redemption. The place He chose for all this to happen is the land God would show to Abraham, the land of Israel. Although Abraham, Isaac and Jacob lived in the Promised Land, they were strangers and sojourners.

> Hebrews 11:13 KJV 13 These all died in faith, not having received the promises, but having seen them afar off, and were persuaded of them, and embraced them, and confessed that they were strangers and pilgrims on the earth.

After them, God chose their descendants, the Israelites, to be His special people and the land He brought them into was the land of Israel. David was not a king anywhere else in the world; he was a king of Israel. Yeshua, the son of David, lived His entire life in the land of Israel. All prophecy centers around Israel and with good reason. Israel is, at least symbolically and perhaps in actuality, the location of the original Garden of Eden. This is the land in which God will dwell with man.

> Psalms 132:13-14 NKJV 13 For the LORD has chosen Zion; He has desired it for His dwelling place: 14 "This is My resting place forever; Here I will dwell, for I have desired it.

How does God show that Israel is the location of the Garden of Eden? God's commandments and dealings with the land of Israel set it apart from all other lands.

**A.** God set the garden apart from the rest of creation. God planted the Garden of Eden before He put Adam there.

> Genesis 2:8 NKJV 8 The LORD God planted a garden eastward in Eden, and there He put the man whom He had formed.

Like Eden, God prepared the land of Israel before bringing Israel into the Land.

> Ezekiel 20:6 NKJV 6 "On that day I raised My hand in an oath to them, to bring them out of the land of Egypt into a land that I had searched out for them, 'flowing with milk and honey,' the glory of all lands.

The Psalmist writes that God took them out of Egypt and planted them in the land.

> Psalms 80:8 KJV 8 Thou hast brought a vine out of Egypt: thou hast cast out the heathen, and planted it.

God planted them in a land that produced more than abundant fruit! The fruit was truly miraculous. When the twelve spies went into the land, they brought back glowing reports of the produce of the land.

> Numbers 13:23 NKJV 23 Then they came to the Valley of Eshcol, and there cut down a branch with one cluster of grapes; they carried it between two of them on a pole. They also brought some of the pomegranates and figs.

As the time when God will once again bring Israel into the Promised Land approaches, the land will begin to produce abundantly in anticipation of their arrival.

> Ezekiel 36:8 NKJV 8 "But you, O mountains of Israel, you shall shoot forth your branches and yield your fruit to My people Israel, for they are about to come.

God will once again plant Israel in the Promised Land who in turn will plant and reap what they plant.

> Isaiah 65:21-22 KJV 21 And they shall build houses, and inhabit them; and they shall plant vineyards, and eat the fruit of them. 22 They shall not build, and another inhabit; they shall not plant, and another eat: for as the days of a tree are the days of my people, and mine elect shall long enjoy the work of their hands.

**B.** God gave Adam charge over the Garden of Eden. He was to tend and keep it. The garden still belonged to God and not to Adam!

> Genesis 2:15 NKJV 15 Then the LORD God took the man and put him in the garden of Eden to tend and keep it.

The Hebrew word for "keep" is shamar.

The Land of Israel

Keep: #8104. שמר shamar, shaw-mar' a primitive root; properly, to hedge about (as with thorns), i.e. guard; generally, to protect, attend to, preserve, regard, reserve, save (self), watch(-man).

Adam was to guard, protect and preserve the Garden of Eden. God's charge to Adam implies that there is something to protect it from. I'm sure that He was to protect it from the serpent and failed miserably.

When God brought Israel into the Land, He made it clear that the Land was His.

> Leviticus 25:23 NKJV 23 'The land shall not be sold permanently, for the land is Mine; for you are strangers and sojourners with Me.

This is an interesting verse. God says that the land is His, but then He goes on to say that He and the Israelites are strangers. The Land is not yet what it was or what it will be. Until the curse is lifted, God even counts Himself as a stranger in the Land.

The Israelites, like Adam were to tend the land acknowledging that God is the source of the abundance of the land.

> Deuteronomy 26:9-10 NKJV 9 'He has brought us to this place and has given us this land, "a land flowing with milk and honey"; 10 'and now, behold, I have brought the firstfruits of the land which you, O LORD, have given me.' Then you shall set it before the LORD your God, and worship before the LORD your God.

They were also to guard and protect the land. Their charge was to guard it from the abominations done in it by the Canaanites.

> Leviticus 18:24-25 NKJV 24 'Do not defile yourselves with any of these things; for by all these the nations are defiled, which I am casting out before you. 25 'For the land is defiled; therefore I visit the punishment of its iniquity upon it, and the land vomits out its inhabitants.

When Adam sinned, he caused a curse to fall on all of the creation and in particular the land itself. The land no longer produced fruit easily on its own; Adam had to work it by the sweat of his brow. If the actions of the Israelites followed after the pattern of the Canaanites, the land of Israel would be defiled and Israel would fail her task. Like with Adam, the danger came from within; it was not an external enemy that would cause the downfall of Israel.

**C.** God gave Adam one commandment; do not eat from the tree in the center of the garden.

> Genesis 2:16-17 NKJV 16 And the LORD God commanded the man, saying, "Of every tree of the garden you may freely eat; 17 "but of the tree of the knowledge of good and evil you shall not eat, for in the day that you eat of it you shall surely die."

The essence of the command was to answer the question, "Will you obey me?" God states His reason for the curse is because Adam disobeyed the command.

> Genesis 3:17 NKJV 17 Then to Adam He said, "Because you have heeded the voice of your wife, and have eaten from the tree of which I commanded you, saying, 'You shall not eat of it': "Cursed is the ground for your sake; In toil you shall eat of it All the days of your life.

Moses instructed the Israelites before they went into the Land about their choices once they were in the land. Their choice is the same as that of Adam, "Will you obey God?" Moses clearly spells out the consequences in terms which call to mind the trees in the Garden of Eden. Choose obedience and receive life. Disobey and receive cursing and death. This warning goes on for several chapters emphasizing its importance.

> Deuteronomy 30:15-19 NKJV 15 "See, I have set before you today life and good, death and evil, 16 "in that I command you today to love the LORD your God, to walk in His ways, and to keep His commandments, His statutes, and His judgments, that you may live and multiply; and the LORD your God will bless you in the land which you go to possess. 17 "But if your heart turns away so that you do not hear, and are drawn away, and worship other gods and serve them, 18 "I announce to you today that you shall surely perish; you shall not prolong your days in the land which you cross over the Jordan to go in and possess. 19 "I call heaven and earth as witnesses today against you, that I have set before you life and death, blessing and cursing; therefore choose life, that both you and your descendants may live;

Adam, also, had a choice of life or death. If Adam had obeyed God's command, he would still have access to the tree of life. Thus, choosing obedience to God is choosing life. Israel, like Adam, was unable to keep God's commandments and, again like Adam, God kicked them out of the land. Jeremiah delivered the words of God to the house of Jacob and the families of the house of Israel.

> Jeremiah 2:7 NKJV 7 I brought you into a bountiful country, To eat its fruit and its goodness. But when you entered, you defiled My land And made My heritage an abomination.

> Jeremiah 21:8-10 NKJV 8 "Now you shall say to this people, 'Thus says the LORD: "Behold, I set before you the way of life and the way of death. 9 "He who remains in this city shall die by the sword, by famine, and by pestilence; but he who goes out and defects to the Chaldeans who besiege you, he shall live, and his life shall be as a prize to him. 10 "For I have set My face against this city for adversity and not for good," says the LORD. "It shall be given into the hand of the king of Babylon, and he shall burn it with fire."'

Like with Adam, staying in the land was not a possibility. God set up cherubim at the entrance of the Garden of Eden to keep Adam from returning. With Israel, those who tried to stay in Israel died; those who went out of the land to Babylon saved their lives. But through Israel and the special provisions for the land itself, God sends a shadow of what the land will be. We see prophecies of Yeshua, the final Adam, who will bring life to man and healing to all of creation.

In the meantime, the Land vomited Israel out just like it did with the Canaanites. Their sins defiled the Land itself.

> Leviticus 18:26-28 NKJV 26 'You shall therefore keep My statutes and My judgments, and shall not commit any of these abominations, either any of your own nation or any stranger who dwells among you 27 '(for all these abominations the men of the land have done, who were before you, and thus the land is defiled), 28 'lest the land vomit you out also when you defile it, as it vomited out the nations that were before you.

When Moses sent the twelve spies into the Promised Land to inspect it, ten of the spies returned with the report that the land devoured its inhabitants.

> Numbers 13:32 NKJV 32 And they gave the children of Israel a bad report of the land which they had spied out, saying, "The land through which we have gone as spies is a land that devours its inhabitants, and all the people whom we saw in it are men of great stature.

Have you ever wondered what was meant by the land devouring its inhabitants? It seems at odds with the rest of their report that the land produced gigantic fruit and was indeed a land of milk and honey. Perhaps they referred to the periodic droughts and the resultant famines that occurred in the Land or perhaps there was sickness in the land. We know that the Canaanites did evil in God's sight which brings judgment and can bring sickness. For example, as God was preparing the children of Israel to go into the Promised Land, He took them by Marah where they encountered the bitter waters. God healed the water and gave them a promise that if they followed His commands, they would not have sickness.

> Exodus 15:26 NKJV 26 and said, "If you diligently heed the voice of the LORD your God and do what is right in His sight, give ear to His commandments and keep all His statutes, I will put none of the diseases on you which I have brought on the Egyptians. For I am the LORD who heals you."

Again, at Mt. Sinai, God promises health in their land if they will serve God.

> Exodus 23:25-26 NKJV 25 "So you shall serve the LORD your God, and He will bless your bread and your water. And I will take sickness away from the midst of you. 26 "No one shall suffer miscarriage or be barren in your land; I will fulfill the number of your days.

God will bless them through the land. The land would not devour its inhabitants! It is as if the Promised Land was waiting for its rightful inhabitants. It produced bountifully in preparation for the coming of the children of Israel. At the same time, the Land devoured those who defiled it. We see this pattern established with the exile and return of Israel.

When the Israelites were exiled from the Land, the land itself became desolate.

> Ezekiel 36:2-3 NKJV 2 'Thus says the Lord GOD: "Because the enemy has said of you, 'Aha! The ancient heights have become our possession,'"' 3 "therefore prophesy, and say, 'Thus says the Lord GOD: "Because they **made you desolate** and swallowed you up on every side, so that you became the possession of the rest of the nations, and you are taken up by the lips of talkers and slandered by the people" -

The Land was desolate and did not produce fruit because the enemy inhabited it. But Ezekiel says there will be a time when the mountains would no longer devour its inhabitants. He goes on to say that the land will freely give of its fruit.

> Ezekiel 36:12-14 NKJV 12 "Yes, I will cause men to walk on you, My people Israel; they shall take possession of you, and you shall be their inheritance; no more shall you bereave them of children." 13 'Thus says the Lord GOD: "Because they say to you, 'You devour men and bereave your nation of children,' 14 "therefore you shall devour men no more, nor bereave your nation anymore," says the Lord GOD.

The nations around Israel will witness this restoration. God removes the desolation of the Land and it becomes like the Garden of Eden.

> Ezekiel 36:35 NKJV 35 "So they will say, 'This land that was desolate has become like the garden of Eden; and the wasted, desolate, and ruined cities are now fortified and inhabited.'

**D.** God makes special provisions for the land of Israel. The land of Israel, like her people, is to observe a Sabbath rest. Every seventh year, the land is not to be plowed, seeded or harvested. The people are to live off the fruit that the land produces naturally as well as the abundance God provides in the sixth year.

> Leviticus 25:1-4 NKJV 1 And the LORD spoke to Moses on Mount Sinai, saying, 2 "Speak to the children of Israel, and say to them: 'When you come into the land which I give you, then the land shall keep a sabbath to the LORD. 3 'Six years you shall sow your field, and six years you shall prune your vineyard, and gather its fruit; 4 'but in the seventh year there shall be a sabbath of solemn rest for the land, a sabbath to the LORD. You shall neither sow your field nor prune your vineyard.

> Leviticus 25:20-21 NKJV 20 'And if you say, "What shall we eat in the seventh year, since we shall not sow nor gather in our produce?" 21 'Then I will command

> My blessing on you in the sixth year, and it will bring forth produce enough for three years.

This is a remembrance of the Garden of Eden before the fall. As a result of Adam's sin, man would have to toil to raise food implying that before the fall, Adam didn't have to toil.

> Genesis 3:19 NKJV 19 In the sweat of your face you shall eat bread Till you return to the ground, For out of it you were taken; For dust you are, And to dust you shall return."

God will bring His people back to the Promised Land and, when He does; God will provide fruit and grain in abundance.

> Ezekiel 36:28-30 NKJV 28 "Then you shall dwell in the land that I gave to your fathers; you shall be My people, and I will be your God. 29 "I will deliver you from all your uncleannesses. I will call for the grain and multiply it, and bring no famine upon you. 30 "And I will multiply the fruit of your trees and the increase of your fields, so that you need never again bear the reproach of famine among the nations.

This foreshadows the Messianic kingdom when the land would freely yield its fruit in contrast to Adam who had to till the earth by the "sweat of his brow."

> Ezekiel 34:26-27 NKJV 26 "I will make them and the places all around My hill a blessing; and I will cause showers to come down in their season; there shall be showers of blessing. 27 "Then the trees of the field shall yield their fruit, and the earth shall yield her increase. They shall be safe in their land; and they shall know that I am the LORD, when I have broken the bands of their yoke and delivered them from the hand of those who enslaved them.

This reminds us of the promise God made to the children of Israel when He broke the chains of their slavery taking them out of Egypt and brought them to a land flowing with milk and honey. When God returns His people to the Promised Land, He says He will make the mountains and all the regions around His temple a blessing. Joel also writes of the restoration of the Land with the water which flows from the temple being the center of that restoration.

> Joel 3:18 NKJV 18 And it will come to pass in that day That the mountains shall drip with new wine, The hills shall flow with milk, And all the brooks of Judah shall be flooded with water; A fountain shall flow from the house of the LORD And water the Valley of Acacias.

During the Messianic kingdom, this will be true only in the land of Israel. God, through Yeshua, is still testing the other nations. If they will worship God, then they will have rain and prosper.

> Zechariah 14:16-17 NKJV 16 And it shall come to pass that everyone who is left of all the nations which came against Jerusalem shall go up from year to year to worship the King, the LORD of hosts, and to keep the Feast of Tabernacles. 17 And it shall be that whichever of the families of the earth do not come up to Jerusalem to worship the King, the LORD of hosts, on them there will be no rain.

The nations will have the nation of Israel with Yeshua as its king for an example. This fulfills what God intended the nation of Israel to be to the other nations—a land ruled with justice and righteousness.

> Deuteronomy 4:5-6 NKJV 5 "Surely I have taught you statutes and judgments, just as the LORD my God commanded me, that you should act according to them in the land which you go to possess. 6 "Therefore be careful to observe them; for this is your wisdom and your understanding in the sight of the peoples who will hear all these statutes, and say, 'Surely this great nation is a wise and understanding people.'

**E.** God is thorough in his prophecies though; He shows an even more vivid picture of the restoration of all things through the image of the year of Jubilee which occurs every fiftieth year. Like the Sabbath year, the Israelites were not to work the land during the year of Jubilee.

> Leviticus 25:11 NKJV 11 'That fiftieth year shall be a Jubilee to you; in it you shall neither sow nor reap what grows of its own accord, nor gather the grapes of your untended vine.

In addition to a Sabbath for the land, the Israelites were to proclaim liberty to all the slaves and the restoration of the land to its original tribe and family

> Leviticus 25:10 NKJV 10'And you shall consecrate the fiftieth year, and proclaim liberty throughout all the land to all its inhabitants. It shall be a Jubilee for you; and each of you shall return to his possession, and each of you shall return to his family.

Yeshua began His ministry by proclaiming liberty for the captives.

> Luke 4:17-19 NKJV 17 And He was handed the book of the prophet Isaiah. And when He had opened the book, He found the place where it was written: 18 "The Spirit of the LORD is upon Me, Because He has anointed Me To preach the gospel to the poor; He has sent Me to heal the brokenhearted, To proclaim liberty to the captives And recovery of sight to the blind, To set at liberty those who are oppressed; 19 To proclaim the acceptable year of the LORD."

Through Adam's sin, mankind became a slave to sin and the sin nature; dominion of the earth passed to Satan. Through Yeshua, those chains of slavery to sin are broken.

> Romans 8:2 NKJV 2 For the law of the Spirit of life in Christ Jesus has made me free from the law of sin and death.

Liberty is now available through faith to all who believe, but we do not yet have our glorious bodies so, we continue to struggle with the flesh. The Land and creation itself is still in bondage. But through Yeshua, Satan has been judged. Yeshua will reclaim His land in the year of Jubilee of His return and we will receive incorruptible bodies like Yeshua's.

> Romans 8:20-23 NKJV 20 For the creation was subjected to futility, not willingly, but because of Him who subjected it in hope; 21 because the creation itself also will be delivered from the bondage of corruption into the glorious liberty of the children of God. 22 For we know that the whole creation groans and labors with birth pangs together until now. 23 Not only that, but we also who have the firstfruits of the Spirit, even we ourselves groan within ourselves, eagerly waiting for the adoption, the redemption of our body.

In the year of Jubilee, the land of Israel reverts to God, its original owner through His son Yeshua the promised seed of Abraham.

> Leviticus 25:28 NKJV 28 'But if he is not able to have it restored to himself, then what was sold shall remain in the hand of him who bought it until the Year of Jubilee; and in the Jubilee it shall be released, and he shall return to his possession.

God told Abraham that his seed, would inherit the land and Paul tells us that Yeshua is that seed.

> Galatians 3:16 NKJV 16 Now to Abraham and his Seed were the promises made. He does not say, "And to seeds," as of many, but as of one, "And to your Seed," who is Christ.

So, the land reverts to the family of its original owner, Yeshua the Son of God. Also, as with the Garden of Eden, it returns to Yeshua, the last Adam, who brings redemption for the land that was cursed because of the sin of Adam.

**F.** And so we come full circle; God will give the Land of Israel into the keeping of His son Yeshua, the final Adam, who spent His entire earthly life in Israel. The land will produce fruit in abundance.

> Isaiah 4:2 NKJV 2 In that day the Branch of the LORD shall be beautiful and glorious; And the fruit of the earth shall be excellent and appealing For those of Israel who have escaped.

And God's Shekinah glory that was with the Israelites in the wilderness, inhabited the tabernacle in the wilderness, and dwelt in the temple in Jerusalem, will cover the Land.

> Isaiah 4:5-6 NKJV 5 then the LORD will create above every dwelling place of Mount Zion, and above her assemblies, a cloud and smoke by day and the shining of a flaming fire by night. For over all the glory there will be a covering. 6 And there will be a tabernacle for shade in the daytime from the heat, for a place of refuge, and for a shelter from storm and rain.

Living water will flow out from the temple in Jerusalem healing the waters of the Dead Sea bringing life to all it touches.

> Ezekiel 47:8-9 NKJV 8 Then he said to me: "This water flows toward the eastern region, goes down into the valley, and enters the sea. When it reaches the sea, its waters are healed. 9 "And it shall be that every living thing that moves, wherever the rivers go, will live. There will be a very great multitude of fish, because these waters go there; for they will be healed, and everything will live wherever the river goes.

The trees along the river are for food like the trees in the Garden of Eden. They produce fruit year round and their leaves are for healing.

> Ezekiel 47:12 NKJV 12 "Along the bank of the river, on this side and that, will grow all kinds of trees used for food; their leaves will not wither, and their fruit will not fail. They will bear fruit every month, because their water flows from the sanctuary. Their fruit will be for food, and their leaves for medicine."

Even the animals will return to eating only vegetation and there will be no killing in Messiah's kingdom.

> Isaiah 11:6-9 NKJV 6 "The wolf also shall dwell with the lamb, The leopard shall lie down with the young goat, The calf and the young lion and the fatling together; And a little child shall lead them. 7 The cow and the bear shall graze; Their young ones shall lie down together; And the lion shall eat straw like the ox. 8 The nursing child shall play by the cobra's hole, And the weaned child shall put his hand in the viper's den. 9 They shall not hurt nor destroy in all My holy mountain, For the earth shall be full of the knowledge of the LORD As the waters cover the sea.

The final restoration of the Garden of Eden will come with the recreation of the heavens and the earth.

> Isaiah 65:17 NKJV 17 "For behold, I create new heavens and a new earth; And the former shall not be remembered or come to mind.

## Student Notes for the Land of Israel

The story of the Land of Israel begins in the Garden of Eden after Adam and Eve ate of the tree of the knowledge of good and evil. With Abraham, God began to enact His plan for redemption. (Gen. 3:17, Gen. 3:15, Heb. 11:13, Psa. 132:13-14)

**A.** God planted the Garden of Eden before He put Adam there. (Gen. 2:8, Eze. 20:6, Psa. 80:8, Num. 13:23, Eze. 36:8, Isa. 65:21-22)

**B.** God gave Adam charge over the Garden of Eden. (Gen. 2:15, Lev. 25:23, Deu. 26:9-10, Lev. 18:24-25)

Keep: #8104. שמר shamar, shaw-mar' a primitive root; properly, to hedge about (as with thorns), i.e. guard; generally, to protect, attend to, preserve, regard, reserve, save (self), watch(-man).

**C.** God gave Adam one commandment. (Gen. 2:16-17, Gen 3:17)

Will you obey God? (Deu. 30:15-19, Jer. 2:7, Jer. 21:8-10, Lev. 18:26-28)

Student Notes for The Land of Israel

The land devoured its inhabitants. (Num. 13:32, Exo. 15:26, Exo. 23:25-26, Eze. 36:2-3, Eze. 36:12-14)

God removes the desolation of the Land and it becomes like the Garden of Eden. (Eze. 36:35)

**D.** The land of Israel, like her people, is to observe a Sabbath rest. (Lev. 25:1-4, Lev. 25:20-21, Gen. 3:19)

God will bring His people back to the Promised Land and when He does, God will provide fruit and grain in abundance. (Eze. 36:28-30, Eze. 34:26-27, Joel 3:18, Zec. 14:16-17, Deu. 4:5-6)

**E.** God shows an even more vivid picture of the restoration of all things in the year of Jubilee which occurs every fiftieth year. (Lev. 25:11, Lev. 25:10, Luke 4:17-19, Rom. 8:2, Rom. 8:20-23, Lev. 25:28, Gal. 3:16)

**F.** God will give the Land of Israel into the keeping of His son Yeshua. (Isa. 4:2, 5-6, Eze. 47:8-9, Eze. 47:12, Isa. 11:6-9, Isa. 65:17)

Student Notes for The Land of Israel

**Discussion Questions for the Land of Israel**

1. The earth and all creation suffered because of Adam's sin. When God creates the new heavens and earth there is no more curse (Rev. 22:3). Read Genesis 9:1-17. How does this covenant reveal that God would redeem both man and all of creation?

2. The curse on the serpent is that he will eat dust. Read the fate of the nations in Micah 7:13-20 and the serpent's fate in Isaiah 65:17-25. What do the nations eat and when does it occur? What does the serpent eat and where does this take place?

3. We have focused our attention on the curse, the serpent, and on Adam. Read Genesis 3:16-20 and Romans 8:18-23. How is the judgment on Eve like the curse on creation? How is it like the desire of creation?

4. In Joel 3:18, we read that a fountain will flow from the house of the LORD and water the Valley of Acacias. Acacia wood is a hardwood that is resistant to decay. How is this additional evidence of the restoration of the Land?

5. God cursed the land because of Adam's disobedience, and cursed it once again at the time of Noah because man's actions were continually evil (Gen. 6:11-12). Read Malachi 3:8-12 and 4:4-6. Discuss the connection between man's spiritual state and the physical reality of the earth.

6. When the high priest went into the Holy of Holies each year on Yom Kippur, he made atonement for both the people and the land (Lev. 16:15-17, 27-34). Based on what we have learned about the connection between the physical and the spiritual, discuss the importance of making atonement for the land.

## Hebron: The Promise of Resurrection

The land of Israel is special to God, and within the land itself, there are special places. Hebron is one of three places in Israel that the Bible mentions was purchased from the Canaanites. Each of these three places has deep spiritual significance. Abraham made the first purchase in Hebron. It represents the promise of resurrection and eternal life. This is the offer extended to all people through Yeshua's death and resurrection. Jacob purchased land outside Shechem next. Shechem represents the location of the tree of the knowledge of good and evil—the place of choosing. We must choose to accept the promise of eternal life or choose death. Finally, David purchased the temple mount in Jerusalem which represents the site of the Tree of Life. Once we choose life, we have the right to eat of the tree of life. We start, then, with Hebron, our promise of resurrection.

**A.** Abraham spent much of his time in the Promised Land at Hebron. He first lived in Hebron after returning to the Promised Land from Egypt where he went to wait out the famine in the Promised Land.

> Genesis 13:18 MKJV 18 And Abram moved his tent and came and lived in the oaks of Mamre, which is in Hebron. And he built an altar to the LORD there.

This verse gives us the first clue that Hebron represents resurrection of the dead. The name Mamre refers to vigor. Strong's Dictionary #4471 defines Mamre as lusty in the sense of vigor. The Brown, Driver, Briggs, Gesenius Lexicon defines it as strength or fatness. While we look at fatness as a negative, fatness of a land means that it is very productive; it brings forth a lot of fruit. The land near Hebron was a very productive region. We see that confirmed when Moses sent the twelve spies into the Promised Land and found the region near Hebron extremely fruitful.

> Numbers 13:22-23 MKJV 22 And they went up by the south and came to Hebron, where Ahiman, Sheshai, and Talmai, the sons of Anak were. (Now Hebron was built seven years before Zoan in Egypt.) 23 And they came to the valley of Eshcol and cut from there a branch with one cluster of grapes. And they carried it between two men upon a staff, and some of the pomegranates and of the figs.

The fruit that the spies brought back as evidence of the fruitfulness of the Promised Land came from a valley near Hebron.

Abraham was living near Hebron when Lot was taken captive by the kings from the area of Babylon. He was still there when God gave him the covenant of circumcision and promised that Sarah would bear a son. This was also when Abraham negotiated for sparing Sodom and Gomorrah if there were ten righteous men in Sodom. After the destruction of Sodom and Gomorrah, Abraham moved to the Negev. We see him returning to Hebron when Sarah dies.

> Genesis 23:2 MKJV 2 And Sarah died in Kirjath-arba; the same is Hebron in the land of Canaan. And Abraham came to mourn for Sarah, and to weep for her.

Abraham buys a field and a cave from Ephron the Hittite for Sarah's burial place. The price demanded by Ephron was too high, but Abraham paid the price without balking.

> Genesis 23:14-18 MKJV 14 And Ephron answered Abraham, saying to him, 15 My lord, listen to me. The land is worth four hundred shekels of silver; what is that between me and you? And bury your dead. 16 And Abraham listened to Ephron. And Abraham weighed to Ephron the silver which he had named in the hearing of the sons of Heth, four hundred shekels of silver, which passes with the merchant. 17 And the field of Ephron was certified, which was Machpelah, which was before Mamre; the field and the cave which was in it, and all the trees in the field, in all the borders round about, 18 to Abraham for a possession in the presence of the sons of Heth, before all that went in at the gate of his city.

One of the many jots and tittles in the Bible is in this passage. It emphasizes the greed of Ephron. Ephron's name is usually spelled עפרון. When Abraham pays Ephron in verse 16, Ephron's name is spelled without the vav, ו. The vav is the number six which represents man or the flesh. His name has been diminished because of his greed, the lust of the flesh. In this context, the greed of Ephron or mankind costs Abraham extra to bury his dead. Overall, the greed of mankind costs God more for our redemption.

Eventually, Abraham, Isaac and Rebecca, Jacob and Leah are all buried in the cave at Machpelah near Hebron. The burial place for all the patriarchs is in a place that produces abundance of life and Abraham willingly paid the price asked for by Ephron.

**B.** After Abraham and Isaac's death, the promise of the land passes on to Jacob. When famine hits the Promised Land, Jacob and his entire household go into Egypt. Jacob, though, is reluctant to leave the Promised Land.

> Genesis 46:2-4 MKJV 2 And God spoke to Israel in the visions of the night, and said, Jacob, Jacob! And he said, Here I am. 3 And He said, I am God, the God of your fathers. Do not fear to go down into Egypt, for I will make of you a great nation. 4 I will go down with you into Egypt, and I will also surely bring you up again. And Joseph shall put his hand on your eyes.

Here is the promise of resurrection! God assures Jacob that He would bring him back to the Promised Land. Instead Jacob dies in Egypt but his body is returned to the Promised Land and buried with Abraham and Isaac.

> Genesis 49:29-31 MKJV 29 And he charged them and said to them, I am to be gathered to my people. Bury me with my fathers in the cave that is in the field of Ephron the Hittite, 30 in the cave that is in the field of Machpelah, which is before Mamre, in the land of Canaan, the field which Abraham bought from Ephron the Hittite for a burying-place. 31 They buried Abraham and his wife Sarah there, and they buried Isaac and his wife Rebekah. And I buried Leah there;

# Hebron: The Promise of Resurrection

Abraham went to live in Hebron after coming out of Egypt. Jacob, in his death, also leaves Egypt and goes to Hebron. Jacob dies believing that God would still fulfill His promise. In fact, God promised all three of the patriarchs that they would inherit the Promised Land. The writer of Hebrews reminds us of their faith in God's promises.

> Hebrews 11:13 MKJV 13 These all died in faith, not having received the promises, but having seen them afar off. And they were persuaded of them and embraced them and confessed that they were strangers and pilgrims on the earth.

The phrase translated "on the earth" could just as easily be translated "in the land," and is in fact translated that way in verse 9.

> Hebrews 11:9 MKJV 9 By faith he lived **in the land** of promise as in a strange country, dwelling in tents with Isaac and Jacob, the heirs of the same promise with him.

Abraham, Isaac, and Jacob lie in Hebron even now awaiting the fulfillment of the promise.

> Hebrews 11:16 MKJV 16 But now they stretch forth to a better fatherland, that is, a heavenly one. Therefore God is not ashamed to be called their God, for He has prepared a city for them.

**C.** When God brought the children of Israel out of Egypt and was getting ready to take them into the Promised Land, Moses sent twelve spies into the Land. They brought back enormous fruit from the region around Hebron. But in addition to the fruit near Hebron, they saw the people. The ten spies who brought the bad report saw only the size of the people.

> Numbers 13:27-28 MKJV 27 And they told him and said, We came to the land where you sent us, and surely it flows with milk and honey. And this is the fruit of it. 28 However, the people that dwell in the land are strong, and the cities are walled, very great. And also we saw the children of Anak there.

> Numbers 13:32-33 MKJV 32 And they brought up an evil report of the land which they had searched to the sons of Israel, saying, The land through which we have gone to search it, is a land that eats up those who live in it. And all the people whom we saw in it were men of stature. 33 And there we saw the giants, the sons of Anak, of the giants. And we were in our own sight like grasshoppers, and so we were in their sight.

Like the fruit of the land, the sons of Anak were also from Hebron. Joshua tells us that there were three sons of Anak in Hebron.

> Joshua 15:14 MKJV 14 And Caleb drove out from there the three sons of Anak, Sheshai, and Ahiman, and Talmai, the sons of Anak.

# Hebron: The Promise of Resurrection

The ten spies saw them as invincible. What the ten spies didn't see were the three men of faith, the three patriarchs, who were buried there at the cave of Machpelah. Caleb and Joshua saw the three spiritual giants and believed along with them that God would do what He promised.

> Numbers 14:6-9 MKJV 6 And Joshua the son of Nun, and Caleb the son of Jephunneh, of those that searched the land, tore their clothes. 7 And they spoke to all the company of the sons of Israel saying, The land which we passed through to search is an exceedingly good land. 8 If the LORD delights in us, then He will bring us into this land and give it to us, a land which flows with milk and honey. 9 Only do not rebel against the LORD, neither fear the people of the land. For they are bread for us. Their protection has moved from them, and the LORD is with us. Do not fear them.

As a result of Caleb's faith in that he wholly followed the LORD his God, he would eventually inherit Hebron. Joshua was the only other man over twenty years of age who was counted in the census of fighting men who would even enter the Promised Land.

> Deuteronomy 1:35-36 MKJV 35 Surely there shall not one of these men of this evil generation see that good land, which I swore to give to your fathers, 36 except Caleb the son of Jephunneh; he shall see it, and to him I will give the land that he has trodden upon, and to his sons, because he has **fully followed the LORD**.

God specifically said that Caleb would inherit the land that he walked on. In the book of Joshua, we read that Moses gave Caleb Hebron

> Joshua 14:7-9 MKJV 7 I was forty years old when Moses the servant of the LORD sent me from Kadesh-barnea to spy out the land. And I brought him word again as it was in my heart. 8 But my brothers that went up with me made the heart of the people melt; yet I **fully followed the LORD** my God. 9 And Moses swore on that day, saying, Surely the land on which your feet have trodden shall be your inheritance, and your sons' forever because you have **fully** followed the LORD my God.

> Joshua 14:12-14 MKJV 12 And now give me this mountain of which the LORD spoke on that day. For you heard in that day how the giants were there, and that the cities were great and fortified. If the LORD will be with me, then I will be able to drive them out, as the LORD said. 13 And Joshua blessed him, and gave Hebron to Caleb the son of Jephunneh for an inheritance. 14 And Hebron became the inheritance of Caleb, the son of Jephunneh the Kenezite, to this day, because he **fully followed the LORD** God of Israel.

We see the phrase "fully followed the LORD" repeated four times in these three passages. The phrase appears one other time in Numbers 32:12 referring to both Caleb and Joshua. The only time this phrase is used is in these five verses. Caleb's faith enabled him to realize his hope of possessing his inheritance. The writer of Hebrews reminds us that it is

## Hebron: The Promise of Resurrection

our continued faith that enables us to realize our inheritance of eternal life.

> Hebrews 10:23 NKJV 23 Let us hold fast the confession of our hope without wavering, for He who promised is faithful.

The word picture for Caleb shows his complete devotion to the LORD.

---

Hebrew Word Picture: Hebrew is read right to left.

Caleb: #3612: כלב: Dog

כ Quph: back of the head, behind, the least, follow

ל Lamed: cattle goad, shepherd's staff, control, authority

ב Beit: tent, house, household, family, into

לב Lev: heart

Caleb is the dog who follows his master with his whole heart into the house and family.

---

Caleb must have walked over many places in the Promised Land as a spy, but it is here at Hebron, the burial place of the Patriarchs, that Caleb claims for his own inheritance. The name Hebron comes from Strong's #2275 meaning the seat of association. It comes from the Hebrew word chaber meaning to join or have fellowship.

#2266. חבר chabar, khaw-bar' a primitive root; to join (literally or figuratively); be compact, couple (together), have fellowship with, heap up, join (self, together), league.

Caleb had a choice when he came to Hebron. He could associate with the three physical giants of the land, the sons of Anak, or he could associate with the three spiritual giants, Abraham, Isaac and Jacob. Caleb chose to join and have fellowship with the spiritual giants receiving Hebron, the place of association, as his inheritance.

---

Hebrew Word Picture: Hebrew is read right to left.

Hebron: #2275: חברון

ח Het: fence, chamber, to separate

ב Bet: house, household, family

ר Resh: head, the highest person

ו Vav: nail, "and", to add, to secure

נ Noon: fish, activity, life

Hebron: The family chamber of the highest person who secures life.

Land. We know that Joshua is a type of Messiah bringing his people into the Promised Land. So, Caleb, as Joshua's follower, is a type of those who believe in Yeshua as Messiah.

> 1 Peter 1:3-5 NKJV 3 Blessed be the God and Father of our Lord Jesus Christ, who according to His abundant mercy has begotten us again to a living hope through the resurrection of Jesus Christ from the dead, 4 to an inheritance incorruptible and undefiled and that does not fade away, reserved in heaven for you, 5 who are kept by the power of God through faith for salvation ready to be revealed in the last time.

Like Caleb, we will realize the hope of our inheritance won for us by the power of God. Our father Abraham paid the price for the field and the cave; Caleb inherited it by the power of his faith in God. Our Father God paid the price for our inheritance; we realize our inheritance through our faith in the power of God that raised Yeshua from the dead. We are the family of God through Yeshua who secures eternal life for us.

**D.** Hebron is one of the six cities set aside as a city of refuge. The penalty for killing someone is death but if he kills accidentally or unintentionally, God set up places of refuge.

> Exodus 21:12-13 NIV 12 "Anyone who strikes a man and kills him shall surely be put to death. 13 However, if he does not do it intentionally, but God lets it happen, he is to flee to a place I will designate.

A person who flees to a city of refuge and is judged to have caused the death by accident must stay in the city until the high priest dies.

> Joshua 20:6 NIV 6 He is to stay in that city until he has stood trial before the assembly and until the death of the high priest who is serving at that time. Then he may go back to his own home in the town from which he fled."

A person who must flee to a city of refuge leaves his life behind. He experiences a death to his old life and must stay for an indefinite period of time in this new city. It is as if he is dead and is awaiting resurrection to return to his life. His resurrection is contingent on the death of the high priest. We also are dead to our old lives and await the resurrection which is made possible by the death of Yeshua our high priest.

> 1 Corinthians 15:42-43 MKJV 42 So also the resurrection of the dead. It is sown in corruption, it is raised in incorruption; 43 it is sown in dishonor, it is raised in glory; it is sown in weakness, it is raised in power;

**E.** Not only was Hebron a city of refuge, it was also a city that was set aside for the sons of Aaron, which is for the families of the priests.

> Joshua 21:9-11 MKJV 9 And they gave out of the tribe of the sons of Judah, and out of the tribe of the sons of Simeon, these cities which are called by name, 10 which the sons of Aaron had, being of the families of the Kohathites, who were of the sons of Levi, for theirs was the first lot. 11 And they gave them the city of Arba, the father of Anak (it is Hebron) in the hills of Judah, with its open lands around it.

It is interesting that a person seeking refuge at Hebron and awaiting the death of the high priest lives among priests and their families as he is waiting. In fact, the assembly of elders who hear his case when he flees to Hebron would consist of priests. But where does that leave Caleb since the sons of Aaron possessed the city itself? Caleb has possession of the fields and villages around the city.

> Joshua 21:12 MKJV 12 But the fields of the city of Arba and its villages they gave to Caleb the son of Jephunneh for his own.

The field and the cave of Machpelah which Abraham purchased were outside the city. They would be a possession of Caleb.

**F.** After the death of King Saul, God directed David to go to Hebron. Abraham, Isaac and Jacob were buried in Hebron, a place that we learned was vigorous with life. In contrast, Saul was buried in Jabesh.

> 1 Samuel 31:11-13 MKJV 11 And when they heard about it, the people of Jabesh-gilead, what the Philistines had done to Saul, 12 then all the brave men arose, and they traveled all night. And they took the body of Saul and the bodies of his sons from the wall of Beth-shan, and came to Jabesh, and burned them there. 13 And they took their bones and buried them under the tamarisk tree at Jabesh. And they fasted seven days.

The name Jabesh comes from yabesh which means dry, to be ashamed.

#3002. יָבֵשׁ yabesh, yaw-bashe'
from 3001; dry:--dried (away), dry.

#3001. יָבֵשׁ yabesh, yaw-bashe' a primitive root; to be ashamed, confused or disappointed; also (as failing) to dry up (as water) or wither (as herbage):--be ashamed.

Unlike Caleb, Saul did not fully follow the LORD.

> 1 Samuel 15:10-11 NKJV 10 Now the word of the LORD came to Samuel, saying, 11 "I greatly regret that I have set up Saul as king, for he has **turned back from following Me**, and has not performed My commandments." And it grieved Samuel, and he cried out to the LORD all night.

Samuel anointed David king of Israel in place of Saul because David was a man after God's own heart.

> Acts 13:22 MKJV 22 And when He had removed him, He raised up David to them to be their king; to whom He also witnessed and said, I have found David the son of Jesse to be a man after My own heart, who shall fulfill all My will.

Now, at the death of Saul, God tells David to go to Hebron where the men of Judah anoint him as king of Judah. The rest of Israel chose Saul's son Ishbosheth, whose name means the man of shame, to be king of Israel.

> 2 Samuel 2:8-11 MKJV 8 But Abner the son of Ner, commander of Saul's army, took Ishbosheth the son of Saul, and brought him over to Mahanaim. 9 And he made him king over Gilead, and over the Ashurites, and over Jezreel, and over Ephraim, and over Benjamin, and over all Israel. 10 Ishbosheth, Saul's son, was forty years old when he began to reign over Israel, and reigned two years. But the house of Judah followed David. 11 And it happened, the number of days that David was king in Hebron over the house of Judah was seven years and six months.

The timing is not yet right for David to go up to Jerusalem and establish his throne there. Instead he waits with Abraham, Isaac and Jacob for the right timing. Even after the death of Ishbosheth, the rest of Israel resists accepting David as king. They wait five and a half more years. David's time as king in Hebron is symbolic of Yeshua's time as king in heaven but not fully realized on earth. (For more about the significance of the seven years and 6 months that David reigned in Hebron, read "David's Reign and Yeshua's Second Coming" in Shadows of Messiah in the Torah, Volume 2.)

Hebron was an Aaronic city; David had priests who followed him including the high priest with the high priest's ephod. When King Saul killed Ahimelech the high priest for giving David and his men bread from the tabernacle, the high priest's son Abiathar fled to David taking the ephod with him.

> 1 Samuel 23:6 MKJV 6 And it happened when Abiathar the son of Ahimelech fled to David to Keilah, he came down with an ephod in his hand.

So David has access to the Urim and Thummim which Abiathar uses on his behalf to inquire of God.

When Yeshua came the first time, only some of the people accepted Him as king. Like David, He waits for the right timing. Among the believers in Yeshua were many of the priests and we have Yeshua Himself as our High Priest with full access to the Father to know His will. At the time of Yeshua, even though Israel had the witness of all the Jewish believers that Yeshua was the Messiah, they did not accept Him even when the temple was destroyed and they were scattered among the nations.

Finally all the tribes of Israel come to David at Hebron and make him their king.

# Hebron: The Promise of Resurrection

> 1 Chronicles 11:1-3 NKJV 1 Then all Israel came together to David at Hebron, saying, "Indeed we are your bone and your flesh. 2 "Also, in time past, even when Saul was king, you were the one who led Israel out and brought them in; and the LORD your God said to you, 'You shall shepherd My people Israel, and be ruler over My people Israel.'" 3 Therefore all the elders of Israel came to the king at Hebron, and David made a covenant with them at Hebron before the LORD. Then they anointed David king over Israel, according to the word of the LORD by Samuel.

Ezekiel prophesies about the Messiah that when Israel is gathered from the nations, God will make His servant David shepherd over all His people.

> Ezekiel 34:23-24 NKJV 23 "I will establish one shepherd over them, and he shall feed them-My servant David. He shall feed them and be their shepherd. 24 "And I, the LORD, will be their God, and My servant David a prince among them; I, the LORD, have spoken.

We see that the end of David's reign in Hebron corresponds to the return of Yeshua and the establishment of the millennial kingdom. The resurrection of the dead will occur at the same time.

> Matthew 24:30-31 NKJV 30 "Then the sign of the Son of Man will appear in heaven, and then all the tribes of the earth will mourn, and they will see the Son of Man coming on the clouds of heaven with power and great glory. 31 "And He will send His angels with a great sound of a trumpet, and they will gather together His elect from the four winds, from one end of heaven to the other.

> 1 Thessalonians 4:16-17 NKJV 16 For the Lord Himself will descend from heaven with a shout, with the voice of an archangel, and with the trumpet of God. And the dead in Christ will rise first. 17 Then we who are alive and remain shall be caught up together with them in the clouds to meet the Lord in the air. And thus we shall always be with the Lord.

When David leaves Hebron, he goes up to Jerusalem with all his armies to take the city. When Yeshua leaves heaven, He goes up to Jerusalem with all His armies including Abraham, Isaac and Jacob.

# Student Notes for Hebron: The Promise of Resurrection

**A.** Abraham spent much of his time in the Promised Land at Hebron. (Gen. 13:18, Num. 13:22-23, Gen 23:2, Gen 23:14-18)

#4471: Mamre: vigor strength or fatness

Jots and tittles:
Ephron's name is usually spelled עפרון.

The burial place for all the patriarchs is in a place that produces abundance of life and Abraham willingly paid the price asked for by Ephron.

**B.** After Abraham and Isaac's death, the promise of the land passes on to Jacob. (Gen. 46:2-4, Gen. 49:29-31, Heb. 11:13, Heb. 11:9, Heb. 11:16)

"On the earth" = "In the land"

**C.** The twelve spies brought back enormous fruit from the region around Hebron. (Num. 13:27-28, Num. 13:32-33, Jos. 15:14, Num. 14:6-9, Deu. 1:35-36, Jos. 14:7-9, Jos. 14:12-14, Heb. 10:23)

Student Notes for Hebron: The Promise of Resurrection

"Fully followed the LORD"

> Hebrew Word Picture: Hebrew is read right to left.
>
> Caleb: #3612: כלב: Dog
>
> כ Quph: back of the head, behind, the least, follow
>
> ל Lamed: cattle goad, shepherd's staff, control, authority
>
> ב Beit: tent, house, household, family, into
>
> לב Lev: heart
>
> Caleb is the dog who follows his master with his whole heart into the house and family.

#2275: Hebron :the seat of association

#2266. חבר chabar, khaw-bar' a primitive root; to join (literally or figuratively); be compact, couple (together), have fellowship with, heap up, join (self, together), league.

> Hebrew Word Picture: Hebrew is read right to left.
>
> Hebron: #2275: חברון
>
> ח Het: fence, chamber, to separate
>
> ב Bet: house, household, family
>
> ר Resh: head, the highest person
>
> ו Vav: nail, "and", to add, to secure
>
> נ Noon: fish, activity, life
>
> Hebron: The family chamber of the highest person who secures life.

Caleb is a type of those who believe in Yeshua haMashiach. (1Pet. 1:3-5)

Student Notes for Hebron: The Promise of Resurrection

**D.** Hebron is one of the six cities set aside as a city of refuge. (Exo. 21:12-13, Jos. 20:6, ICor. 15:42-43)

**E.** Hebron was also a city that was set aside for the sons of Aaron. (Jos. 21:9-11, Jos. 21:12)

**F.** After the death of Saul, God directed David to go to Hebron. (1Sam. 31:11-13, 1Sam. 15:10-11, Acts 13:22, 2Sam. 2:8-11, 1Sam. 23:6,)

#3002. יבש yabesh, yaw-bashe'
from 3001; dry:--dried (away), dry.

#3001. יבש yabesh, yaw-bashe' a primitive root; to be ashamed, confused or disappointed; also (as failing) to dry up (as water) or wither (as herbage):--be ashamed.

All the tribes of Israel come to David at Hebron and make him king. (1Chr. 11:1-3, Eze. 34:23-24, Mat. 24:30-31, 1The. 4:16-17)

Student Notes for Hebron: The Promise of Resurrection

**Discussion Questions for Hebron: The Promise of Resurrection**

1. David used the ephod to inquire of God. Read 1 Samuel 23:9-13; 2 Samuel 2:1-7; and 2 Samuel 5:17-25. How do these events show that David wholly followed the LORD? What are the significances of these events?

2. Read Matthew 22:31-32 and Luke 20:37-38. What did Yeshua say about the resurrection of the dead? How does this apply to Hebron and the promise of resurrection?

3. Caleb and Joshua wholly followed the LORD unlike the other ten spies. Read Numbers 13:26-33; James 1:6-8; and James 4:8. What does James say about the double-minded man? How does this apply to the ten spies and the children of Israel in regards to going into the Land?

4. Caleb kept his eyes on God's promise to give them the Land and on the patriarchs. Read Hebrews 11. What is implied about the resurrection of these men of faith?

5. Compare the word picture for Caleb with the greatest commandment in Deuteronomy 4:4-6.

6. Compare Isaiah 26:19-21 with the word picture for Hebron.

7. When Jacob returned to his father in the Promised Land after His exile, where did he "come home?" (Gen. 31:17-18, Gen. 35:27) Discuss the significance of the homecoming.

## Shechem: Choose Life

Shechem is one of three places in Israel that the Bible records the children of Israel purchasing land. These three places, Hebron, Shechem and Jerusalem, all have incredible prophetic significance. Hebron, the burial place of Abraham, Isaac, and Jacob, is the promise of resurrection. Shechem is the symbolic equivalent of the location of the tree of knowledge of good and evil. When we come to Shechem, we must choose to follow God or to follow our own way. Jerusalem, the eternal city, represents the tree of life. Israel, as a whole, represents the Garden of Eden.

One of the most recognized phrases from the Bible are the words spoken by Joshua just before his death in front of the gathered tribes of Israel. We usually quote just part of the verse, "Choose this day whom you will serve, as for me and my house, we will serve the LORD." These words are popular adornments to hang in our houses. The actual verse from which we take these words reads as follows:

> Joshua 24:15 NKJV 15 "And if it seems evil to you to serve the LORD, choose for yourselves this day whom you will serve, whether the gods which your fathers served that were on the other side of the River, or the gods of the Amorites, in whose land you dwell. But as for me and my house, we will serve the LORD."

The gathering where Joshua spoke these words took place at Shechem. As we examine the events that take place at Shechem, we will see that Shechem is the place of choosing. When God brought Abraham, Jacob and the children of Israel into the Promised Land, their first stop for each of them was at Shechem. The city of Shechem is located at the northern edge of the mountains of Israel. These mountains are called the spine of Israel with Shechem located at the neck or shoulders. The name Shechem means the base of the neck, the place of burdens, a portion. It is, also, an idiom for consent.

#7926. שכם shakem shek-em' from 7925; the neck (between the shoulders) as the place of burdens; figuratively, the spur of a hill:--back, X consent, portion, shoulder.

Shechem is also a city of refuge and a city set aside for the Levites. Specifically, it is a city given to the Kohathites whose duty it was to carry the sacred furnishings of the Tabernacle, including the Ark of the Covenant, on their shoulders whenever the Tabernacle of God moved.

> Numbers 3:31 KJV 31 And their charge shall be the ark, and the table, and the candlestick, and the altars, and the vessels of the sanctuary wherewith they minister, and the hanging, and all the service thereof.

Yeshua's words about bearing his burden come to mind.

> Matthew 11:28-30 NKJV 28 "Come to Me, all you who labor and are heavy laden, and I will give you rest. 29 "Take My yoke upon you and learn from Me, for I am

> gentle and lowly in heart, and you will find rest for your souls. 30 "For My yoke is easy and My burden is light."

Shechem is the place between the shoulders where a burden is carried. As we arrive at Shechem with our lives burdened by sin, we have a choice. We can exchange our burdens for the yoke of Yeshua or continue in our lives of sin. We can choose to be yoked to Yeshua, letting Him take control and bring us fully into the Promised Land, the place of rest. Jerusalem, halfway down the mountain range, represents the navel, the place of nourishment. It is only through Shechem that one can finally arrive at Jerusalem.

So, we see Israel as the Garden of Eden and Jerusalem as the place of nourishment through the Tree of Life. Shechem, as the place of decision, represents the tree of the knowledge of good and evil. Joshua's words in our verse even phrase the question of who to serve in terms of good and evil. He says, "If it seems evil to you…"

Adam and Eve had a choice there in the Garden of Eden. They could choose to obey God and trust that He had their best interests at heart, or they could choose to disobey God and seek their own best interests. That is, they could choose for themselves what actions are good and what actions are evil.

> Genesis 3:4-6 NKJV 4 Then the serpent said to the woman, "You will not surely die. 5 "For God knows that in the day you eat of it your eyes will be opened, and you will be like God, knowing good and evil." 6 So when the woman saw that the tree was good for food, that it was pleasant to the eyes, and a tree desirable to make one wise, she took of its fruit and ate. She also gave to her husband with her, and he ate.

Eve made the decision that she knew better than God. She gave in to the lust of the flesh, the lust of the eyes, and the pride of life, choosing to decide "good and evil." Adam, who was with her, went along with her choice instead of disavowing it as a husband had the option to do.

> Numbers 30:10-11 NIV 10 "If a woman living with her husband makes a vow or obligates herself by a pledge under oath 11 and her husband hears about it but says nothing to her and does not forbid her, then all her vows or the pledges by which she obligated herself will stand.

Yeshua faced the same choice as Eve when Satan tempted Him in the wilderness. When Abraham, Jacob, and the children of Israel entered the Promised Land, they each faced one of the three aspects of the same temptation at Shechem. Abraham faced the lust of the eyes; Jacob faced the lust of the flesh; and the children of Israel faced the pride of life.

**A.** When Abraham enters the Promised Land for the first time, God speaks to him when he is near Shechem.

# Shechem: Choose Life

> Genesis 12:6-7 NKJV 6 Abram passed through the land to the place of Shechem, as far as the terebinth tree of Moreh. And the Canaanites were then in the land. 7 Then the LORD appeared to Abram and said, "To your descendants I will give this land." And there he built an altar to the LORD, who had appeared to him.

God told Abraham that He would give this land to Abraham's seed. Abraham looks and sees all the land around him. He reacted to this news by building an altar to the LORD. He chose to worship God. Abraham's actions are similar to the actions of Yeshua when Satan tempted Him. Satan took Him to a high mountain and promised Him all the kingdoms of the world.

> Matthew 4:8-10 NKJV 8 Again, the devil took Him up on an exceedingly high mountain, and showed Him all the kingdoms of the world and their glory. 9 And he said to Him, "All these things I will give You if You will fall down and worship me." 10 Then Jesus said to him, "Away with you, Satan! For it is written, 'You shall worship the LORD your God, and Him only you shall serve.'"

Abraham built an altar to God at the terebinth tree at Shechem. Like Yeshua, Abraham chose to worship God.

**B.** When Jacob entered the Promised Land after his exile, his first stop is also at Shechem. Jacob settled down there; he bought land and dug a well. Life was comfortable and the living was good. Then Shechem the son of Hamor raped his daughter Dinah. Jacob could have compromised; Shechem wished to marry Dinah thus restoring her honor, but that would mean mingling with the Canaanites of the land. When Joshua spoke to the gathered children of Israel at Shechem, he contrasted the choice of serving God with the choice to serve the gods of the Amorites. God described the Amorite branch of Canaanites to Abraham as sinful, and that He would drive them out to give the land to Abraham.

> Genesis 15:16 NKJV 16 "But in the fourth generation they shall return here, for the iniquity of the Amorites is not yet complete."

So, compromising and melding into Shechem society as the Shechemites wanted was not God's plan. Shechem explained his plan for assimilating the sons of Jacob to his fellow townsmen.

> Genesis 34:23 NKJV 23 "Will not their livestock, their property, and every animal of theirs be ours? Only let us consent to them, and they will dwell with us."

Jacob's sons Simeon and Levi respond in the flesh and wipe out all the people of Shechem. Jacob finally awakens to his situation and God calls out to him. God reminded Jacob of their encounter at Bethel before Jacob left the land fleeing from Esau.

> Genesis 35:1 NKJV 1 Then God said to Jacob, "Arise, go up to Bethel and dwell there; and make an altar there to God, who appeared to you when you fled from the face of Esau your brother."

# Shechem: Choose Life

God's promise was to be with Jacob and to accomplish what God spoke to Jacob. God had promised Jacob to be with him in his exile and to return him to the Promised Land. Jacob responded with the promise to build God an altar at Bethel when he returned and to give him a tenth of everything that God had given him.

> Genesis 28:15 NKJV 15 "Behold, I am with you and will keep you wherever you go, and will bring you back to this land; for I will not leave you until I have done what I have spoken to you."

> Genesis 28:20-22 KJV 20 And Jacob vowed a vow, saying, If God will be with me, and will keep me in this way that I go, and will give me bread to eat, and raiment to put on, 21 So that I come again to my father's house in peace; then shall the LORD be my God: 22 And this stone, which I have set for a pillar, shall be God's house: and of all that thou shalt give me I will surely give the tenth unto thee.

Jacob had apparently forgotten this vow as he settled in near Shechem. The comfort of the things of this world had him reluctant to move on. This calls to mind another of Yeshua's temptations, the lust of the flesh.

> Matthew 4:3-4 NKJV 3 Now when the tempter came to Him, he said, "If You are the Son of God, command that these stones become bread." 4 But He answered and said, "It is written, 'Man shall not live by bread alone, but by every word that proceeds from the mouth of God.'"

Jacob nearly gave in to the lust of the flesh, but the incident with Dinah jolted him out of his complacency. Jacob chose instead to listen and obey the words of God, to live by the words God had given him.

> Genesis 35:2-4 NKJV 2 And Jacob said to his household and to all who were with him, "Put away the foreign gods that are among you, purify yourselves, and change your garments. 3 "Then let us arise and go up to Bethel; and I will make an altar there to God, **who answered me in the day of my distress and has been with me in the way which I have gone."** 4 So they gave Jacob all the foreign gods which were in their hands, and the earrings which were in their ears; and Jacob hid them under the terebinth tree which was by Shechem.

Abraham built an altar by the terebinth tree; Jacob buried his idols under the same tree.

**C.** When Joshua led the Israelites into the Promised Land, God told him even before he entered the Land to make his first stop at Shechem. The underlying theme throughout God's instructions to Joshua is that it is God, and not the power of the Israelites, that will conquer the land. They are not to get puffed up in their own pride and strength of arms.

Moses delivers God's message by starting with a recitation of what God did for the Israelites. He reminds them of the mighty works that God did.

# Shechem: Choose Life

> Deuteronomy 11:1-7 NKJV 1 "Therefore you shall love the LORD your God, and keep His charge, His statutes, His judgments, and His commandments always. 2 "Know today that I do not speak with your children, who have not known and who have not seen the chastening of the LORD your God, His greatness and His mighty hand and His outstretched arm- 3 "His signs and His acts which He did in the midst of Egypt, to Pharaoh king of Egypt, and to all his land; 4 "what He did to the army of Egypt, to their horses and their chariots: how He made the waters of the Red Sea overflow them as they pursued you, and how the LORD has destroyed them to this day; 5 "what He did for you in the wilderness until you came to this place; 6 "and what He did to Dathan and Abiram the sons of Eliab, the son of Reuben: how the earth opened its mouth and swallowed them up, their households, their tents, and all the substance that was in their possession, in the midst of all Israel- 7 "but your eyes have seen every great act of the LORD which He did.

Moses continues with God's promise to drive out the inhabitants of the Promised Land as long as Israel continues to obey God. He concludes with stating the choice they will face at Shechem which is nestled between Mount Gerizim and Mount Ebal.

> Deuteronomy 11:26-29 NKJV 26 "Behold, I set before you today a blessing and a curse: 27 "the blessing, if you obey the commandments of the LORD your God which I command you today; 28 "and the curse, if you do not obey the commandments of the LORD your God, but turn aside from the way which I command you today, to go after other gods which you have not known. 29 "Now it shall be, when the LORD your God has brought you into the land which you go to possess, that you shall put the blessing on Mount Gerizim and the curse on Mount Ebal.

A summary of God's promises as they go into the Promised Land are that He would send His angel before them to drive out the inhabitants, that no man would be able to stand against them, and that God would set them high above all the other nations.

> Exodus 33:2 NKJV 2 "And I will send My Angel before you, and I will drive out the Canaanite and the Amorite and the Hittite and the Perizzite and the Hivite and the Jebusite.

> Deuteronomy 11:25 NKJV 25 "No man shall be able to stand against you; the LORD your God will put the dread of you and the fear of you upon all the land where you tread, just as He has said to you.

> Deuteronomy 28:1 NKJV 1 "Now it shall come to pass, if you diligently obey the voice of the LORD your God, to observe carefully all His commandments which I command you today, that the LORD your God will set you high above all nations of the earth.

Satan promises variations of these same things to Yeshua.

Shechem: Choose Life

> Matthew 4:5-7 NKJV 5 Then the devil took Him up into the holy city, set Him on the pinnacle of the temple, 6 and said to Him, "If You are the Son of God, throw Yourself down. For it is written: 'He shall give His angels charge over you,' and, 'In their hands they shall bear you up, Lest you dash your foot against a stone.'" 7 Jesus said to him, "It is written again, 'You shall not tempt the LORD your God.'"

Satan set Yeshua high above the city, tempting Yeshua to test the presence of God's angels and His promise of protection. Yeshua responds from the book of Deuteronomy which contains God's instructions to Israel in the last month before they enter the Promised Land. The rest of the passage Yeshua quotes here goes on to say that God gives them this warning so that they will go on to possess the land God promised to them.

> Deuteronomy 6:16-19 NKJV 16 "You shall not tempt the LORD your God as you tempted Him in Massah. 17 "You shall diligently keep the commandments of the LORD your God, His testimonies, and His statutes which He has commanded you. 18 "And you shall do what is right and good in the sight of the LORD, that it may be well with you, and that you may go in and possess the good land of which the LORD swore to your fathers, 19 "to cast out all your enemies from before you, as the LORD has spoken.

Again, this is in the context of the children of Israel entering the Promised Land and God defeating all their enemies. They are to do what is right in God's sight.

**D.** The details of this ceremony at Shechem further connect this to Adam and Eve's decision at the foot of the tree of the knowledge of good and evil. Satan's opening words to Eve are "Has God really said…?" There in Shechem, there can be no doubt about what God said. The first thing the Israelites were to do was to write all the words of the Torah on white-washed stones and set them on Mount Ebal.

> Deuteronomy 27:2-4 NKJV 2 "And it shall be, on the day when you cross over the Jordan to the land which the LORD your God is giving you, that you shall set up for yourselves large stones, and whitewash them with lime. 3 "You shall write on them all the words of this law, when you have crossed over, that you may enter the land which the LORD your God is giving you, 'a land flowing with milk and honey,' just as the LORD God of your fathers promised you. 4 "Therefore it shall be, when you have crossed over the Jordan, that on Mount Ebal you shall set up these stones, which I command you today, and you shall whitewash them with lime.

The stones are set up on Mount Ebal, the mount of cursing. It is there on Mt. Ebal that, when they are tempted with the words of Satan that would lead to the curse, they need to be reminded of God's very words! There, right in front of them, in the form of two mountains, are the choices. Obey God and be blessed with a Land flowing with milk and honey, or follow after other gods and be afflicted with the curse which would (and did) lead to their ejection from the Land.

They also set up an altar on Mount Ebal.

> Deuteronomy 27:5-7 NKJV 5 "And there you shall build an altar to the LORD your God, an altar of stones; you shall not use an iron tool on them. 6 "You shall build with whole stones the altar of the LORD your God, and offer burnt offerings on it to the LORD your God. 7 "You shall offer peace offerings, and shall eat there, and rejoice before the LORD your God.

The location is again on the mount of cursing because it is there, that when they have overcome the temptations of Satan, they are to bring their burnt offerings and peace offerings. Notice the absence of the mention of a sin or guilt offering. The burnt offerings are those given entirely to God and are meant to draw the one who offers them near to God. The peace offerings, also called fellowship offerings, are a shared meal with God. The reward for obedience is to enter into the very presence of God.

Before Adam and Eve ate from the tree of the knowledge of good and evil, they walked with God daily enjoying fellowship with their creator. After eating from the tree, they hid from God. When God came to fellowship with them in the cool of the evening, that fellowship was no longer possible; their choice to listen to Satan broke that fellowship. They couldn't draw near to God.

The altar itself was made of unhewn stone; they weren't to make it with ornately decorated stones or with precious metals. The altar in no way lifts up or glorifies the acts of man. They could take no pride in the construction of the altar; it was all about God and not about them. The unhewn stone of the altar represents Yeshua Himself. Like the altar, Yeshua was not beautiful in man's eyes.

> Isaiah 53:2 NKJV 2b He has no form or comeliness; And when we see Him, There is no beauty that we should desire Him.

In the book of Daniel, an unhewn stone represents the Messiah who would destroy the kingdoms of this world and establish the everlasting kingdom of Messiah.

> Daniel 2:31-35 NKJV 31 "You, O king, were watching; and behold, a great image! This great image, whose splendor was excellent, stood before you; and its form was awesome. 32 "This image's head was of fine gold, its chest and arms of silver, its belly and thighs of bronze, 33 "its legs of iron, its feet partly of iron and partly of clay. 34 "You watched while a stone was cut out without hands, which struck the image on its feet of iron and clay, and broke them in pieces. 35 "Then the iron, the clay, the bronze, the silver, and the gold were crushed together, and became like chaff from the summer threshing floors; the wind carried them away so that no trace of them was found. And the stone that struck the image became a great mountain and filled the whole earth.

The image, described as great and splendorous, represents the kingdoms of man, that is, their own achievements. In contrast, the stone that destroys them is not the work of man and it lacks the outward splendor of the image. Judgment is coming on those who give in to the temptation of the pride of life. The works of men will be blown away like chaff on the wind.

The Israelites carried out the ceremony as Moses instructed them, building the altar, writing the Torah on the stones and reading the Torah in front of all the people. Joshua gathered the Israelites again at Shechem just before he died. He recites all that God had done for them starting with bringing Abraham to the Promised Land and ending with God giving them the land. The emphasis is, again, that God is the one who acted. They did not achieve any of their victories by their own strength.

> Joshua 24:13 NKJV 13 'I have given you a land for which you did not labor, and cities which you did not build, and you dwell in them; you eat of the vineyards and olive groves which you did not plant.'

Joshua then follows this statement with the famous instructions for the Israelites to choose whom they would serve. They choose to serve God.

> Joshua 24:24-27 NKJV 24 And the people said to Joshua, "The LORD our God we will serve, and His voice we will obey!" 25 So Joshua made a covenant with the people that day, and made for them a statute and an ordinance in Shechem. 26 Then Joshua wrote these words in the Book of the Law of God. And he took a large stone, and set it up there under the oak (terebinth) that was by the sanctuary of the LORD. 27 And Joshua said to all the people, "Behold, this stone shall be a witness to us, for it has heard all the words of the LORD which He spoke to us. It shall therefore be a witness to you, lest you deny your God."

Abraham built an altar under the terebinth tree; Jacob buried all his idols under the terebinth tree. Joshua set up a stone under the terebinth tree as a witness to their decision to serve the LORD. The Israelites continued to serve God as long as there were elders alive who had personally experienced God's miracles.

> Joshua 24:31 NKJV 31 Israel served the LORD all the days of Joshua, and all the days of the elders who outlived Joshua, who had known all the works of the LORD which He had done for Israel.

After their death, as we enter the book of Judges, the recurring theme is that the people did what was right in their own eyes. The last verse in the book of Judges states this summation.

> Judges 21:25 NKJV 25 In those days there was no king in Israel; everyone did what was right in his own eyes.

# Shechem: Choose Life

One day there will be a king in Israel. He shall not judge by the sight of His eyes, but shall rule with righteousness.

> Isaiah 11:1-5 NKJV 1 There shall come forth a Rod from the stem of Jesse, And a Branch shall grow out of his roots. 2 The Spirit of the LORD shall rest upon Him, The Spirit of wisdom and understanding, The Spirit of counsel and might, The Spirit of knowledge and of the fear of the LORD. 3 His delight is in the fear of the LORD, And He shall not judge by the sight of His eyes, Nor decide by the hearing of His ears; 4 But with righteousness He shall judge the poor, And decide with equity for the meek of the earth; He shall strike the earth with the rod of His mouth, And with the breath of His lips He shall slay the wicked. 5 Righteousness shall be the belt of His loins, And faithfulness the belt of His waist.

**E.** The journey of the Israelites from Egypt to the Promised Land mirrors our life's journey. It begins with life in Egypt representing our lives in the world. God sent redemption on Passover. The Israelites had the choice to participate by eating the Passover Lamb and following Moses, their redeemer out of Egypt leading to a new life. We have the choice to participate in the death of Yeshua and follow Him out of Egypt into a new life. As the Israelites began their new life, they first passed through the Sea and met with God at Mt. Sinai. We, too, pass through the Sea through baptism, the outward profession of our faith, and meet with God at our Mt. Sinai. At Mt. Sinai, the Israelites received the Covenant written by the finger of God on tablets of stone. At our Mt. Sinai, we receive the New Covenant written by the finger of God on the tablets of our hearts.

At the altar of unhewn stone, the Israelites bring their burnt offerings and their fellowship offerings. We too are to bring our burnt offerings and fellowship offerings.

> Romans 12:1-2 NKJV 1 I beseech you therefore, brethren, by the mercies of God, that you present your bodies a living sacrifice, holy, acceptable to God, which is your reasonable service. 2 And do not be conformed to this world, but be transformed by the renewing of your mind, that you may prove what is that good and acceptable and perfect will of God.

We bring our offerings to the altar of unhewn stone on the mount of cursing that represents Yeshua who has redeemed us from the curse of the Law.

> Galatians 3:13 NKJV 13 Christ has redeemed us from the curse of the law, having become a curse for us (for it is written, "Cursed is everyone who hangs on a tree"),

Literally, Yeshua died on the wooden cross; He was displayed on a tree. Symbolically, there is the witness of the stone Joshua set up under the Terebinth tree near Shechem. Through Yeshua, we can draw near to God and have fellowship with Him.

> Hebrews 10:16-22 NKJV 16 "This is the covenant that I will make with them after those days, says the LORD: I will put My laws into their hearts, and in their minds I will write them," 17 then He adds, "Their sins and their lawless deeds I will

> remember no more." 18 Now where there is remission of these, there is no longer an offering for sin. 19 Therefore, brethren, having boldness to enter the Holiest by the blood of Jesus, 20 by a new and living way which He consecrated for us, through the veil, that is, His flesh, 21 and having a High Priest over the house of God, 22 let us draw near with a true heart in full assurance of faith, having our hearts sprinkled from an evil conscience and our bodies washed with pure water.

God says He writes His laws in our hearts. John tells us that the outward evidence of knowing God is to obey Him.

> 1 John 2:3-6 NKJV 3 Now by this we know that we know Him, if we keep His commandments. 4 He who says, "I know Him," and does not keep His commandments, is a liar, and the truth is not in him. 5 But whoever keeps His word, truly the love of God is perfected in him. By this we know that we are in Him. 6 He who says he abides in Him ought himself also to walk just as He walked.

The whole book of 1 John is about recognizing and making the right choices so that we may have fellowship with the Father and His son Yeshua.

> 1 John 1:3-5 NKJV 3 that which we have seen and heard we declare to you, that you also may have fellowship with us; and truly our fellowship is with the Father and with His Son Jesus Christ. 4 And these things we write to you that your joy may be full. 5 This is the message which we have heard from Him and declare to you, that God is light and in Him is no darkness at all.

The result of making the choices John will lay out in his letter is that our joy may be full. Joshua sets out the choice of who to serve that they may have abundant life in the Promised Land. John contrasts the choice of light and darkness. Choose good by choosing light and life, or choose evil by choosing darkness and death.

John contrasts love and hate, truth and lies, righteousness and sin, and the spirit of truth and error. John goes on to warn us against falling prey to those same temptations faced by Adam and Eve in the Garden of Eden; and by Abraham, Jacob and the children of Israel as they entered the Promised Land; and by Yeshua when Satan tempted Him in the wilderness.

> 1 John 2:15-16 NKJV 15 Do not love the world or the things in the world. If anyone loves the world, the love of the Father is not in him. 16 For all that is in the world--the lust of the flesh, the lust of the eyes, and the pride of life--is not of the Father but is of the world.

How then should we live? The Israelites had to choose each day how they would live. We also have a daily decision to make. Yeshua tells us to take up our crosses every day and follow Him.

> Luke 9:23 NKJV 23 Then He said to them all, "If anyone desires to come after Me, let him deny himself, and take up his cross daily, and follow Me.

If we make this choice, our reward, like the reward of the Israelites, is to live in the Promised Land of milk and honey.

> 1 John 5:11-12 NKJV 11 And this is the testimony: that God has given us eternal life, and this life is in His Son. 12 He who has the Son has life; he who does not have the Son of God does not have life.

John closes his letter with the same theme as Joshua's words. He exhorts us to know the truth and reject the false, to worship only God.

> 1 John 5:18-21 NKJV 18 We know that whoever is born of God does not sin; but he who has been born of God keeps himself, and the wicked one does not touch him. 19 We know that we are of God, and the whole world lies under the sway of the wicked one. 20 And we know that the Son of God has come and has given us an understanding, that we may know Him who is true; and we are in Him who is true, in His Son Jesus Christ. This is the true God and eternal life. 21 Little children, keep yourselves from idols. Amen.

Will you choose to follow the wicked one and worship the idols set up in imitation of God or will you choose to worship God and receive life through His Son Yeshua? Choose life.

# Student Notes for Shechem: Choose Life

Joshua 24:15 NKJV 15 "And if it seems evil to you to serve the LORD, choose for yourselves this day whom you will serve, whether the gods which your fathers served that were on the other side of the River, or the gods of the Amorites, in whose land you dwell. But as for me and my house, we will serve the LORD."

Shechem is the place of choice. (Num. 3:31)

Shechem: #7926. שכם shakem, shek-em' from 7925; the neck (between the shoulders) as the place of burdens; figuratively, the spur of a hill:--back, X consent, portion, shoulder.

Yeshua's words about bearing his burden come to mind. (Mat. 11:28-30)

Shechem represents the tree of the knowledge of good and evil. (Gen. 3:4-6, Num. 30:10-11)

**A.** When Abraham enters the Promised Land for the first time, God speaks to him when he is near Shechem. (Gen. 12:6-7, Mat. 4:8-10)

Like Yeshua, Abraham chose to worship God.

**B.** When Jacob entered the Promised Land after his exile, his first stop is also at Shechem. (Gen. 15:16, Gen. 34:23, Gen. 35:1, Gen. 28:15, Gen. 28:20-22, Mat. 4:3-4, Gen. 35:2-4)

Abraham built an altar by the terebinth tree; Jacob buried his idols under the same tree.

**C.** When Joshua led the Israelites into the Promised Land, God told him even before he entered the Land to make his first stop at Shechem. (Deu. 11:1-7, Deu. 11:26-29, Exo. 33:2, Deu. 11:25, Deu. 28:1, Mat. 4:5-7, Deu. 6:16-19)

They are to do what is right in God's sight.

**D.** Satan's opening words to Eve are "Has God really said...?" There in Shechem, there can be no doubt about what God said. (Deu. 27:2-4, Deu. 27:5-7, Isa. 53:2b, Dan 2:31-35, Jos. 24:13, Jos. 24:24-27)

Abraham built an altar under the terebinth tree; Jacob buried all his idols under the terebinth tree. Joshua set up a stone under the terebinth tree as a witness to their decision to serve the LORD.

The Israelites continued to serve God as long as there were elders alive who had personally experienced God's work. (Jos. 24:31, Jdg. 21:25)

One day there will be a king in Israel. He shall not judge by the sight of His eyes, but shall rule with righteousness. (Isa. 11:1-5)

**E.** The journey of the Israelites from Egypt to the Promised Land mirrors our life's journey. At the altar of unhewn stone: (Rom. 12:1-2, Gal. 3:13, Heb. 10:16-22, 1John 2:3-6)

The whole book of 1 John is about recognizing and making the right choices so that we may have fellowship with the Father and His son Yeshua. (1John 1:3-5, 1John 2:15-16, Luke 9:23, 1John 5:11-12, 1John 5:18-21)

Will you choose to follow the wicked one and worship the idols set up in imitation of God or will you choose to worship God and receive life through His Son Yeshua? Choose life.

**Discussion Questions Shechem: Choose Life**

1. In John's closing words of his first epistle, he describes Yeshua as "true." We tend to think of false as the opposite of true, but true also means real as opposed to an imitation, illusion or replica. Discuss 1 John 5:18-21 with this understanding of the word "true."

2. The book of Judges ends with the words that there was no king in Israel. Who was supposed to be king of Israel (1 Sam. 8:4-9)? What does this say about the spiritual state of Israel at this time?

3. Read Genesis 34 about Simeon and Levi's choice to slaughter the inhabitants of Shechem. How was their action reflected in Jacob's "blessing" on them in Genesis 49:5-7?

4. The study ended by comparing Joshua's final words in Joshua 24:14-28 with the closing words of John's first epistle in 1 John 5:18-21. What is one common exhortation and one common warning in these two passages?

5. Before the children of Israel went into the Promised Land, Moses recited God's deeds from the exodus from Egypt to the current time. Joshua recited God's actions on their behalf twice at Shechem (Josh. 8:30-33 and Josh. 24). What was the purpose of this recital? How can we apply this in our lives?

## Shechem: Decisions, Decisions!

Shechem is the location of crucial decisions that altered the course of Israel. We will look at three incidents involving decisions that influenced the history of Israel as well as having prophetic significance. These are the decisions of Jacob's sons, Gideon's son Abimelech and the residents of Shechem, and Solomon's son Rehoboam and the leaders of the other tribes of Israel.

**A.** The first incident involves Jacob's sons. The life of Jacob's son Joseph is one of the strongest Shadows of Messiah in the Bible. The Jewish people say one of the titles of the Messiah is the Son of Joseph. The study of Joseph as a type of Messiah is so large it needs its own book. For this study, we will focus on Joseph's leaving and returning to the Promised Land. Shechem has a role to play in both events.

When Jacob and his children returned to the Promised Land, they settled in Shechem. When Shechem, the son of the ruler of the city of Shechem, raped Dinah, Simeon and Levi took it upon themselves to avenge her by slaughtering all the men of Shechem, taking the women and children captive, and plundering the city. While it was true that Dinah was raped and they were not to intermarry with the Canaanites of Shechem, the judgment against the city and inhabitants of Shechem rightly belonged to their father. They usurped his authority by planning and executing judgment behind their father's back.

> Genesis 49:5-7 NKJV 5 "Simeon and Levi are brothers; Instruments of cruelty are in their dwelling place. 6 Let not my soul enter their council; Let not my honor be united to their assembly; For in their anger they slew a man, And in their self-will they hamstrung an ox. 7 Cursed be their anger, for it is fierce; And their wrath, for it is cruel! I will divide them in Jacob And scatter them in Israel.

In their anger, their actions exceed the concept of measure for measure. They took vengeance on the entire city of Shechem. They made a wrong decision about what would be an appropriate punishment for the rape of their sister Dinah. Jacob left the Shechem area and settled near Hebron.

Jacob's sons returned to Shechem while they were tending their father's flocks. They don't seem to have learned anything from the events that led to the slaughter of all the Shechemites because it was just after this that they made the decision to sell their brother Joseph into slavery.

> Genesis 37:12-13 NKJV 12 Then his brothers went to feed their father's flock in Shechem. 13 And Israel said to Joseph, "Are not your brothers feeding the flock in Shechem? Come, I will send you to them." So he said to him, "Here I am."

Although the actual act of selling Joseph did not happen in Shechem, the Torah links these events by stating that the brothers were feeding Jacob's flock in Shechem and that Jacob sent Joseph to them at Shechem. Jacob's stated purpose was to check on their welfare.

## Shechem: Decisions, Decisions!

> Genesis 37:14 NKJV 14 Then he said to him, "Please go and see if it is well with your brothers and well with the flocks, and bring back word to me." So he sent him out of the Valley of Hebron, and he went to Shechem.

The Hebrew word for "well" is Shalom.

> #7965. שלום shalowm, shaw-lome' or shalom {shaw-lome'}; from 7999; safe, i.e. (figuratively) well, happy, friendly; also (abstractly) welfare, i.e. health, prosperity, peace, (X perfect, such as be at) peace(-able, -ably), prosper(-ity, -ous), rest, safe(-ty), welfare

Joseph was to see if they were safe, well, at peace or at rest. The only way they could be all of those things was if they accepted Joseph. The only way we can have "shalom" is if we accept Yeshua.

Joseph's brothers had actually moved on to Dothan when Joseph caught up with them. Even as Joseph approached, they conspired to kill him. It was certainly not well with them!

> Genesis 37:18 NKJV 18 Now when they saw him afar off, even before he came near them, they conspired against him to kill him.

Why did they want to kill Joseph? He was certainly their father's favorite but the final factor that spurred them to action was Joseph's dream in which they bowed down to Joseph. The brothers rejected the idea that Joseph would rule over them. In the same way, the Jews of Yeshua's time rejected the very thought that Yeshua had any authority over them. The inhabitants of Yeshua's hometown of Nazareth could not accept that Yeshua, a man who had grown up in Nazareth, could speak with such authority and perform mighty miracles.

> Luke 4:22 NKJV 22 So all bore witness to Him, and marveled at the gracious words which proceeded out of His mouth. And they said, "Is this not Joseph's son?"

> Luke 4:28-29 NKJV 28 So all those in the synagogue, when they heard these things, were filled with wrath, 29 and rose up and thrust Him out of the city; and they led Him to the brow of the hill on which their city was built, that they might throw Him down over the cliff.

The Pharisees questioned by what authority He spoke. Unlike other teachers, Yeshua did not rise through the ranks of the school of the Pharisees. In his teaching, He did not quote the Rabbis who went before Him citing their authority. He spoke with His own authority given Him by the Father.

Joseph's brothers, spear-headed by Judah, ended up selling him into slavery instead of killing him. He ends up in Egypt where he would eventually hold his brothers' futures in his hand. He had the authority under pharaoh to sit in judgment over his brothers.

# Shechem: Decisions, Decisions!

> Genesis 44:16 NKJV 16 Then Judah said, "What shall we say to my lord? What shall we speak? Or how shall we clear ourselves? God has found out the iniquity of your servants; here we are, my lord's slaves, both we and he also with whom the cup was found."

Joseph tests his brothers, once again giving them the choice to betray their brother. Joseph sets Benjamin up to be falsely accused of stealing. Will his other brothers stand with Benjamin or desert him? Judah chooses differently this time. Instead of selling out Benjamin, he offers his life in exchange for Benjamin's life. Joseph, as our type of Messiah, chooses to extend mercy to his brothers. Their actions in selling Joseph into slavery which they intended for evil, God meant for good.

> Genesis 50:20 NKJV 20 "But as for you, you meant evil against me; but God meant it for good, in order to bring it about as it is this day, to save many people alive.

When Jacob is close to death, he splits the blessing of the firstborn between Joseph and Judah. Reuben is disqualified from the blessing because he slept with Bilhah. Simeon and Levi are disqualified because of their violence against Shechem. Instead, Jacob splits the blessing of the firstborn. Judah, the fourth son of Leah, receives the promise of the Seed of Abraham, and Joseph, the firstborn son of Rachel, receives the double portion of the firstborn.

> Genesis 48:21-22 NKJV 21 Then Israel said to Joseph, "Behold, I am dying, but God will be with you and bring you back to the land of your fathers. 22 "Moreover I have given to you one **portion** above your brothers, which I took from the hand of the Amorite with my sword and my bow."

The word portion in this verse is "shekem" bringing the double meaning that Joseph receives the double portion of the firstborn as well as the land of Shechem. God would indeed bring Joseph back to the Promised Land linking both his exile and his return to Shechem.

> Joshua 24:32 NKJV 32 The bones of Joseph, which the children of Israel had brought up out of Egypt, they buried at Shechem, in the plot of ground which Jacob had bought from the sons of Hamor the father of Shechem for one hundred pieces of silver, and which had become an inheritance of the children of Joseph.

The presence of Joseph's bones in Shechem is also a witness that God fulfills His promises. Joseph's last words to his brothers were to take his bones with them when God visited them and took them out of Egypt back to the Promised Land.

> Genesis 50:24 NKJV 24 And Joseph said to his brethren, "I am dying; but God will surely visit you, and bring you out of this land to the land of which He swore to Abraham, to Isaac, and to Jacob."

Joseph is buried there at Shechem where Jacob sent him to check if it was "well" with his brothers and Jacob's flocks. But although his bones are buried there in Shechem, in a sense, Joseph has been resurrected. His tomb in Egypt is empty. So, the presence of Joseph's bones there in Shechem testifies to Yeshua's death and resurrection. Before we can enter into God's rest, His Shalom, we must accept that Yeshua, our Joseph, died for us and that He lives again. God sends His son Yeshua to us every day to check if it is well with us. Do we have His Shalom, His peace? In the words of Joshua to the children of Israel, "Choose THIS day whom you will serve." We are not to choose yesterday or tomorrow, but today, this day.

**B.** The second incident at Shechem involves Gideon's sons and the inhabitants of Shechem. One of Gideon's sons, Abimelech, lived in Shechem. Unlike Gideon's other sons, Abimelech's mother was not one of Gideon's wives but his concubine who was a Shechemite. Predictably, there is friction between Abimelech and his brothers. Abimelech convinces his fellow Shechemites to help him kill his brothers.

> Judges 9:2 NKJV 2 "Please speak in the hearing of all the men of Shechem: 'Which is better for you, that all seventy of the sons of Jerubbaal reign over you, or that one reign over you?' Remember that I am your own flesh and bone."

(Jerubbaal is a nickname for Gideon given to him by his father when he tore down the altar to Baal. It means let Baal contend with him. Judges 6:31-32)

We hear elements of the serpent's question to Eve in Abimelech's question to the Shechemites. When the Israelites tried to make Abimelech's father Gideon king, Gideon declined both on his own behalf and that of his sons.

> Judges 8:23 NKJV 23 But Gideon said to them, "I will not rule over you, nor shall my son rule over you; the LORD shall rule over you."

Gideon's sons were not to be kings over Israel. Abimelech, whose name means my father is king, twisted the truth just like the serpent did with Eve. He played on mankind's aversion to submitting to any ruler. In the Garden of Eden, the serpent promised Eve that she would be like God. She would no longer have to submit to God as king, but could do what she wanted. Like Eve with the serpent, the Shechemites listen to Abimelech's lies. They chose to make one like themselves king once again rejecting God as king. There at the terebinth tree where Abraham built an altar, Jacob buried his idols, and Joshua erected the stone as witness, the Sechemites made Abilmelech their king. The symbolism of Abimelech as a type of serpent and the terebinth tree as a symbol of the tree of the knowledge of good and evil is irresistible here.

> Judges 9:6 NKJV 6 And all the men of Shechem gathered together, all of Beth Millo, and they went and made Abimelech king beside the terebinth tree at the pillar that was in Shechem.

## Shechem: Decisions, Decisions!

The people of Shechem join with Abimelech to kill all of Gideon's sons. Only Gideon's youngest son Jotham escapes the slaughter. Jotham climbs to the top of Mt. Gerizim, the mount of blessing, and there he tells a parable and curses Abimelich and Shechem. His parable is about the trees going to anoint a king over them.

> Judges 9:7-15 NKJV 7 Now when they told Jotham, he went and stood on top of Mount Gerizim, and lifted his voice and cried out. And he said to them: "Listen to me, you men of Shechem, That God may listen to you! 8 "The trees once went forth to anoint a king over them. And they said to the olive tree, 'Reign over us!' 9 But the olive tree said to them, 'Should I cease giving my oil, With which they honor God and men, And go to sway over trees?' 10 "Then the trees said to the fig tree, 'You come and reign over us!' 11 But the fig tree said to them, 'Should I cease my sweetness and my good fruit, And go to sway over trees?' 12 "Then the trees said to the vine, 'You come and reign over us!' 13 But the vine said to them, 'Should I cease my new wine, Which cheers both God and men, And go to sway over trees?' 14 "Then all the trees said to the bramble, 'You come and reign over us!' 15 And the bramble said to the trees, 'If in truth you anoint me as king over you, Then come and take shelter in my shade; But if not, let fire come out of the bramble And devour the cedars of Lebanon!'

So, in the parable, the trees first go to the olive tree, the fig tree, and the vine. Each of these trees produces fruit that is symbolic of God's blessings, the oil, the fruit and the new wine. Each recognizes their place in God's kingdom, not as a ruler but as a blessing to both God and men. Like Gideon, they reject the offer of the kingship in favor of accepting God as king.

The trees then go to the bramble and offer to make the bramble king. The word bramble means to pierce.

> #329.  אטד  'atad, aw-tawd' from an unused root probably meaning to pierce or make fast; a thorn-tree (especially the buckthorn):--Atad, bramble, thorn.

The bramble's response to their request is to command the trees to take shelter in its shade. Imagine taking shelter in a thorn bush! Have you ever stepped on a thorn with your heel? It pierces into the heel and bruises it making it painful to walk on. God's curse on the serpent says that the serpent would bruise the heel of the Seed of the woman.

> Genesis 3:15 NKJV 15 And I will put enmity Between you and the woman, And between your seed and her Seed; He shall bruise your head, And you shall bruise His heel."

If the trees' request is not in truth, the bramble promises fire and destruction, specifically against the cedars of Lebanon. Lebanon was famous for her cedars and took pride in them. Jotham's parable warns against the destructive nature of Abimelech. If the people of Shechem choose Abimelech as king, they will get nothing but pain and misery. And if they change their minds, Abimelech will destroy them and all that they take pride in.

Jotham concludes with a curse on both Abimelech and the people of Shechem.

> Judges 9:19-20 NKJV 19 "if then you have acted in truth and sincerity with Jerubbaal and with his house this day, then rejoice in Abimelech, and let him also rejoice in you. 20 "But if not, let fire come from Abimelech and devour the men of Shechem and Beth Millo; and let fire come from the men of Shechem and from Beth Millo and devour Abimelech!"

Both Shechem and Abimelech have acted deceitfully against the house of Gideon. And so, Jotham calls down God's judgment on Shechem and Abimelech. Eventually, Abimelech kills all the people of Shechem by the sword and by fire. Abimelech's end comes at the hand of a woman similar to the end foretold for the serpent.

> Judges 9:52-53 NKJV 52 So Abimelech came as far as the tower and fought against it; and he drew near the door of the tower to burn it with fire. 53 But a certain woman dropped an upper millstone on Abimelech's head and crushed his skull.

A stone from the hand of a woman crushes Abimelech's head. Again, we see in Abimelech a type of serpent.

Both the name of the person leading the rebellion and the timing of the rebellion against Abimelech are interesting. First, the man who leads the revolt is named Gaal which means loathing or to vilely cast away.

#1603. געל Ga`al, gah'-al from 1602; loathing;

#1602. געל ga`al, gaw-al' a primitive root; to detest; by implication, to reject:--abhor, fail, loathe, vilely cast away

Gaal encourages the Shechemites to completely reject the God of Israel and embrace the gods of the Canaanites.

> Judges 9:28-29 NIV 28 Then Gaal son of Ebed said, "Who is Abimelech, and who is Shechem, that we should be subject to him? Isn't he Jerub-Baal's son, and isn't Zebul his deputy? Serve the men of Hamor, Shechem's father! Why should we serve Abimelech? 29 If only this people were under my command! Then I would get rid of him. I would say to Abimelech, 'Call out your whole army!' Then he said to Abimelech, "Call out your whole army!"

Hamor was the Canaanite ruler of Shechem that Simeon and Levi killed in vengeance for the rape of Dinah. Gaal is calling the Shechemites to reject Abimelech because he is Gideon's son and instead elevate the Canaanites to power! Gaal wants loathing and total rejection of God.

Secondly, this revolt occurred at the time of the grape harvest.

> Judges 9:27 NKJV 27 So they went out into the fields, and gathered grapes from their vineyards and trod them, and made merry. And they went into the house of their god, and ate and drank, and cursed Abimelech.

They were celebrating the harvest of the grapes in the temple of the god they were worshipping, Ba-al Berith, instead of God. They began their worship of Ba-al Berith as soon as Gideon died.

> Judges 8:33 NKJV 33 So it was, as soon as Gideon was dead, that the children of Israel again played the harlot with the Baals, and made Baal-Berith their god.

The name Ba-al Berith means god of covenant.

#1170. בעל ברות Ba`al Bahriyth, bah'-al ber-eeth from 1168 and 1285; Baal of (the) covenant;

There at Shechem, the location of the stones with the words of the Commandments and God's Covenant on them, the location of the stone altar built by Joshua, and the location of the pillar under the terebinth tree, they set up a god they called the god of the covenant! Oh how far they have fallen!

They should have gone to Shiloh, the current location of the Ark of the Covenant of God, and celebrated the Feast of Tabernacles bringing their offerings to God.

> Deuteronomy 16:13 NKJV 13 "You shall observe the Feast of Tabernacles seven days, when you have gathered from your threshing floor and from your winepress.

> Deuteronomy 16:17 NKJV 17 "Every man shall give as he is able, according to the blessing of the LORD your God which He has given you.

When Yeshua comes again, He will bring judgment at the time of the grape harvest and the celebration afterwards at the Feast of Tabernacles is the wedding supper of the lamb.

> Joel 3:12-14 NKJV 12 "Let the nations be wakened, and come up to the Valley of Jehoshaphat; For there I will sit to judge all the surrounding nations. 13 Put in the sickle, for the harvest is ripe. Come, go down; For the winepress is full, The vats overflow-For their wickedness is great." 14 Multitudes, multitudes in the valley of decision! For the day of the LORD is near in the valley of decision.

It is likely that God's judgment will begin there at Shechem and move on to Jerusalem where the final battle will take place.

**C.** The third incident centers around Solomon's son Rehoboam, Jereboam and all the leaders of the twelve tribes of Israel. In Solomon's later years, he turned away from God and worshipped the idols introduced by his foreign wives. Because of this, God took the kingdom away from his son Rehoboam and gave it to Solomon's servant Jeroboam (1 Kings 11:9-13). The fulfillment of this judgment occurred at Shechem.

> 2 Chronicles 10:1-4 NKJV 1 And Rehoboam went to Shechem, for all Israel had gone to Shechem to make him king. 2 So it happened, when Jeroboam the son of Nebat heard it (he was in Egypt, where he had fled from the presence of King Solomon), that Jeroboam returned from Egypt. 3 Then they sent for him and called him. And Jeroboam and all Israel came and spoke to Rehoboam, saying, 4 "Your father made our yoke heavy; now therefore, lighten the burdensome service of your father and his heavy yoke which he put on us, and we will serve you."

Remember, Shechem means between the shoulders, the place where a burden is carried. The discussion here is about carrying a heavy yoke. Yeshua told us His burden is light.

> Matthew 11:29-30 NKJV 29 "Take My yoke upon you and learn from Me, for I am gentle and lowly in heart, and you will find rest for your souls. 30 "For My yoke is easy and My burden is light."

Rehoboam is the opposite of Yeshua. Influenced by the young men who had grown up with him, Rehoboam promised to make his yoke even more burdensome than Solomon's yoke.

> 2 Chronicles 10:13-14 NKJV 13 Then the king answered them roughly. King Rehoboam rejected the advice of the elders, 14 and he spoke to them according to the advice of the young men, saying, "My father made your yoke heavy, but I will add to it; my father chastised you with whips, but I will chastise you with scourges!"

Rehoboam chose to reject the wise counsel of the elders and instead listen to men who grew up with him. As a result, the ten tribes of Israel rejected Rehoboam and the house of David.

> 2 Chronicles 10:16 NKJV 16 Now when all Israel saw that the king did not listen to them, the people answered the king, saying: "What share have we in David? We have no inheritance in the son of Jesse. Every man to your tents, O Israel! Now see to your own house, O David!" So all Israel departed to their tents.

Only Judah and Benjamin chose to follow Rehoboam as their king. The chronicler reports that Israel has been and continues to be in rebellion against the house of David.

> 2 Chronicles 10:19 NKJV 19 So Israel has been in rebellion against the house of David to this day.

They followed after Jeroboam of the tribe of Ephraim who took them from rebellion to idolatry. Jeroboam set up his capital in Shechem.

# Shechem: Decisions, Decisions!

> 1 Kings 12:25 NKJV 25 Then Jeroboam built Shechem in the mountains of Ephraim, and dwelt there. Also he went out from there and built Penuel.

We see here that Shechem is described as being in the mountains of Ephraim. Besides Mount Ebal and Mount Garazim, there are many other hills around Shechem. To the east in the tribal lands of Manasseh are Elon More and Mount Itamar. Mount Itamar is the traditional location of the tomb of Gideon, as well as the location of the tombs of Eleazar and Itamar the sons of Aaron.

Jeroboam set up two golden calves to worship and changed the day of the Feast of Tabernacles. He did not want the Israelites to go up to Jerusalem to worship and be reminded that Rehoboam was their rightful king.

> 1 Kings 12:26-27 NKJV 26 And Jeroboam said in his heart, "Now the kingdom may return to the house of David: 27 "If these people go up to offer sacrifices in the house of the LORD at Jerusalem, then the heart of this people will turn back to their lord, Rehoboam king of Judah, and they will kill me and go back to Rehoboam king of Judah."

There will come a day though when the Israelites turn from their rebellion. The prophet Jeremiah writes of a day when the watchmen of these mountains will sound the cry to return to the LORD.

> Jeremiah 31:6-7 NKJV 6 For there shall be a day When the watchmen will cry on Mount Ephraim, 'Arise, and let us go up to Zion, To the LORD our God.'" 7 For thus says the LORD: "Sing with gladness for Jacob, And shout among the chief of the nations; Proclaim, give praise, and say, 'O LORD, save Your people, The remnant of Israel!'

God says that He will hear the voice of Ephraim when he declares, like Joshua and the Israelites before him, that God is the LORD.

> Jeremiah 31:18 KJV 18 I have surely heard Ephraim bemoaning himself thus; Thou hast chastised me, and I was chastised, as a bullock unaccustomed to the yoke: turn thou me, and I shall be turned; for thou art the LORD my God.

Ephraim, who led the rebellion against the house of David through his descendant Jereboam, shall turn and take on the yoke God places on them. There on the mountains of Israel that stretch from Shechem in the north to Hebron in the south, God will reunite Ephraim and Judah. Ephraim and the tribes that followed him will no longer be in rebellion against the house of David. God tells Ezekiel to take two sticks and write Judah on one stick and Ephraim on the other and to bring them together in one hand.

> Ezekiel 37:21-24 NKJV 21 "Then say to them, 'Thus says the Lord GOD: "Surely I will take the children of Israel from among the nations, wherever they have gone,

and will gather them from every side and bring them into their own land; 22 "and I will make them one nation in the land, on the mountains of Israel; and one king shall be king over them all; they shall no longer be two nations, nor shall they ever be divided into two kingdoms again. 23 "They shall not defile themselves anymore with their idols, nor with their detestable things, nor with any of their transgressions; but I will deliver them from all their dwelling places in which they have sinned, and will cleanse them. Then they shall be My people, and I will be their God. 24 "David My servant shall be king over them, and they shall all have one shepherd; they shall also walk in My judgments and observe My statutes, and do them.

This reverses the choice made at Shechem in the time of Rehoboam and Jereboam. Israel and Judah will be made one nation on the mountains of Israel starting at Shechem. Like Joshua, they will bury their idols and choose to serve God. Like the sons of Jacob, they will accept Joseph, a type of Yeshua who died and rose again as their brother and one to whom they bow down. They will accept Yeshua, the son of David, as their rightful king and will no longer be in rebellion against the house of David. They will come back into covenant with God and follow the statutes and commandments which were written on the stones on top of Mount Ebal.

# Student Notes for Shechem: Decisions, Decisions!

**A.** Shechem has a role to play in both Joseph's exile and return to the Promised Land. (Gen. 49:5-7, Gen. 37:12-13)

Jacob's stated purpose was to check on their welfare. (Gen. 37:14, Gen. 37:18)

Well: #7965. שלום shalowm, shaw-lome' or shalom {shaw-lome'}; from 7999; safe, i.e. (figuratively) well, happy, friendly; also (abstractly) welfare, i.e. health, prosperity, peace, (X perfect, such as be at) peace(-able, -ably), prosper(-ity, -ous), rest, safe(-ty), welfare

The Jews of Yeshua's time rejected the very thought that Yeshua had any authority over them. (Luke 4:22, Luke 4:28-29, Gen. 44:16, Gen. 50:20, Gen. 48:21-22, Jos. 24:32, Gen. 50:24)

Portion: shekem

**B.** One of Gideon's sons, Abimelech, lived in Shechem. Abimelech convinces his fellow Shechemites to help him kill his brothers. (Jdg. 9:2, Jdg. 8:23, Jdg. 9:6)

Jotham climbs to the top of Mt. Gerizim, the mount of blessing, and there he tells a parable and curses Abimelich and Shechem. (Jdg. 9:7-15, Gen. 3:15, Jdg. 9:19-20, Jdg. 9:52-53)

Bramble: #329 אטד 'atad, aw-tawd' from an unused root probably meaning to pierce or make fast; a thorn-tree (especially the buckthorn):--Atad, bramble, thorn.

Student Notes for Shechem: Decisions, Decisions!

The person who leads the revolt is named Gaal (Jdg. 9:28-29)

Gaal: #1603. גַעַל Ga`al, gah'-al from 1602; loathing;

#1602. גָעַל ga`al, gaw-al' a primitive root; to detest; by implication, to reject:--abhor, fail, loathe, vilely cast away

This revolt occurred at the time of the grape harvest. (Jdg. 9:27, Jdg. 8:33, Deu. 16:13, 17, Joel 3:12-14)

Ba-al Berith: #1170. בַּעַל בְּרִית Ba`al Bahriyth, bah'-al ber-eeth from 1168 and 1285; Baal of (the) covenant;

**C.** God took Solomon's kingdom away from his son Rehoboam and gave it to Solomon's servant Jeroboam. The fulfillment of this judgment occurred at Shechem. (2Chr. 10:1-4, Mat. 11:29-30, 2Chr. 10:13-14, 2Chr. 10:16, 19)

They followed after Jeroboam of the tribe of Ephraim who took them from rebellion to idolatry. (1 Kin. 12:26-27, Jer. 31:6-7, Jer. 31:18)

There on the mountains of Israel that stretch from Shechem in the north to Hebron in the south, God will reunite Ephraim and Judah. (Eze. 37:21-24)

Student Notes for Shechem: Decisions, Decisions!

**Discussion Questions for Shechem: Decisions, Decisions!**

1. Hebron represents the promise of resurrection. How is God sending Yeshua to His Jewish brothers like Jacob sending Joseph from Hebron to Shechem to check on his brothers' well-being? (Mat. 15:22-28, John 3:17)

2. How is returning Joseph's bones to Shechem a promise of Yeshua's resurrection and return?

3. The word "today" appears fifty times and the phrase "this day" appears twenty four times in the book of Deuteronomy. Read Deuteronomy 11:8-28 and 26:16-19, and Matthew 10:37-39. How should we approach and live each day?

4. Rehoboam rejected the wise counsel of the elders. Jereboam rejected God's injunction to follow His instructions, instead deciding to follow his own "wisdom." The Shechemites listened to the "wisdom" of Abimelech. Read each of the following scriptures and discuss the importance, source, and application of wisdom.

    a. Importance: Psa. 111:10, Prov. 3:13-18, Prov. 9:10-12, Prov. 13:14

    b. Source: Deut. 4:5-7, Prov. 2:1-6, Prov. 13:20, Eph. 1:17, James 1:5

    c. Application: Prov. 19:11, Prov. 29:3, Eph. 5:15-20, James 3:13-18

5. The disagreement between Rehoboam and the ten tribes of Israel was over the yoke that Rehoboam would place on them. When God brought Israel out from Egypt, He broke the yoke of their bondage (Lev. 26:13). When they disobeyed, God allowed them to once again be placed under bondage (Deu. 28:36-48). What will God do in the latter days (Eze. 34:24-27)? Discuss the spiritual implications of Rehoboam and Jeroboam's actions that day at Shechem. Discuss the overall spiritual aspects of the "yoke."

## Bethlehem: The City of Yeshua's Birth

The location of Yeshua's birth has deep symbolic meaning. He was born in Bethlehem in the region called Ephratah. Micah prophesies that His birth would be in Bethlehem and Luke records the fulfillment in his gospel.

> Micah 5:2 MKJV 2 And you, Bethlehem Ephratah, you being least among the thousands of Judah, out of you He shall come forth to Me, to become Ruler in Israel, He whose goings forth have been from of old, from the days of eternity.

> Luke 2:4 KJV 4 And Joseph also went up from Galilee, out of the city of Nazareth, into Judaea, unto the city of David, which is called Bethlehem; (because he was of the house and lineage of David:)

> Luke 2:6-7 KJV 6 And so it was, that, while they were there, the days were accomplished that she should be delivered. 7 And she brought forth her firstborn son, and wrapped him in swaddling clothes, and laid him in a manger; because there was no room for them in the inn.

Luke calls Bethlehem the city of David because it was the city of David's birth, but elsewhere in the scriptures, Zion or Jerusalem is called the city of David.

> 2 Samuel 5:7 KJV 7 Nevertheless David took the strong hold of Zion: the same is the city of David.

So, which one is the city of David? We will see is that these two cities are linked. First, Bethlehem is a mere five miles from Jerusalem and many of the events associated with Bethlehem happen in the area around it. For instance, most of the events in the book of Ruth take place in the fields around Bethlehem. Also, Jacob's wife Rachel dies in childbirth on the way to Bethlehem and David watched his father's sheep in the pastures around Bethlehem. As we look at each of these situations, we will see how they link Bethlehem to Jerusalem through the broader prophecy in Micah 4:6 through Micah 5:5.

**A.** Bethlehem means the house of bread and Ephratah means fruitfulness. Yeshua was born in the house of bread in the region of fruitfulness. He is the Bread of Life.

> John 6:33-35 MKJV 33 For the bread of God is He who comes down from Heaven and gives life to the world. 34 Then they said to him, Lord, evermore give us this bread. 35 And Jesus said to them, I am the bread of life. He who comes to Me shall never hunger, and he who believes on Me shall never thirst.

He tells His followers that those who remain in Him will be fruitful.

> John 15:1-2 MKJV 1 I am the True Vine, and My Father is the Vinedresser. 2 Every branch in Me that does not bear fruit, He takes away. And every one that bears fruit, He prunes it so that it may bring forth more fruit.

**B.** Scripture first mentions Bethlehem in connection with Rachel. Rachel's name means ewe lamb. Yeshua is the Lamb of God.

> John 1:29 MKJV 29 The next day John sees Jesus coming to him and says, Behold the Lamb of God who takes away the sin of the world!

Not only is the name Rachel associated with a lamb, she was a shepherdess taking care of her father's sheep when she met Jacob.

> Genesis 29:9-10 NKJV 9 Now while he was still speaking with them, Rachel came with her father's sheep, for she was a shepherdess. 10 And it came to pass, when Jacob saw Rachel the daughter of Laban his mother's brother, and the sheep of Laban his mother's brother, that Jacob went near and rolled the stone from the well's mouth, and watered the flock of Laban his mother's brother.

It is interesting that the stone covering the well needed to be rolled away in order to access the water for the sheep. There would be another stone rolled away that would provide access to the Living Water for Yeshua's flock.

> Luke 24:2-7 NKJV 2 But they found the stone rolled away from the tomb. 3 Then they went in and did not find the body of the Lord Jesus. 4 And it happened, as they were greatly perplexed about this, that behold, two men stood by them in shining garments. 5 Then, as they were afraid and bowed their faces to the earth, they said to them, "Why do you seek the living among the dead? 6 "He is not here, but is risen! Remember how He spoke to you when He was still in Galilee, 7 "saying, 'The Son of Man must be delivered into the hands of sinful men, and be crucified, and the third day rise again.'"

Jacob is the one who rolled away the stone and watered Rachel's sheep, and it was at a well called Jacob's well near Shechem that Yeshua spoke of being the living water.

> John 4:5-6 NKJV 5 So He came to a city of Samaria which is called Sychar, near the plot of ground that Jacob gave to his son Joseph. 6 Now Jacob's well was there. Jesus therefore, being wearied from His journey, sat thus by the well. It was about the sixth hour.

> John 4:13-14 NKJV 13 Jesus answered and said to her, "Whoever drinks of this water will thirst again, 14 "but whoever drinks of the water that I shall give him will never thirst. But the water that I shall give him will become in him a fountain of water springing up into everlasting life."

As Jacob and Rachel were traveling from Bethel which is about ten miles north of Jerusalem to Bethlehem or Ephrath which is about five miles southwest of Jersualem, Rachel gave birth to her son Benjamin. She died as she gave birth but not before giving him the name Benoni.

## Bethlehem: The City of Yeshua's Birth

> Genesis 35:16-21 MKJV 16 And they moved from Bethel. And there was only a length of land to come to Ephrath. And Rachel travailed, and she had hard labor in her bearing. 17 And it happened when she was in hard labor in her bearing, the midwife said to her, Do not fear, you shall have this son also. 18 And it happened as her soul was departing (for she died) that she called his name Benoni. But his father called him Benjamin. 19 And Rachel died and was buried in the way to Ephrath, which is Bethlehem. 20 And Jacob set up a pillar upon her grave. That is the pillar of Rachel's grave to this day. 21 And Israel moved, and spread his tent beyond the tower of Edar.

Benjamin's name foreshadows Yeshua's mission. Rachel called him Benoni which means son of my sorrow referring to Yeshua's first coming as a man of sorrows.

#1126. בן אוני Ben-'Owniy, ben-o-nee' from 1121 and 205; son of my sorrow; Ben-Oni, the original name of Benjamin:--Ben-oni.

> Isaiah 53:3 MKJV 3 He is despised and rejected of men; a Man of sorrows, and acquainted with grief; and as it were a hiding of faces from Him, He being despised, and we esteemed Him not.

Interestingly, it is Rachel's sorrow that foreshadows the sorrow of Yeshua. He expresses that sorrow over Jerusalem. Jeremiah attributes Rachel's sorrow to the captivity of Jerusalem and the death of the sons of Jerusalem.

> Jeremiah 31:15-17 MKJV 15 So says the LORD: A voice was heard in Ramah, wailing and bitter weeping; Rachel weeping for her sons; she refuses to be comforted for her sons, because they are not. 16 So says the LORD: Hold back your voice from weeping and your eyes from tears; for your work shall be rewarded, says the LORD. And they shall come again from the land of the enemy. 17 And there is hope for your future, says the LORD, that your sons shall come again to their own border.

Rachel's weeping was heard in Ramah, a town north of Jerusalem. At the time of the Babylonian exile, the people of Jerusalem were led through Ramah on their way to Babylon.

> Jeremiah 40:1 MKJV 1 This is the word that came to Jeremiah from the LORD, after Nebu-zaradan the chief of the executioners had let him go from Ramah, when he had taken him, being bound in chains, among all the captives of Jerusalem and Judah, who were being exiled to Babylon.

Matthew states that the passage of Rachel weeping over her children is fulfilled when Herod killed the sons of Bethlehem after the birth of Yeshua.

> Matthew 2:16-18 MKJV 16 Then Herod, when he saw that he was mocked by the wise men, was greatly enraged. And he sent and killed all the boys in Bethlehem, and in all its districts, from two years old and under, according to the time which he had carefully inquired of the wise men. 17 Then was fulfilled that which was spoken by Jeremiah the prophet, saying, 18 "A voice was heard in Ramah, wailing and weeping and great mourning, Rachel weeping for her children, and would not be comforted, because they are not."

Rachel's sorrow is one of many links between Bethlehem and Jerusalem. Yeshua, also, expresses sorrow over Jerusalem at their rejection of Him and over the upcoming exile that would follow that rejection. This sorrow matches the sorrow Jeremiah attributed to Rachel over the earlier captivity of Jerusalem.

> Luke 13:34 MKJV 34 Jerusalem! Jerusalem! The one killing the prophets, and stoning those having been sent to her; how often I desired to gather your children in the way a hen gathers her brood under the wings, and you did not desire it.

> Luke 19:41-42 MKJV 41 And as He drew near, He beheld the city and wept over it, 42 saying, If you had known, even you, even at least in this day of yours, the things for your peace! But now they are hidden from your eyes.

Yeshua goes on to say that He will return when they can say "Blessed is He who comes in the name of the LORD.

> Luke 13:35 MKJV 35 Behold, your house is left to you desolate. And truly I say to you, You will not see Me until it come when you say, Blessed is He who comes in the name of the Lord.

Jacob, who was also called Israel, took the son whom Rachel named son of my sorrow and gave him a new name. He named his son Benjamin which means son of my right hand.

#1144. בנימין Binyamiyn, bin-yaw-mene' from 1121 and 3225; son of (the) right hand

This speaks of His resurrection and second coming. When Yeshua returns, it will be as the son of my right hand. Yeshua even now sits at God's right hand waiting for His enemies to be put under His feet.

> Hebrews 12:2 MKJV 2 looking to Jesus the Author and Finisher of our faith, who for the joy that was set before Him endured the cross, despising the shame, and sat down at the right of the throne of God.

So, through Rachel, we see the affliction and sorrow of Yeshua the suffering servant. He is the bread of life broken for us. Through Jacob, we see the living water who is the son at the right hand of the Father.

Bethlehem: The City of Yeshua's Birth

When Yeshua returns, He will be the ruler on David's throne. Isaiah 9, which is also about Yeshua's birth, refers to His second coming just like the dual names of Benoni and Benjamin refer to Yeshua's first and second comings.

> Isaiah 9:6-7 NKJV 6 For unto us a Child is born, Unto us a Son is given; And the government will be upon His shoulder. And His name will be called Wonderful, Counselor, Mighty God, Everlasting Father, Prince of Peace. 7 Of the increase of His government and peace There will be no end, Upon the throne of David and over His kingdom, To order it and establish it with judgment and justice From that time forward, even forever. The zeal of the LORD of hosts will perform this.

The government of Yeshua will be established when He comes again.

Rachel was buried where she gave birth there on the way to Bethlehem. This is the time of Jacob's trouble. His beloved wife died to give birth to his son, the son at his right hand. Jacob placed a memorial pillar on her grave and moved on to Migdal Edar, the tower of Edar. The tower of Edar is the "Tower of the Flock" built to watch over the sheep around Bethlehem. The flocks around Bethlehem at the time of Yeshua's birth were the temple flocks and the shepherds were all Levites. It was from these flocks that the sacrifices were chosen. There on the same fields where David watched his father's sheep and Levites watched over the temple flocks, Yeshua, the lamb of God was born. It is to these Levitical shepherds set aside for service to God that an angel announces the birth of a very special lamb.

> Luke 2:8-10 NKJV 8 Now there were in the same country shepherds living out in the fields, keeping watch over their flock by night. 9 And behold, an angel of the Lord stood before them, and the glory of the Lord shone around them, and they were greatly afraid. 10 Then the angel said to them, "Do not be afraid, for behold, I bring you good tidings of great joy which will be to all people.

Great joy accompanied Yeshua's birth as the suffering servant. Jacob's trouble will precede Yeshua's coming as the ruling king and the son at the right hand of the Father.

The prophet Micah mentions the same tower of Edar in the verses leading up to the prophecy that Bethlehem would be the birthplace of the Messiah. But he mentions the tower of Edar in connection with Jerusalem not Bethlehem. The prophecy begins with the phrase "In that day" in verse six which always refers to the end times.

> Micah 4:6-7 NKJV 6 "In that day," says the LORD, "I will assemble the lame, I will gather the outcast And those whom I have afflicted; 7 I will make the lame a remnant, And the outcast a strong nation; So the LORD will reign over them in Mount Zion From now on, even forever.

The end result will be God as king ruling from Jerusalem. The next verses are about what leads up to this victory. We see a time of suffering and confusion. There is no king in their midst!

> Micah 4:8-10 NKJV 8 And you, O tower of the flock, The stronghold of the daughter of Zion, To you shall it come, Even the former dominion shall come, The kingdom of the daughter of Jerusalem." 9 Now why do you cry aloud? Is there no king in your midst? Has your counselor perished? For pangs have seized you like a woman in labor. 10 Be in pain, and labor to bring forth, O daughter of Zion, Like a woman in birth pangs. For now you shall go forth from the city, You shall dwell in the field, And to Babylon you shall go. There you shall be delivered; There the LORD will redeem you From the hand of your enemies.

The daughter of Zion will labor to bring forth a son but that will be "In that day;" for now they are exiled to Babylon. Even though the official exile to Babylon ended when Cyrus allowed the Jewish people to return to Jerusalem and rebuild the temple, the promise of God through Micah has not yet been fulfilled. God is not yet King in Mount Zion. The Romans once again exiled the Jewish people from Jerusalem and are waiting for God's deliverance.

**C.** David, like Yeshua, was born in Bethlehem and would become the King of Israel and reign from Jerusalem. When God rejected Saul as king, he sent Samuel to Bethlehem where God said, "He would provide for Himself a king."

> 1 Samuel 16:1b NKJV 1b Fill your horn with oil, and go; I am sending you to Jesse the Bethlehemite. For I have provided Myself a king among his sons."

This expression is similar to the words of Abraham when Isaac asked where the sacrifice lamb was.

> Genesis 22:7-8 NKJV 7 But Isaac spoke to Abraham his father and said, "My father!" And he said, "Here I am, my son." Then he said, "Look, the fire and the wood, but where is the lamb for a burnt offering?" 8 And Abraham said, "My son, God will provide for Himself the lamb for a burnt offering." So the two of them went together.

Abraham said that God would provide for Himself the offering. Yeshua is both the lamb and the king provided by God and for Him.

David, like Rachel, is one who took care of the sheep. He was a good and protective shepherd frequently saving his father's sheep from predators.

> 1 Samuel 17:34-35 NKJV 34 But David said to Saul, "Your servant used to keep his father's sheep, and when a lion or a bear came and took a lamb out of the flock, 35 I went out after it and struck it, and delivered the lamb from its mouth; and when it arose against me, I caught it by its beard, and struck and killed it.

Ezekiel describes the negligent shepherds of Israel and the good shepherd that God would provide.

> Ezekiel 34:8 NKJV 8 "as I live," says the Lord GOD, "surely because My flock became a prey, and My flock became food for every beast of the field, because there was no shepherd, nor did My shepherds search for My flock, but the shepherds fed themselves and did not feed My flock"
>
> Ezekiel 34:11-14 NKJV 11 'For thus says the Lord GOD: "Indeed I Myself will search for My sheep and seek them out. 12 "As a shepherd seeks out his flock on the day he is among his scattered sheep, so will I seek out My sheep and deliver them from all the places where they were scattered on a cloudy and dark day. 13 "And I will bring them out from the peoples and gather them from the countries, and will bring them to their own land; I will feed them on the mountains of Israel, in the valleys and in all the inhabited places of the country. 14 "I will feed them in good pasture, and their fold shall be on the high mountains of Israel. There they shall lie down in a good fold and feed in rich pasture on the mountains of Israel.

Yeshua says that He is the Good Shepherd of both the flock of Israel and another flock.

> John 10:14-16 NKJV 14 "I am the good shepherd; and I know My sheep, and am known by My own. 15 "As the Father knows Me, even so I know the Father; and I lay down My life for the sheep. 16 "And other sheep I have which are not of this fold; them also I must bring, and they will hear My voice; and there will be one flock and one shepherd.

Yeshua says that He would bring those two flocks together as one. The book of Ruth foreshadows this event and also takes place in Bethlehem.

**D.** Ruth represents those sheep from another fold. Naomi represents exiled Israel tasting the bitterness of affliction.

> Ruth 1:20-21 MKJV 20 And she said to them, Do not call me Naomi, call me Mara. For the Almighty has dealt very bitterly with me. 21 I went out full, and the LORD has brought me back empty. Why do you call me Naomi, since the LORD has testified against me, and the Almighty has afflicted me?

Boaz is a type of Messiah. He is of the line of Judah through Perez and is an ancestor of David.

> Ruth 4:18-22 MKJV 18 And these are the generations of Pharez. Pharez fathered Hezron, 19 and Hezron fathered Ram, and Ram fathered Amminadab, 20 and Amminadab fathered Nahshon, and Nahshon fathered Salmon, 21 and Salmon fathered Boaz, and Boaz fathered Obed, 22 and Obed fathered Jesse, and Jesse fathered David.

Ruth is a Moabite who married into an Israelite family. When her mother-in-law Naomi tries to send her back to her own family, Ruth "clings" to Naomi.

> Ruth 1:14 NKJV 14 Then they lifted up their voices and wept again; and Orpah kissed her mother-in-law, but Ruth clung to her.

The word for cling is dabak. This is the same word used by Moses instructing the Israelites to cling or hold fast to God.

#1692. דבק dabaq, daw-bak' a primitive root; properly, to impinge, i.e. cling or adhere; figuratively, to catch by pursuit:--abide fast, cleave (fast together), follow close (hard after), be joined (together), keep (fast), overtake, pursue hard, stick, take.

> Deuteronomy 10:20 NKJV 20 "You shall fear the LORD your God; you shall serve Him, and to Him you shall **hold fast**, and take oaths in His name.

Ruth is holding fast to her allegiance to Naomi who is a representative of Israel. After stating her determination to stay with Naomi, Ruth concludes with the well-known passage stating her allegiance to Naomi's God, the God of Israel.

> Ruth 1:16-17 NKJV 16 But Ruth said: "Entreat me not to leave you, Or to turn back from following after you; For wherever you go, I will go; And wherever you lodge, I will lodge; Your people shall be my people, And your God, my God. 17 Where you die, I will die, And there will I be buried. The LORD do so to me, and more also, If anything but death parts you and me."

Paul says that the Gentiles, like Ruth, are grafted into Israel.

> Romans 11:17-18 MKJV 17 And if some of the branches were broken off, and you, being a wild olive tree, were grafted in among them, and became a sharer of the root and the fatness of the olive tree with them, 18 do not boast against the branches. But if you boast, it is not you that bears the root, but the root bears you.

Gentiles are not to boast but to come with the attitude of Ruth supporting Israel in their affliction. Ruth didn't abandon or replace Naomi; she worked to take care of Naomi.

> Ruth 2:5-7 MKJV 5 And Boaz said to his servant who was set over the reapers, Whose girl is this? 6 And the servant who was set over the reapers answered and said, It is the girl from Moab who came back with Naomi out of the country of Moab. 7 And she said, Please let me glean and gather after the reapers among the sheaves. And she came, and has kept on from the morning until now, but that she stayed a little in the house.

Boaz' words to Ruth praising her for taking care of Naomi foreshadow the words Yeshua speaks to those who will believe in Him.

> Ruth 2:11-12 NKJV 11 And Boaz answered and said to her, "It has been fully reported to me, all that you have done for your mother-in-law since the death of

your husband, and how you have left your father and your mother and the land of your birth, and have come to a people whom you did not know before. 12 "The LORD repay your work, and a full reward be given you by the LORD God of Israel, under whose wings you have come for refuge."

First, Boaz says he knows her and the deeds that she has done. Yeshua says over and over that "I know your works" in his messages to the churches in the book of Revelation chapters two and three. In contrast, there are those Yeshua says He doesn't know.

> Matthew 7:22-23 MKJV 22 Many will say to Me in that day, Lord! Lord! Did we not prophesy in Your name, and through Your name throw out demons, and through Your name do many wonderful works? 23 And then I will say to them I never knew you! Depart from Me, those working lawlessness!

Who are those that He knows? They are the ones, like Ruth, who took care of His people.

> Matthew 25:37-40 MKJV 37 Then the righteous shall answer Him, saying, Lord, when did we see You hungry, and fed You? Or thirsty, and gave You drink? 38 When did we see You a stranger, and took You in? Or naked, and clothed You? 39 Or when did we see You sick, or in prison, and came to You? 40 And the King shall answer and say to them, Truly I say to you, Inasmuch as you did it to one of the least of these My brothers, you have done it to Me.

Second, Boaz says God will reward her. When Yeshua comes again, He will bring His reward with Him.

> Isaiah 62:11 MKJV 11 Behold, the LORD has sent a message to the end of the earth, Tell the daughter of Zion, Behold, your salvation comes. Behold, His reward is with Him, and His work before Him.

> Revelation 22:12 MKJV 12 And behold, I am coming quickly, and My reward is with Me, to give to each according as his work is.

Third, he states that she has taken refuge under the wings of the LORD God of Israel. The word for wings is kanaph.

#3671. כנף kanaph, kaw-nawf' from 3670; an edge or extremity; specifically (of a bird or army) a wing, (of a garment or bed-clothing) a flap, (of the earth) a quarter, (of a building) a pinnacle:--+ bird, border, corner, end, feather(-ed).

The Psalmists frequently speak of God taking His people under "the shadow of His wings."

> Psalms 17:8 NKJV 8 Keep me as the apple of Your eye; Hide me under the shadow of Your wings,

Later in the story, Ruth goes to Boaz on the threshing floor and repeats those words back to him. This is the same Hebrew word Kanaph even though many translations use the word skirt or garment instead of wings.

> Ruth 3:8-9 NKJV 8 Now it happened at midnight that the man was startled, and turned himself; and there, a woman was lying at his feet. 9 And he said, "Who are you?" So she answered, "I am Ruth, your maidservant. Take your maidservant under your wing, for you are a close relative."

Boaz said that she took refuge under God's wings; Ruth asks for protection under Boaz's wings! Ruth is asking that Boaz act as kinsman redeemer to her, taking her as his bride, just like the church or congregation is the bride of Christ.

> Isaiah 54:5 NKJV 5 For your Maker is your husband, The LORD of hosts is His name; And your Redeemer is the Holy One of Israel; He is called the God of the whole earth.

> Ephesians 5:30-32 NKJV 30 For we are members of His body, of His flesh and of His bones. 31 "For this reason a man shall leave his father and mother and be joined to his wife, and the two shall become one flesh." 32 This is a great mystery, but I speak concerning Christ and the church.

The location of Ruth's meeting with Boaz is the threshing floor. Solomon built the temple of God on a threshing floor that David, our shepherd from Bethlehem, purchased from the Jebusite.

> 2 Chronicles 3:1 MKJV 1 And Solomon began to build the house of the LORD at Jerusalem in Mount Moriah, where He appeared to David his father, in the place that David had prepared in the threshing-floor of Ornan the Jebusite.

This takes us back to the prophecy in Micah about "that day." The prophecy continues describing the nations that come against the daughter of Zion.

> Micah 4:11-13 NKJV 11 Now also many nations have gathered against you, Who say, "Let her be defiled, And let our eye look upon Zion." 12 But they do not know the thoughts of the LORD, Nor do they understand His counsel; For He will gather them like sheaves to the threshing floor. 13 "Arise and thresh, O daughter of Zion; For I will make your horn iron, And I will make your hooves bronze; You shall beat in pieces many peoples; I will consecrate their gain to the LORD, And their substance to the Lord of the whole earth."

The nations are brought to the threshing floor of judgment. There on the threshing floor, the nations will either be brought into God's barn as His grain or burned up like the chaff. John the Baptist says that Yeshua will bring the wheat into the barn and burn the chaff.

> Matthew 3:12 NKJV 12 "His winnowing fan is in His hand, and He will thoroughly clean out His threshing floor, and gather His wheat into the barn; but He will burn up the chaff with unquenchable fire."

This emphasizes the difference between those who are known by Him and those He doesn't know. Ruth is there on the floor of judgment. Will she be accepted or rejected? Boaz declares that he will do as she asked; he will be her kinsman redeemer.

> Ruth 4:9-10 MKJV 9 And Boaz said to the elders and all the people, You are witnesses this day that I have bought all that was Elimelech's and all that was Chilion's and Mahlon's, from the hand of Naomi. 10 And also Ruth of Moab, the wife of Mahlon, I have purchased to be my wife, to raise up the name of the dead on his inheritance, so that the name of the dead may not be cut off from among his brothers and from the gate of his place. You are witnesses this day.

The people in the gate reply with two blessings.

> Ruth 4:11 KJV 11 And all the people that were in the gate, and the elders, said, We are witnesses. The LORD make the woman that is come into thine house like Rachel and like Leah, which two did build the house of Israel: and do thou worthily in Ephratah, and be famous in Bethlehem:

The first blessing is that she be like Rachael and Leah, the two "mothers" who built up the house of Israel. This blessing is fulfilled in Ruth in two ways. The literal and obvious way is that she is an ancestor of David and God promised David to build his house forever.

> 2 Samuel 7:25-26 MKJV 25 And now, O LORD God, the word that You have spoken concerning Your servant, and concerning his house: establish it forever, and do as You have said. 26 And let Your name be magnified forever, saying, The LORD of hosts is the God over Israel. And let the house of Your servant David be established before You.

The second way is that Ruth, the Gentile, provides a son for Naomi, the Israelite, who has lost her sons.

> Ruth 4:14-16 MKJV 14 And the women said to Naomi, Blessed be the LORD, who has not left you this day without a redeemer, so that his name may be famous in Israel. 15 And he shall be to you as a restorer of life, and one who cheers your old age. For your daughter-in-law who loves you has borne him, she who is better to you than seven sons. 16 And Naomi took the child and laid it in her bosom, and became nurse to it.

This son is described as Naomi's kinsman redeemer not Boaz. Further, this son's name will be famous not just in Bethlehem, but in Israel. The word famous is the Hebrew word "kara" which means to call out.

#7121. קרא qara', kaw-raw' a primitive root (rather identical with 7122 through the idea of accosting a person met); to call out to

The name of this son, this kinsman redeemer will be called out in all Israel.

Isaiah speaks of Zion as a bereaved mother mourning for her sons who is suddenly presented with new sons.

> Isaiah 49:20-22 MKJV 20 The sons of your bereavement shall yet say in your ears, The place is too narrow for me; come near to me so that I may dwell. 21 Then you shall say in your heart, Who has borne me these, since I am bereaved, and desolate, turned aside and an exile, and who has brought up these? Behold, I was left alone; these, where were they? 22 So says the Lord Jehovah, Behold, I will lift up My hand to the nations, and have set up My banner to the people; and they shall bring your sons in their bosom, and your daughters shall be carried on their shoulders.

Naomi is that bereaved mother who is unexpectedly presented with a new son. Those Gentiles who are grafted into Israel will bring the sons and daughters of Israel home in their arms.

This takes us back once again to the prophecy in Micah.

> Micah 5:3-5 NKJV 3 Therefore He shall give them up, Until the time that she who is in labor has given birth; Then the remnant of His brethren Shall return to the children of Israel. 4 And He shall stand and feed His flock In the strength of the LORD, In the majesty of the name of the LORD His God; And they shall abide, For now He shall be great To the ends of the earth; 5 And this One shall be peace.

God will give up the Jewish people until the daughter of Zion gives birth—until Yeshua comes again. Then we, as His brothers, will return and be joined once again to the children of Israel. His name will be called out in all the earth. And He will be our shepherd watching and guarding from the Tower of Edar as we feed from His pasture.

The name of Naomi's son Obed means to serve.

#5744. עובד `Owbed, o-bade' active participle of 5647; serving; Obed, the name of five Israelites:--Obed.

Yeshua showed us how to be a servant. He says that those who would be great would serve others.

> Matthew 23:11 MKJV 11 But he who is greatest among you shall be your servant.

The second blessing given to Ruth in Ruth 4:11 is that she will do worthily in Ephratah and be famous in Bethlehem. This takes us full circle back to the beginning of our lesson, the meaning of Bethlehem in Ephrata. May Ruth, as she represents Gentile believers, do worthily in Ephrata (fruitfulless) and be famous (as a servant) in the house of bread. The word famous is actually two words in Hebrew, kara shem which means to call out a name. We saw kara earlier and the word shem means name.

#8034 שם shem, an appellation, name.

Yeshua commanded all His disciples to be fruitful by sharing the good news of salvation that comes through Him, the Bread of Life.

> Matthew 28:19-20 MKJV 19 Therefore go and teach all nations, baptizing them in the name of the Father and of the Son and of the Holy Spirit, 20 teaching them to observe all things, whatever I commanded you. And, behold, I am with you all the days until the end of the world.

When we do so, we can anticipate that He will call out our names, "Well done thy good and faithful servant."

> Matthew 25:23 KJV 23 His lord said unto him, Well done, good and faithful servant; thou hast been faithful over a few things, I will make thee ruler over many things: enter thou into the joy of thy lord.

**Student Notes for Bethlehem: The City of Yeshua's Birth**

The location of Yeshua's birth has deep symbolic meaning. He was born in the City of David, Bethlehem, in the region called Ephratah. His birth in Bethlehem is prophesied by Micah and the fulfillment is recorded in the gospel of Luke. (Micah 5:2, Luke 2:4, Luke 2:6-7, 2Sam. 5:7)

**A.** Bethlehem means the house of bread and Ephratah means fruitfulness. (John 6:33-35, John 15:1-2)

**B.** Bethlehem is first mentioned in scripture in connection with Rachel. Rachel's name means ewe lamb. Yeshua is the Lamb of God. (John 1:29, Gen. 29:9-10, Luke 24:2-7, John 4:5-6, John 4:13-14)

Rachel, like Mary, gave birth at Bethlehem. Her son Benjamin was born as she died. (Gen. 35:16-21)

Benoni: #1126. בן אוני Ben-'Owniy, ben-o-nee' from 1121 and 205; son of my sorrow; Ben-Oni, the original name of Benjamin:--Ben-oni.

The sorrow of Rachel foreshadows the sorrow of Yeshua. (Isa. 53:3, Jer. 31:15-17, Jer. 40:1, Mat. 2:16-18, Luke 13:34, Luke 19:41-42, Luke 13:35)

Jacob, also called Israel, named him Benjamin which means son of my right hand.

Benjamin: #1144. בנימין Binyamiyn, bin-yaw-mene' from 1121 and 3225; son of (the) right hand

This speaks of His resurrection and second coming. (Heb. 12:2, Isa. 9:6-7)

Jesus, the Lamb of God was born among the sheep of God's pasture. (Luke 2:8-10, Mic. 4:6-7, Mic. 4:8-10)

**C.** Bethlehem is also the City of David. When God rejected Saul as king, he sent Samuel to Bethlehem where God said, "He would provide for Himself a king." (1Sam. 16:1b, Gen. 22:7-8)

David, like Rachel, is one who took care of the sheep. (1Sam. 16:11-12, 1Sam. 17:34-35, Eze. 34:8, Eze. 34:11-14, John 10:14-16)

**D.** Finally, Bethlehem is the setting for the book of Ruth. Boaz is a type of Messiah in this story.

First, he is of the line of Judah through Perez and is an ancestor of David. (Ruth 1:20-21, Ruth 4:18-22)

Ruth marries into Israel. (Ruth 1:14, Deu. 10:20, Ruth 1:16-17, Rom. 11:17-18, Ruth 2:5-7)

Cling: #1692. דבק dabaq, daw-bak' a primitive root; properly, to impinge, i.e. cling or adhere; figuratively, to catch by pursuit:--abide fast, cleave (fast together), follow close (hard after), be joined (together), keep (fast), overtake, pursue hard, stick, take.

Boaz' words to Ruth foreshadow the words of Yeshua to those who will believe in Him. (Ruth 2:11-12, Mat. 7:22-23, Mat. 25:37-40)

Second, Boaz says God will reward her. When Yeshua comes again, He will bring His reward with Him. (Isa. 62:11, Rev. 22:12)

Third, he states that she has taken refuge under the wings of the LORD God of Israel. The word for wings is kanaph. (Ruth 3:8-9, Ps. 17:8, Is 54:5, Is. 44:6)

Wings: #3671. כנף kanaph, kaw-nawf' from 3670; an edge or extremity; specifically (of a bird or army) a wing, (of a garment or bed-clothing) a flap, (of the earth) a quarter, (of a building) a pinnacle:--+ bird, border, corner, end, feather(-ed).

The location of Ruth's meeting with Boaz is the threshing floor. (Mat. 3:12, Ruth 4:9-10)

The blessings from the people of Bethlehem (Ruth 4:11)

The first blessing is that she be like Rachael and Leah, the two "mothers" who built up the house of Israel. (2Sam. 7:25-26, Ruth 4:15-17, Isa. 49:20-22)

The second blessing takes us back to the beginning. May Ruth, as she represents Gentile believers, be blessed in Ephratah (fruitfulness) and be famous in Bethlehem the house of bread. (Mat. 28:19-20)

Student Notes for Bethlehem: The City of Yeshua's Birth

**Discussion Questions for Bethlehem: The City of Yeshua's Birth**

1. When the Jewish people bless their sons, they bless them with the words "May you be like Ephraim and Manasseh." The idea is that they be so fruitful (Ephraim) that they forget (Manasseh) the iniquities of the past. How is that fulfilled in us through Yeshua?

2. Jacob's Trouble occurred when Rachel died laboring to give birth to Benjamin. Read Jeremiah 31:8, Isaiah 54:1, and Isaiah 26:16-218 about Jacob's Trouble and the latter days. What do they all have in common?

3. Read Psalm 23 and compare it to the good shepherd in Ezekiel 34:11-14 and Yeshua's description of Himself as the good shepherd in John 10:11-16.

4. Read Revelation 2 and 3 focusing on the verses that begin "I know your works." Summarize the works that Yeshua sees each of the churches doing. How do these apply to us?

5. Read Boaz's words to Ruth on the threshing floor in Ruth 3:10. Compare Boaz's testimony about Ruth with Jeremiah's words about Israel in Jeremiah 3:1-5. Even though Israel has strayed, what is God's desire for them? Even though we stray, what is God's desire for us? (1 John 1:5 through 1 John 2:2)

6. This lesson concludes with the injunction by Yeshua to be His faithful servants. He has a task for each of His servants. Take a few minutes to write or discuss the task Yeshua has given to you. Pray for God's strength to help you carry out your task.

## Jerusalem: The Eternal City

Jerusalem is the city God has chosen to put His name. He made His choice of Jerusalem known at the time of David. Then, when Solomon built the temple, He placed His name there.

> 1 Kings 9:3 NKJV 3 And the LORD said to him: "I have heard your prayer and your supplication that you have made before Me; I have consecrated this house which you have built **to put My name there forever**, and My eyes and My heart will be there perpetually.

But the history of Jerusalem goes back beyond even the days of Abraham. What is it about this Jerusalem that God would place His name there?

**A.** The first mention of Jerusalem is when Abraham meets Melchizedek after Abraham rescues Lot. Abraham shares bread and wine with Melchizedek, the King of Salem. Melchizedek means King of righteousness.

#4442. מלכי צדק Malkiy-Tsedeq, mal-kee-tseh'-dek from 4428 a king:--king, royal and 6664 meaning the right or righteous; king of right; Malki-Tsedek,

The name of the city, Salem, means peace but not just peace. It means complete, full, made ready, perfected, whole.

#8004. שלם Shalem, shaw-lame' the same as 8003; peaceful; Shalem, an early name of Jerusalem:--Salem.

#8003 שלם shalem from 7999; complete full, just, made ready, peaceable, perfect(-ed), quiet, whole.

Isaiah prophesies over Jerusalem stating that one day she will indeed be the city of righteousness.

> Isaiah 1:26-27 NKJV 26 I will restore your judges as at the first, And your counselors as at the beginning. Afterward you shall be called the city of righteousness, the faithful city." 27 Zion shall be redeemed with justice, And her penitents with righteousness.

He goes on to write of her that her children will see peace.

> Isaiah 54:11-13 NKJV 11 "O you afflicted one, Tossed with tempest, and not comforted, Behold, I will lay your stones with colorful gems, And lay your foundations with sapphires. 12 I will make your pinnacles of rubies, Your gates of crystal, And all your walls of precious stones. 13 All your children shall be taught by the LORD, And great shall be the peace of your children.

Right now, the eternal Jerusalem which will be populated with the saints of God is being made ready and being perfected.

**B.** The Bible's next mention of Jerusalem is actually of a mount just outside the actual city of that time. God tells Abraham to bring his son Isaac to a place in the land of Moriah. He was to offer Isaac as a burnt offering to God.

> Genesis 22:2 NKJV 2 Then He said, "Take now your son, your only son Isaac, whom you love, and go to the land of Moriah, and offer him there as a burnt offering on one of the mountains of which I shall tell you."

The name Moriah means seen or provided of God. It is a compound word consisting of "Yah," the name of God, and ra'ah meaning to see or provide. God weaves this word ra'ah throughout this account of the offering of Isaac beginning with the name Moriah.

#4179. מוריה Mowriyah, mo-ree-yaw' or Moriyah {mo-ree-yaw'}; from 7200 ra-ah to see or provide and 3050 Jah a shortened form of the name of God; seen of Jah;

Moriah, the place seen of God and provided of God, is the mount just outside of Jerusalem where Solomon would eventually build the temple where God would place His name.

> 2 Chronicles 3:1 MKJV 1 And Solomon began to build the house of the LORD at Jerusalem in Mount Moriah, where He appeared to David his father, in the place that David had prepared in the threshing-floor of Ornan the Jebusite.

The word play with the word "see" #7200 ra-ah continues as Abraham nears the end of his journey to Moriah. On the third day of their journey, Abraham "lifted his eyes and saw the place." After binding Isaac to the altar, God called out and Abraham "lifted his eyes and saw the ram." Finally, Abraham names the place Jehovahjireh, The LORD will see or provide.

> Genesis 22:14 KJV 14 And Abraham called the name of that place Jehovahjireh: as it is said to this day, In the mount of the LORD it shall be seen.

This word play with the word "see" or "ra-ah" is not finished yet. Ra-ah also means to provide. Abraham saw the ram God provided. When the Israelites came into the Promised Land, God instructed them to bring all their sacrifices to the place where He would place His name. The requirements for the sacrifices were that they were to be done before God's face; He would see them.

> Deuteronomy 12:11 NKJV 11 "then there will be the place where the LORD your God chooses to make His name abide. There you shall bring all that I command you: your burnt offerings, your sacrifices, your tithes, the heave offerings of your hand, and all your choice offerings which you vow to the LORD.

> Leviticus 1:5a NKJV 5a 'He shall kill the bull before the LORD;

The phrase translated "before the LORD" is literally before the face of the LORD. God will see each sacrifice brought before Him. There at Mount Moriah, the place that God both provided and sees, and that would eventually become the site of the temple, God would see all the sacrifices brought before Him. The first of these sacrifices was Abraham's offering of the ram in Isaac's place. With the dual meaning of ra'ah, God also provides all the sacrifices brought to the mount He provided. God would see and provide a specific sacrifice in that place, the sacrifice of His Son Yeshua.

**C.** The next time we visit Jerusalem is about 800 years later. David reigns as king over all Israel from Jerusalem. Late in his reign, Satan tempts him to count the men who can bear arms.

> 1 Chronicles 21:1 NKJV 1 Now Satan stood up against Israel, and moved David to number Israel.

This doesn't sound like such a bad idea. It would be helpful to know how many troops one could muster if they were needed. But God has other ideas. He specifically forbids the numbering of the troops unless it is done for the purpose of raising funds for the community as a whole so there would be no plague.

> Exodus 30:12 NKJV 12 "When you take the census of the children of Israel for their number, then every man shall give a ransom for himself to the LORD, when you number them, that there may be no plague among them when you number them.

The literal reading is "when you elevate the heads of the children of Israel" indicating that the entire community is elevated by the contributions. This de-emphasizes the numbering itself and emphasizes the common good of the community.

Samuel recounts David's numbering of Israel a little differently than the chronicler. Samuel records that God was angered against David and Israel and so allowed Satan to tempt David into the sin of numbering the Israelites.

> 2 Samuel 24:1 NKJV 1 Again the anger of the LORD was aroused against Israel, and He moved David against them to say, "Go, number Israel and Judah."

The sin of Israel and David is not specified but the numbering of Israel reveals that David is relying on his own strength and the strength of the numbers of Israel instead of relying on God. He is in essence elevating himself and the strength of man above God. This reminds me of Scrooge in <u>The Christmas Carol</u>. Scrooge loved counting his money, glorying in his great accumulation of wealth. David apparently gloried in the great strength of the armies of Israel.

When David is confronted with his sin, he repents but the nation is still punished for his actions. A plague is determined on Israel for three days during which 70,000 people die.

The great number of the dead reinforces that David's sin was taking pride in the numbers of Israel. Further, David actually saw the angel who was striking the people. What a humbling experience! God sent the prophet Gad, whose name means troop, to tell David to build an altar on the threshing floor of Ornan or Araunah the Jebusite. The chronicler calls him Ornan while the book of Samuel refers to him as Araunah.

> 2 Samuel 24:18 NKJV 18 And Gad came that day to David and said to him, "Go up, erect an altar to the LORD on the threshing floor of Araunah the Jebusite."

Although Araunah offers to give David all that is needed to build an altar and offer sacrifices, David refuses. He insists on paying for what he offers to God. King David, the ancestor of Yeshua willingly provides the sacrifice.

> 2 Samuel 24:24-25 NKJV 24 Then the king said to Araunah, "No, but I will surely buy it from you for a price; nor will I offer burnt offerings to the LORD my God with that which costs me nothing." So David bought the threshing floor and the oxen for fifty shekels of silver. 25 And David built there an altar to the LORD, and offered burnt offerings and peace offerings. So the LORD heeded the prayers for the land, and the plague was withdrawn from Israel.

This entire episode is filled with symbolism of the final judgment. First, the Antichrist elevates Himself above God, declaring that He is God. In this incident, David and the Israelites took pride in their own strength of arms. (We are not saying that David is a symbol of the Antichrist. It is only in this incident that he elevates himself in such a way. Also, David repents of his actions and provides the atoning sacrifice; the Antichrist will not.)

> Daniel 11:36 NKJV 36 "Then the king shall do according to his own will: he shall exalt and magnify himself above every god, shall speak blasphemies against the God of gods, and shall prosper till the wrath has been accomplished; for what has been determined shall be done.

> 2 Thessalonians 2:3-4 NKJV 3 Let no one deceive you by any means; for that Day will not come unless the falling away comes first, and the man of sin is revealed, the son of perdition, 4 who opposes and exalts himself above all that is called God or that is worshiped, so that he sits as God in the temple of God, showing himself that he is God.

Before judgment, God sends out his angels to proclaim the gospel one last time.

> Revelation 14:6-7 NKJV 6 Then I saw another angel flying in the midst of heaven, having the everlasting gospel to preach to those who dwell on the earth--to every nation, tribe, tongue, and people-- 7 saying with a loud voice, "Fear God and give glory to Him, for the hour of His judgment has come; and worship Him who made heaven and earth, the sea and springs of water."

The people are instructed to worship God who made heaven and earth, not man and man's works!

Second, the agent of judgment against David was an angel from the LORD. It was not another nation raised up against Israel but God Himself who exacted punishment. In Revelation, judgment comes from the angel of the LORD.

> Revelation 14:18-20 NKJV 18 And another angel came out from the altar, who had power over fire, and he cried with a loud cry to him who had the sharp sickle, saying, "Thrust in your sharp sickle and gather the clusters of the vine of the earth, for her grapes are fully ripe." 19 So the angel thrust his sickle into the earth and gathered the vine of the earth, and threw it into the great winepress of the wrath of God. 20 And the winepress was trampled outside the city, and blood came out of the winepress, up to the horses' bridles, for one thousand six hundred furlongs.

Third, David is instructed to build the altar on a threshing floor during the time of the wheat harvest.

> 1 Chronicles 21:20 NKJV 20 Now Ornan turned and saw the angel; and his four sons who were with him hid themselves, but Ornan continued threshing wheat.

The judgment in Revelation is in terms of the harvest. Yeshua describes the harvest as consisting of wheat and tares. The wheat goes into God's barn and the tares are burned in the fire.

> Matthew 13:40-43 NKJV 40 "Therefore as the tares are gathered and burned in the fire, so it will be at the end of this age. 41 "The Son of Man will send out His angels, and they will gather out of His kingdom all things that offend, and those who practice lawlessness, 42 "and will cast them into the furnace of fire. There will be wailing and gnashing of teeth. 43 "Then the righteous will shine forth as the sun in the kingdom of their Father. He who has ears to hear, let him hear!

Fourth, the location of the threshing floor is where Solomon will build the temple and God will put his name.

> 1 Chronicles 22:1 NKJV 1 Then David said, "This is the house of the LORD God, and this is the altar of burnt offering for Israel."

> 1 Chronicles 22:6 NKJV 6 Then he called for his son Solomon, and charged him to build a house for the LORD God of Israel.

At the same place where Abraham brought Isaac, David brings offerings to God with a repentant heart.

Finally, the threshing floor itself is at Jerusalem where God will gather the nations for the final judgment.

> Zechariah 12:8-9 NKJV 8 "In that day the LORD will defend the inhabitants of Jerusalem; the one who is feeble among them in that day shall be like David, and the house of David shall be like God, like the Angel of the LORD before them. 9 "It shall be in that day that I will seek to destroy all the nations that come against Jerusalem.

Joel describes this place as both the valley of Jehoshaphat and the valley of decision. The name Jehoshaphat means God's judgment. David decided for God and for repentance. The Anti-Christ will decide in favor of himself. What will the nations decide?

> Joel 3:12-14 NKJV 12 "Let the nations be wakened, and come up to the Valley of Jehoshaphat; For there I will sit to judge all the surrounding nations. 13 Put in the sickle, for the harvest is ripe. Come, go down; For the winepress is full, The vats overflow-For their wickedness is great." 14 Multitudes, multitudes in the valley of decision! For the day of the LORD is near in the valley of decision.

**D.** Yeshua's sacrifice, ascension and return are all at Jerusalem. The Mount of Olives is due east of the Temple Mount. Since the Temple faces east, God symbolically "sees" what happens on the Mount of Olives. Since all the sacrifices were to be brought before the LORD, literally before His face, Yeshua's crucifixion must have been to the east of the temple which places it on the Mount of Olives. We do know that His crucifixion was outside of the city.

> Hebrews 13:11-12 NKJV 11 For the bodies of those animals, whose blood is brought into the sanctuary by the high priest for sin, are burned outside the camp. 12 Therefore Jesus also, that He might sanctify the people with His own blood, suffered outside the gate.

Yeshua ascended from the Mount of Olives, the place of so many of His teachings and also His arrest.

> John 18:1-2 NKJV 1 When Jesus had spoken these words, He went out with His disciples over the Brook Kidron, where there was a garden, which He and His disciples entered. 2 And Judas, who betrayed Him, also knew the place; for Jesus often met there with His disciples.

> Acts 1:10-12 NKJV 10 And while they looked steadfastly toward heaven as He went up, behold, two men stood by them in white apparel, 11 who also said, "Men of Galilee, why do you stand gazing up into heaven? This same Jesus, who was taken up from you into heaven, will so come in like manner as you saw Him go into heaven." 12 Then they returned to Jerusalem from the mount called Olivet, which is near Jerusalem, a Sabbath day's journey.

Zechariah writes of Yeshua's return as He steps down on the Mount of Olives with a sword of judgment. This again recalls the actions of the Angel bringing judgment against

Israel and Judah. This time judgment will be against those nations who come against Jersualem and Israel.

> Zechariah 14:3-4 NKJV 3 Then the LORD will go forth And fight against those nations, As He fights in the day of battle. 4 And in that day His feet will stand on the Mount of Olives, Which faces Jerusalem on the east. And the Mount of Olives shall be split in two, From east to west, Making a very large valley; Half of the mountain shall move toward the north And half of it toward the south.

**E.** Yeshua will reign from Jerusalem on David's throne. In that day both His name and the name of the city are the same. Jeremiah writes that Jerusalem will be called the LORD our righteousness.

> Jeremiah 33:15-16 KJV 15 In those days, and at that time, will I cause the **Branch of righteousness to grow up unto David**; and he shall execute judgment and righteousness in the land. 16 In those days shall Judah be saved, and Jerusalem shall dwell safely: and this is the name wherewith **she shall be called**, The LORD our righteousness.

The name "the LORD our righteousness" incorporates the very name of God, יהוה , sometimes pronounced Yah-weh or Yehovah. In most of our Bibles, it is translated LORD with all the letters capitalized. Interestingly enough, when Yeshua comes as King, He will also be called the LORD our righteousness.

> Jeremiah 23:5-6 NKJV 5 "Behold, the days are coming," says the LORD, "That I will raise to David a Branch of righteousness; A King shall reign and prosper, And execute judgment and righteousness in the earth. 6 In His days Judah will be saved, And Israel will dwell safely; Now this is His name by which **He will be called**: THE LORD OUR RIGHTEOUSNESS.

Ezekiel writes about the time of the millennial reign of Messiah. At that time, God will establish His throne in Jerusalem forever.

> Ezekiel 43:7 NKJV 7 And He said to me, "Son of man, this is the place of My throne and the place of the soles of My feet, where I will dwell in the midst of the children of Israel forever. No more shall the house of Israel defile My holy name, they nor their kings, by their harlotry or with the carcasses of their kings on their high places.

**F.** According to the sages, Jerusalem was the sight of the original Garden of Eden. If the whole land of Israel, though, represents the Garden of Eden, Jerusalem is the sight of the tree of life in the midst of the garden. The Bible does not actually state the location of the Garden of Eden. So, what evidence do we have to support this idea? It may surprise you to find that there is an incredible amount of evidence.

1. There was a single river coming out of the Garden of Eden that split into four rivers as it left the garden. The names of the rivers coming out of the Garden of Eden were the Pishon, Gihon, Hiddekel, and Euphrates.

> Genesis 2:10-14 NKJV 10 Now a river went out of Eden to water the garden, and from there it parted and became four riverheads. 11 The name of the first is Pishon; it is the one which skirts the whole land of Havilah, where there is gold. 12 And the gold of that land is good. Bdellium and the onyx stone are there. 13 The name of the second river is Gihon; it is the one which goes around the whole land of Cush. 14 The name of the third river is Hiddekel; it is the one which goes toward the east of Assyria. The fourth river is the Euphrates.

Today, all of these rivers have different sources since they have been cutoff from the Garden of Eden, and the flood changed the geography of the earth drastically.

In Jerusalem, the spring of Gihon feeds the Pool of Siloam. The word Siloam means sent out.

> John 9:6-7 NKJV 6 When He had said these things, He spat on the ground and made clay with the saliva; and He anointed the eyes of the blind man with the clay. 7 And He said to him, "Go, wash in the pool of Siloam" (which is translated, Sent). So he went and washed, and came back seeing.

The Pool of Siloam was the source of water for the Ceremony of Water Pouring during the Feast of Tabernacles which represented the water from the wells of salvation spoken of by Isaiah. Any water that flows from a natural source is called living water. The water from the Pool of Siloam was both living water and the water of salvation.

> Isaiah 12:3 NKJV 3 Therefore with joy you will draw water From the wells of salvation.

The Living Water is sent out to bring healing and salvation to those who wash themselves in it.

2. When Yeshua returns there will be living water flowing from the temple.

> Zechariah 14:8 NKJV 8 And in that day it shall be That living waters shall flow from Jerusalem, Half of them toward the eastern sea And half of them toward the western sea; In both summer and winter it shall occur.

> Ezekiel 47:1 NKJV 1 Then he brought me back to the door of the temple; and there was water, flowing from under the threshold of the temple toward the east, for the front of the temple faced east; the water was flowing from under the right side of the temple, south of the altar.

> Ezekiel 47:6-9,12 NKJV 6 He said to me, "Son of man, have you seen this?" Then he brought me and returned me to the bank of the river. 7 When I returned, there, along the bank of the river, were very many trees on one side and the other. 8 Then he said to me: "This water flows toward the eastern region, goes down into the valley, and enters the sea. When it reaches the sea, its waters are healed. 9 "And it shall be that every living thing that moves, wherever the rivers go, will live. There will be a very great multitude of fish, because these waters go there; for they will be healed, and everything will live wherever the river goes. 12 "Along the bank of the river, on this side and that, will grow all kinds of trees used for food; their leaves will not wither, and their fruit will not fail. They will bear fruit every month, because their water flows from the sanctuary. Their fruit will be for food, and their leaves for medicine."

The living water "heals" the waters of the Dead Sea returning life to it. The river itself teems with life. The trees that grow along the banks of the river are for food and for healing. They don't lose their leaves and they produce fruit year round. This is reminiscent of the trees in the Garden of Eden.

In fact, Isaiah compares the restoration of Jerusalem and, by extension, the whole of Israel to the Garden of Eden both in fruitfulness and in joy.

> Isaiah 51:3 NKJV 3 For the LORD will comfort Zion, He will comfort all her waste places; He will make her wilderness like Eden, And her desert like the garden of the LORD; Joy and gladness will be found in it, Thanksgiving and the voice of melody.

3. God placed Cherubim at the east entrance to the Garden of Eden to guard it.

> Genesis 3:24 NKJV 24 So He drove out the man; and He placed cherubim at the east of the Garden of Eden, and a flaming sword which turned every way, to guard the way to the tree of life.

Cherubim were embroidered into the curtains of the Tabernacle and the veil separating the Holy of Holies. Only priests could enter the Tabernacle itself and the High priest was the only one who could enter into the Holy of Holies once a year. So, the cherubim guarded the entrance to both the Garden of Eden and the Holy of Holies.

> Exodus 36:35 NKJV 35 And he made a veil of blue, purple, and scarlet thread, and fine woven linen; it was worked with an artistic design of cherubim.

The entrance to the Temple in Jerusalem and the Holy of Holies, like the entrance to the Garden of Eden faces east. When Yeshua comes, He will enter Jerusalem from the east.

4. The name of Jerusalem is in the plural. In Hebrew the name is pronounced "Yerushaliyim." The "iyim" ending indicates a special plural form called a dual. It is

used to indicate two of something especially pairs of items that go together like two hands. There is not one Jerusalem, but two. This indicates the dual nature of Jerusalem as both physical and spiritual, as both earthly and heavenly. The spiritual nature of Jerusalem will become more evident during the millennial reign of Yeshua. The heavenly Jerusalem that comes down from heaven when the earth and heavens are recreated at the end of the millennial reign of Messiah will embody the dual nature. It will be the bridge joining heaven and earth; it will be entirely physical and entirely spiritual.

> Revelation 21:1-2 NKJV 1 Now I saw a new heaven and a new earth, for the first heaven and the first earth had passed away. Also there was no more sea. 2 Then I, John, saw the holy city, New Jerusalem, coming down out of heaven from God, prepared as a bride adorned for her husband.

There is a river of Living Water coming out from the throne of God in the city and on both sides of the river is the tree of Life.

> Revelation 22:1-2 NKJV 1 And he showed me a pure river of water of life, clear as crystal, proceeding from the throne of God and of the Lamb. 2 In the middle of its street, and on either side of the river, was the tree of life, which bore twelve fruits, each tree yielding its fruit every month. The leaves of the tree were for the healing of the nations.

Jerusalem is indeed God's city where He will place His name forever.

> Ezekiel 48:35 NKJV 35 "All the way around shall be eighteen thousand cubits; and the name of the city from that day shall be: THE LORD IS THERE."

**Student Notes for Jerusalem: The Eternal City**

Jerusalem is the city God has chosen to put His name.

> 1 Kings 9:3 NKJV 3 And the LORD said to him: "I have heard your prayer and your supplication that you have made before Me; I have consecrated this house which you have built **to put My name there forever**, and My eyes and My heart will be there perpetually.

**A.** The first mention of Jerusalem is when Abraham meets Melchizedek after Abraham rescues Lot. (Isa. 1:26-27, Isa. 54:11-13)

#4442. מלכי צדק Malkiy-Tsedeq, mal-kee-tseh'-dek from 4428 a king:--king, royal and 6664 meaning the right or righteous; king of right; Malki-Tsedek,

#8004. שלם Shalem, shaw-lame' the same as 8003; peaceful; Shalem, an early name of Jerusalem:--Salem.

#8003 שלם shalem from 7999; complete full, just, made ready, peaceable, perfect(-ed), quiet, whole.

**B.** The land of Moriah. (Gen 22:2, 2Chron. 3:1, Gen 22:14, Deu. 12:11, Lev. 1:5a)

#4179. מוריה Mowriyah, mo-ree-yaw' or Moriyah {mo-ree-yaw'}; from 7200 ra-ah to see or provide and 3050 Jah a shortened form of the name of God; seen of Jah;

**C.** David is king over all Israel in Jerusalem. (1Chr. 21:1, Exo. 30:12, 2Sam. 24:1, 2Sam. 24:18, 2Sam. 24:24-25)

This entire episode is filled with symbolism of the final judgment.
    1. First, the Antichrist elevates Himself above God, declaring that He is God. (Dan. 11:36, 2The. 2:3-4, Rev. 14:6-7)

    2. The agent of judgment was an angel from the LORD. (Rev. 14:18-20)

    3. David is instructed to build the altar on a threshing floor during the time of the wheat harvest. (1Chr. 21:20, Mat. 13:40-43)

    4. The location of the threshing floor is where Solomon will build the temple and God will put his name. (1Chr. 22:1, 1Chr. 22:6, Zech. 12:8-9, Joel 3:12-14)

**D.** Yeshua's sacrifice, ascension and return are all at Jerusalem. (Heb. 13:11-12, John 18:1-2, Acts 1:10-12, Zec. 14:3-4)

**E.** Yeshua will reign from Jerusalem on David's throne. (Jer. 33: 15-16, Jer. 23:5-6, Eze. 43:7)

**F.** According to the sages, Jerusalem was the sight of the original Garden of Eden.

    1. There was a single river coming out of the Garden of Eden. (Gen. 2:10-14, John 9:6-7, Isa. 12:3)

    2. When Yeshua returns there will be living water flowing from the temple. (Zec. 14:8, Eze. 47:1, Eze. 47:6-9, 12, Isa. 51:3)

    3. God placed Cherubim at the east entrance to the Garden of Eden to guard it. (Gen. 3:24, Ex. 36:35)

    4. The name of Jerusalem is in the plural. (Rev. 21:1-2, Rev. 22:1-2, Eze. 48:35)

**Discussion Questions for Jerusalem: the eternal City**

1. David began to rely on his own strength and the strength of the armies of Israel, so he counted the armies. Read Judges 7:1-8 and 1 Chronicles 21:1-8. Compare David's actions and attitudes in this situation with Gideon's actions and attitudes.

2. The name of the spring in Jerusalem that feeds the pool of Siloam is Gihon. The name Gihon means to gush forth and the name Siloam means sent one. How is this a picture of the water that will flow out from beneath the temple?

3. When we first encounter Jerusalem in scripture, Melchizedek is her king. Compare Yeshua and Melchizedek. (Gen. 14, Psa. 110, Heb. 7:1-18)

4. The Mount of Olives is east of Jerusalem. Since Yeshua will return from the east to step down on the Mount of Olives, it serves as a gateway to Jerusalem. Describe how each situation applies either physically, spiritually or both to the Mount of Olives being a gateway to Jerusalem.

    a) Solomon set up idols on the Mount of Olives (1Kin. 11:5-7, 2Kin. 23:13)

    b) Josiah tore down the altars on the Mount of Olives and throughout all of Israel. (2Kin. 23)

    c) The ashes of the red heifer used to cleanse a person after touching a dead body were prepared on the Mount of Olives. (Num. 19)

    d) The Shekinah Glory left Jerusalem by way of the Mount of Olives. (Eze. 10:1-9, Eze. 11:22-24)

    e) Yeshua's triumphal entry into Jerusalem was from the Mount of Olives. (Luke 19:28-44)

    f) Judas betrayed Yeshua into the hands of the high priest on the Mount of Olives. (Luke 22:39-55)

    g) Yeshua ascended from the Mount of Olives blessing the disciples as He rose. (Acts 1:1-10)

    h) Yeshua will return by way of the Mount of Olives. (Acts 1:9-11, Zec. 14)

# Appendix A: The Hebrew Alphabet

The Hebrew alphabet started out in the form of pictographs with each character representing a specific picture. Words were constructed by putting pictures together illustrating a characteristic of a word. An example is the word "father." The Hebrew word for father is spelled "ab" in English. In Hebrew it consists of the letters aleph, א, and bet, ב written from right to left, אב. From the Hebrew alphabet chart we see that the aleph represents an ox for strength or leadership and the bet represents a family or house. A father, therefore, is the strength and leader of his house and family.

The Hebrew letters also stand for numbers. There weren't different symbols for numbers. Many numbers have significance in scripture. We see numbers repeated over and over. For example, one is the number for God; seven is the number of completion, eight is the number of new beginnings; and forty is the number of testing or trial.

Even as the shape of the letters changed and became more abstract, the connection to the original picture language remains. Moses would have written in the pictograph or early ancient Hebrew form; David in the mid ancient Hebrew; and Yeshua would have written in the late ancient Hebrew form. The Modern Hebrew script was not established until the 15th century A.D. and was strongly influenced by the Aramaic form of the letters.

When we read the Old Testament of the Bible, we need to realize that it was originally written in ancient Hebrew and each of the letters in the words represents a picture. Many words and names carry extra, deeper meaning by examining the word picture presented by the original pictographs. Yeshua said that "not one jot or tittle" would pass away from the word of God.

> Mt 5:18 "For assuredly, I say to you, till heaven and earth pass away, one jot or one tittle will by no means pass from the law till all is fulfilled. (NKJV)

The jot refers to the smallest Hebrew letter the yad or yood, י. A tittle is a variation in how a letter is written. Some examples of a "tittle" would be a letter that is written larger or smaller than normal, a gap in the text, a word spelled with an additional letter or a letter left out, as well as embellishments of a letter. All those variations in text are for a purpose with the ultimate purpose to further reveal the character of God.

> 2Ti 2:15 Study to shew thyself approved unto God, a workman that needeth not to be ashamed, rightly dividing the word of truth. (KJV)

> Pr 25:2 It is the glory of God to conceal a matter, But the glory of kings to search out a matter. (NKJV)

> 2Ti 3:16 All Scripture is given by inspiration of God, and is profitable for doctrine, for reproof, for correction, for instruction in righteousness, (NKJV)

# Hebrew Alphabet Chart

| Ancient Hebrew | | | Sound | Name | Literal and symbolic meaning | Modern Script | End of Word | Numeric value | End of word character |
|---|---|---|---|---|---|---|---|---|---|
| Early | Mid | Late | | | | | | | |
| 🐂 | 𐤀 | א | silent | aleph | ox, bull - strength, leader, first | א | | 1 | |
| 🏠 | 𐤁 | ב | b,bh,v | beyt (bet) | tent, house - household, into, family | ב | | 2 | |
| 𐤂 | 𐤂 | ג | g | gimel | camel - pride, to lift up, animal | ג | | 3 | |
| 𐤃 | 𐤃 | ד | d | dalet | door - pathway, enter | ד | | 4 | |
| 𐤄 | 𐤄 | ה | h,e | hey | window, lattice - "the", to reveal | ה | | 5 | |
| 𐤅 | 𐤅 | ו | w,o,u | vav | nail - "and", to secure, to add | ו | | 6 | |
| 𐤆 | 𐤆 | ז | z | zayin | weapon - cut, to cut off | ז | | 7 | |
| 𐤇 | 𐤇 | ח | h | het | fence, a chamber - private, to separate | ח | | 8 | |
| ⊗ | 𐤈 | ט | th | tet | to twist, a snake - to surround | ט | | 9 | |
| 𐤉 | 𐤉 | י | y,i | yad (yood) | hand, closed hand - a deed, to make, work | י | | 10 | |
| 𐤊 | 𐤊 | כ | k,kh | kaph | arm, open hand - to cover, to allow, to open | כ | ך | 20 | 500 |
| 𐤋 | 𐤋 | ל | l | lamed | cattle goad, staff - prod, toward, control, authority | ל | | 30 | |
| 𐤌 | 𐤌 | מ | m | Mem | water - massive, chaos, liquid | מ | ם | 40 | 600 |
| 𐤍 | 𐤍 | נ | n | nun (noon) | fish (moving) - activity, life | נ | ן | 50 | 700 |
| 𐤎 | 𐤎 | ס | s | samech | a prop - support, turn | ס | | 60 | |
| 𐤏 | 𐤏 | ע | silent | ayin | eye - to see, know, experience | ע | | 70 | |
| 𐤐 | 𐤐 | פ | p,ph | pey | mouth - to speak, to open, a word | פ | ף | 80 | 800 |
| 𐤑 | 𐤑 | צ | ts | tsadik | fish hook - harvest, need, desire | צ | ץ | 90 | 900 |
| 𐤒 | 𐤒 | ק | q | quph (koof) | back of the head - behind, the last, the least | ק | | 100 | |
| 𐤓 | 𐤓 | ר | r | resh | head - a person, highest, the head | ר | | 200 | |
| 𐤔 | 𐤔 | ש | sh | shin | teeth - consume, destroy | ש | | 300 | |
| 𐤕 | 𐤕 | ת | t | tav | a sign, a cross - to covenant, to seal | ת | | 400 | |

## Appendix B: List of the Meanings of Names for Naomi and Ruth: Jew and Gentile

**Elimelech**: #458. אלימלך 'Eliymelek, el-ee-meh'-lek from 410 and 4428; God of (the) king; Elimelek, an Israelite:--Elimelech.

**Naomi**: #5281. נעמי No`omiy, no-om-ee' from 5278; pleasant;

#5278. נעם no`am, no'-am from 5276; agreeableness, i.e. delight, suitableness, splendor or grace:--beauty, pleasant(-ness).

**Lot**: #3875. לשט lowt, from 3874; a veil:--covering

**Mahlon**: #4248. מחלון Machlown, makh-lone' from 2470; sick, weak, afflicted, to grieve; Machlon, an Israelite:--Mahlon.

**Chilion**: #3630. כליון Kilyown, kil-yone' a form of 3631 pining, destruction: -consumption, failing.

**Judah**: #3063. יהודה Yahuwdah from #3064 praised; God is praised.

**Ephrathites**: #673. אפרתי 'Ephrathiy, from 6509; fruitfulness

**Bethlehem**: #1035. בית לחם Beyth Lechem, bayth leh'-khem from 1004 and 3899; house of bread;

**Moab**: #4124. מואב Mow'ab, mo-awb from a prolonged form of the prepositional prefix m- and ab; from (her (the mother's)) father; Moab, an incestuous son of Lot

**Almighty**: #7706. שדי Shadday, shad-dah'-ee from 7703; the Almighty:--Almighty.

#7703. שדד shadad, shaw-dad' a primitive root; properly, to be burly, i.e. (figuratively) powerful (passively, impregnable); by implication, to ravage:--dead, destroy(-er), oppress, robber, spoil(-er), X utterly, (lay) waste.

Other sources say Shaddai is from #7736:

#7736. שוד shuwd, shood a primitive root; properly, to swell up, i.e. figuratively (by implication of insolence) to devastate:--waste.

**Boaz**: Boaz comes from an unused Hebrew root the meaning of which is in doubt. Some same it means fleetness (Brown, Driver, Griggs, Gesenius Lexicon) others say it means strength. The two pillars next to the door of Solomon's Temple were named Jachin and Boaz. Jachin means Yah establishes. The Septuagint renders Boaz as a Greek word meaning "with strength" in 2 Chron. 3:17. (Source Jewish Encyclopedia) So the pillars would read "Yah establishes with strength."

**Obed**: #5744. עובד `Owbed, o-bade' active participle of 5647; serving, servant, worshiper

# Appendix C: These are the Generations: the Story of Our Redemption

After God created the heavens and sanctified the seventh day, He concludes with the words, "These are the generations of the heavens and of the earth when they were created." The Hebrew word translated as generations is toledot, תולדות, spelled from right to left with tav, vav, lamed, dalet, vav, tav beginning and ending with a vav and tav. The next time the scriptures use the phrase "these are the generations," it is about the generations of Adam after Adam and Eve sin and are kicked out of the Garden of Eden. This time the word toledot is spelled with the second "vav" missing from the word, like so: תולדת. This is called a defective spelling. This is one of the "jots and tittles" spoken of by Yeshua in Matthew chapter 5. Yeshua tells us that these jots and tittles are important and that not one of them will pass away from the scriptures. Jots and Tittles are only found in the original Hebrew language and are not translated to your English Bible. So what is the meaning of this particular defective spelling?

In Hebrew, each letter began as a pictogram and each word is made up of a set of pictures. The word picture of the complete spelling of toledot shows that the covenant is attached on both sides of the shepherd leading the way through the doorway. With the second "vav" missing in the defective spelling, our side of the covenant is blocked off. Sin has disconnected us from the doorway to the Shepherd. We can do nothing to restore our relationship with God. We need a redeemer that only He can provide.

The meanings of the names of the ten generations of Adam tell us of God's plan to bring a redeemer.

(# references are from the Strong's Concordance and Dictionary)

### Adam: mankind:
#120 from #119; ruddy i.e. a human being (an individual or the species, mankind, etc.

### Seth: appointed to
#8352. Sheth, (shayth) from #7896; put, i.e. substituted;
#7896. shiyth, (sheeth) a primitive root; to place (in a very wide application):--apply, appoint, array, bring, consider, lay (up), let alone

### Enos: feeble, frail, mortality
#582. 'enowsh, en-oshe' a mortal (and thus differing from the more dignified #120); hence, a man in general (singly or collectively):
#605. 'anash, aw-nash' a primitive root; to be frail, feeble

### Cainan: a fixed dwelling place
#7018. Qeynan, kay-nawn' from the same as #7064; fixed
#7064. qen, kane contracted from #7077; a nest (as fixed), sometimes including the nestlings; figuratively, a chamber or dwelling:--nest, room.

### Mahalaleel: God who is praised
#4111. Mahalal'el, mah-hal-al-ale' from #4110 and #410; praise of God

### Jared: come down, descends
#3382. Yered, yeh'-red from #3381; a descent
#3381. dry yarad, yaw-rad' a primitive root; to descend

### Enoch: instruct, train up
#2585. Chanowk, khan-oke' from #2596; initiated
#2596. chanak, khaw-nak' a primitive root; properly, to narrow (compare 2614); figuratively, to initiate or discipline:--dedicate, train up.

### Methusalah: a man sent forth
#4968. Methuwshelach, (meth-oo-sheh'-lakh) from #4962 and #7973; man of a dart
#4962 math: from the same as #4970; properly, an adult (as of full length); by implication, a man
#37973. shelach, from #7971; a missile of attack #7971. shalach, (shaw-lakh') a primitive root; to send away, for, or out

### Lamech: beaten, smitten, and tortured
#3929 from #4347. makkah, mak-kaw' or (masculine) makkeh {muk-keh'}; (plural only) from #5221; a blow; by implication, a wound; figuratively, carnage, also pestilence:--beaten, blow, plague, slaughter, smote, X sore, stripe, stroke, wound((-ed))

### Noah: rest, a quiet peace
#5146 Noach, (no'-akh) the same as #5118; rest
#5118 nuwach, (noo'-akh) or nowach {no'-akh}; from #5117; quiet peace

**The generations of Adam read, "Mankind is appointed to feeble, frail mortality, a fixed dwelling place. God who is praised comes down to instruct as a man sent forth to be beaten, smitten, tortured bringing comfort, a quiet peace."**

God promises a redeemer who will come and take our punishment for sin on Himself bringing us into God's rest. But each time the Bible uses the phrase "these are the generations" the spelling remains defective. The Bible uses the defective spelling a total of eleven times, ten times in Genesis and once in Numbers. Eleven is the number of defect, disorder or imperfection. We see this in the twelve sons of Jacob. When Joseph was in slavery in Egypt there were only eleven sons. In the words of Judah, "one is no more" and Jacob continued to grieve. When Judas Iscariot betrayed Yeshua, the perfect number of twelve disciples dropped to eleven. Before the Holy Spirit fell on the Feast of Weeks, the remaining eleven appointed a man to take Judas' place so they would be prepared to be witnesses to all they had seen. (Acts 1:16-22)

The defective spelling remained until the line of the redeemer was in sight and God was ready to reveal more of His redemption plan. We see the first glimmer of the redeemer in the book of Ruth which is all about a kinsman redeemer named Boaz. As the book of Ruth closes, the Bible uses the phrase "these are the generations" once again in relation to the generations of Peretz.

The original Hebrew manuscripts now spell Toledot with the full spelling, the second Vav is restored. The meanings of the names of the generations of Perez to David, speak of Yeshua as the firstborn of the resurrection, continue with the promise of our resurrection and eternity with God and Yeshua.

**Peretz: The one who breaks out**
#6556 from #6555; a break (literally or figuratively):--breach, breaking forth

**Hezron: a walled courtyard**
#2696. from #2691; court-yard;
#2691. a yard (as enclosed by a fence); also a hamlet (as similarly surrounded with walls)

**Ram: high, exalted**
#7410 active participle of #7311; high, from #7311 a primitive root; to be high actively, to rise or raise bring up, exalt

**Aminidab: a people impelled, a people who volunteer freely**
#5992. from #5971 and #5068; people of liberality:
#5068: to impel; hence, to volunteer (as a soldier), to present spontaneously:--offer freely

**Nahshon: the one who whispers, prognosticate, predict from the signs**
#5177. enchant, whisper from #5172
#5172: to prognosticate: predict from the signs (Dictionary.com definition for prognosticate)

**Salmon: invested with garments**
#8012 from #8008; investiture
#8008: a dress, clothes, garment, raiment

**Boaz: with strength** (According to Jewish Encyclopedia)

**Obed: servant, worshiper**
#5744 active participle of #5647; serving
#5647: to work, bondsmen, servant, worshipper

**Jesse: exist, to be**
#3448 from the same as #3426
#3426: exist; entity; used adverbially or as a copula for the substantive verb, there is or are, or any other form of the verb to be

**David: beloved**
#1732. from the same as #1730; loving
#1730: to love; by implication, a love- token, lover, friend; (well-) beloved

The generations of Peretz read, "One who breaks out of the walled courtyard, high and exalted, (with) a people impelled, a people who offer themselves freely (to) the one who whispers, predicted from the signs. (They are) invested with garments of strength, servants and worshippers, existing to be beloved."

Yeshua breaks out of the grave into new life. When He comes again, we will go with Him experiencing our own resurrection and our transformation. And we will forever be with the LORD.

> Micah 2:12-13 NKJV 12 "I will surely assemble all of you, O Jacob, I will surely gather the remnant of Israel; I will put them together like sheep of the fold, Like a flock in the midst of their pasture; They shall make a loud noise because of so many people. 13 The one who breaks open will come up before them; They will break out, Pass through the gate, And go out by it; Their king will pass before them, With the LORD at their head."

*This information is from the lesson "The Kingdom of Heaven Suffers Violence?" in <u>Shadows of Messiah Vol. 1</u>. It also appears in this form as a blog on our blogsite at www.moedtorah.blogspot.com.*

| | Appendix D: THE THIRTEEN ATTRIBUTES OF GOD Ex 34:6,7 | | | |
|---|---|---|---|---|
| 1 | יהוה | YHVH | The LORD | His Covenant Keeping Unchanging Nature |
| 2 | יהוה | YHVH | The LORD | Emphasizes His Unchanging Character and His Mercy |
| 3 | אל | EL | GOD | The Creator/King Underscoring His Capacity For Mercy |
| 4 | רחום | RACHUM | Compassionate | As For a Child in the Womb |
| 5 | חנון | CHANAN | Gracious | Showers Grace and Favor to the Undeserving |
| 6 | ארך אפים | EREK APAYIM | Slow to Anger | Patiently Waits For You To Repent |
| 7 | רב חסד | RAV CHESED | Abounding in Lovinkindness | To Both the Righteous and the Unrighteous |
| 8 | אמת | EMET | Truth | He's Fair and Equitable in His Justice |
| 9 | נצר חסד לאלפים | NOTZEIR CHESED L'ALAFIM | Keeps Lovinkindness for Thousands | His Generational Covenant Devotion is Boundless |
| 10 | נשא עון | NOSEI AVON | Forgives Iniquity | Intentional Sins |
| 11 | נשא פשע | NOSEI PESHA | Forgives Transgression | Rebellious Sins |
| 12 | נשא חטאה | NOSEI CHATAAH | Forgives Sin | Inadvertant Sins |
| 13 | נקה | NAKEH | Who Cleanses | He Cleanses Sin |

# Glossary

Brit Chadashah: New covenant, renewed covenant, the New Testament

Gemara: Written commentary on the Oral Law. Part of the Talmud

Ketuvim: The part of the Tanakh consisting of the writings. In our Protestant Bibles, these are the books of Joshua through The Song of Solomon.

Meshiach: Messiah, anointed one, Christ

Miqra: Convocation, assembly, dress rehearsal

Mincha: gift, offering, present, voluntary offering

Mishna: the written collection of the Oral Law. Part of the Talmud

Moed: appointed time or place, appointment, festival. Plural: Moedim

Navi'im: The books of the Prophets

Olah: to ascend or go up, a burnt offering

Owth: sign, signal, as an appearing

Talmud: A record of rabbinic discussions pertaining to Jewish law, ethics, customs, and history. It consists of two parts, the Mishnah and the Gemara.

Tanakh: An acronym for the Hebrew Scriptures. The T stands for the Torah which consists of the Books of Moses, the N stands for Navi'im which are the books of the prophets, and the K stands for the Ketuvim which are the writings.

Tallit: cloak, prayer shawl

Targum: Aramaic translation and interpretation of the Tanakh.

Torah: a precept or statute, especially the Decalogue or Pentateuch, teaching, law.

Year of Jubilee: Observed every $50^{th}$ year. All the land in Israel was returned to its original tribe and family. All Israelite slaves were set free.

Yehoshua: Joshua. God (Yah) will save.

Yeshua: Given Hebrew name of Jesus. It means he will save.

## Additional recommended resources

This is not intended to be an exhaustive list but it is some of the primary research resources that we have used and it will give you a good place to start.

**Online resources:**
    www.biblestudytools.com
    Multiple Bible versions, commentaries and other on-line reference tools.
    www.elshaddaiministries.us
    Weekly Torah teachings and other teaching sessions available free on-line.
    www.jewishencyclopedia.com

**CD and DVD's by Pastor Mark Biltz**
    The Feasts of the LORD
    Song of Solomon
    Spots, Wrinkles and Blemishes
    Hebrew Roots, Volumes 1 and 2

**Computer software**

**Power Bible**
    Available at www.powerbible.com

**E-Sword**
    www.e-sword.net

**Printed books or ebooks**
**E. W. Bullinger:**
    Numbers in Scripture
    The Witness of the Stars
    Figures of Speech Used in the Bible

**Alfred Edersheim:**
    The Temple – Its Ministry and Services
    The Bible History: Old Testament
    Sketches of Jewish Social life in the Time of Christ
    The Life and Times of Jesus the Messiah

**Daniel Gruber**
    The Separation of Church and Faith, Volume 1—Copernicus and the Jews

**Dr. Frank Seekins:**
    Hebrew Word Pictures
    The Gospel in Ancient Hebrew
    The Ten Commandments

Strong's Exhaustive Concordance and Dictionary